# WHAT A GAME THEY PLAYED

*Stories of the early days*

*of pro football by those*

*who were there*

# WHAT A GAME THEY PLAYED

## Richard Whittingham

HARPER & ROW, PUBLISHERS, New York
*Cambridge, Philadelphia, San Francisco, London*
*Mexico City, São Paulo, Singapore, Sydney*

1817

Grateful acknowledgment is made for permission to reprint:

Excerpt from *Pro Football's Hall of Fame* by Arthur Daley. Copyright © 1963 by Arthur Daley. Reprinted by permission of Times Books/Quadrangle, The New York Times Book Company.

Excerpt from *Pro Football's Rag Days* by Bob Curran. Copyright © 1969 by Bob Curran. Reprinted by permission of Prentice-Hall, Inc.

The 1938 article reporting the NFL Championship game between the New York Giants and the Green Bay Packers. Copyright 1938 by The New York Times Company. Reprinted by permission of The New York Times Company.

"Great Moments in Pro Football: The First Televised NFL Game" by Jim Campbell first appeared in *Football Digest,* 1975. Reprinted by permission of the author.

FIRST EDITION

*Designer: Sidney Feinberg*

Library of Congress Cataloging in Publication Data

Whittingham, Richard, 1939–
  What a game they played.

  1. Football—United States—History.  2. Football
players—United States—Biography.  I. Title.
GV954.P35   1984       796.332'092'2 [B]       84-47610
ISBN 0-06-015355-5

84 85 86 87 88 10 9 8 7 6 5 4 3 2 1

For
the Rev. Gilbert Hartke, O.P.
One-time quarterback and fullback,
long-time football fan,
who may indeed have been the first
practitioner of the Hail Mary pass

# Contents

# *Illustrations*

# Acknowledgments

The author and publisher would like to extend sincere appreciation to those former NFL players who so generously cooperated by submitting to lengthy interviews in which they shared their fascinating remembrances of the earliest days of professional football on and off the field.

Our thanks are also offered to the Pro Football Hall of Fame in Canton, Ohio, especially for the counsel and cooperation provided by Joe Horrigan, curator and chief researcher; and to the NFL Alumni Association, Fort Lauderdale, Florida, especially to Jim Campbell, director of communications. Special help was also provided by the Professional Football Researchers Association and their publications, and by authors David S. Neft, Richard M. Cohen, and Jordan A. Deutsch through their book *Pro Football: The Early Years* (Sports Products, Inc., 1978), which enabled the author to ascertain and verify many of the facts, statistics, and scores contained in this book.

# WHAT A GAME THEY PLAYED

# *Joey Sternaman*

Joey Sternaman joined the ranks of professional football in 1922, the same year that the assembly of teams from cities like Chicago, Green Bay, Columbus, Buffalo, Akron, Hammond, and even Canton and Marion, Ohio, officially adopted the name the National Football League. A quarterback, he was the little brother of Dutch Sternaman, who was co-founder, co-owner, and co-coach, along with George Halas, of the Chicago Bears.

Born in 1900, Joey was small for football even in those early days, standing a mere 5 feet 6 inches and weighing only 150 pounds. But, as one Chicago sportswriter noted, he had the "unique characteristics of a combined bantam rooster and a pit bulldog." He was a fast, shifty runner and a talented dropkicker in that age of the much rounder ball.

After being kicked off the University of Illinois football team for playing in the infamous Taylorville-Carlinville game—where a number of players from the Illinois and Notre Dame teams received money for their efforts on the field—he signed with the Chicago Bears. He won the starting job at quarterback immediately on a team that included his brother Dutch as one halfback, George Halas at one end, and Hunk Anderson as a guard. The team ended up in second place with a record of 9–3.

Joey Sternaman accounted for seventy-five points in the 1924 season, by far the most in the NFL that year and only three points shy of the record then held by Paddy Driscoll of the Chicago Cardinals. In 1925, he was joined in the Bear backfield by Red Grange and went on C. C. Pyle's legendary postseason tour. And he outgained and outscored the great Grange by using a play he designed himself, faking to Grange—on whom everyone was keying—and bootlegging the ball around the other end.

The next year, like Grange, he left the Bears to start his own team, the

Chicago Bulls, in the new American Football League. After the AFL's collapse, he returned to the Bears in 1927 and played there through the 1930 season. Pint-size Joey was considered one of the finest quarterbacks and kickers of the 1920s.

I got started in athletics early in life. I was born in Springfield, Illinois, and that was in 1900. As a young boy, I delivered newspapers around town, got $2.10 a week, and I used a bicycle to get from house to house. It led me to enter my first athletic contest, a bike race at the state fair. It was a one-mile race for kids and I won it. Later I won a twenty-five-mile race and got this fancy, silver plated cup for it.

I also played tennis as a boy, although it was not a well-known sport back then. I practiced by hitting a ball up against the side of our house, hours on end. I spent a lot of time at it and my mother never complained about all the thumping it made. A friend of mine's father put up a net in a field behind his house and we had a kind of grass court. When we got a little better, we played in the city. I think I once won some elimination tournament in town as a boy.

Football I took to very early also and it became my favorite sport. We had a tree in our backyard with a big fork in it, and I'd go out there every day, for hours, and kick a ball through it. Drop-kicking was the thing in those days, and I'd practice it, getting farther and farther away. I also practiced my passing by throwing at the tree. This was all when I was very young.

Things were very different in those days. Where we lived, there was a lot of space. We had a house with vacant lots on each side of it. There was a cherry tree, a pear tree, apple trees, and grape arbors. We had an outhouse out back. I guess I was about ten years old when the family first put a bathroom in upstairs and a toilet off the kitchen. We had stove heat and a wood pile. In the cellar my mother kept hundreds of jars of fruits and vegetables. There was a big vegetable garden in the back and from that and the fruit trees was where my mother got the food for canning. We had a chicken coop with loads of chickens, and it was my job to kill the chickens for Sunday dinners. I remember how I'd have to be sure to pull all the feathers off right away. Later I got a job firing furnaces during the winter. I got a dollar a week from each family. It was quite a job. I got up about 4:30 in the morning and would go to each house and clean out the ashes from the furnace. I'd carry them out and if the fire was out I'd build a new one. The house would then be comfortably warm when the people got up. I guess you could say I was the forerunner of automatic heat. I managed to handle about seven customers and therefore made seven dollars a week. It was enough to enable me to buy all my clothes and it paid for a lot of other things as well. As I said, things were a lot different then.

But I always had time for sports. The person who got me most interested in football was my older brother Ed, who everybody called Dutch. He was very good at the game himself and was about four years older than I. He encouraged me all along. I also learned a lot from our high school coach in Springfield, a man by the name of Johnny Merriman. Dutch had told him I was a pretty good dropkicker and might be able to help the team, even though I think I was only about 100 pounds when I started high school. Merriman said to Dutch that I had better be a good runner in the open field, too, if I expected to play, especially because of my size. Well, Dutch got me together with Merriman and he took some time to explain to me a lot of things about running. The most important was that when you were running with the ball and you saw someone coming at you, you should take a step to the right or to the left and spin away. He taught me all kinds of twirls and side steps. I kept practicing them, at school and at home in the vacant lot next door, and they really helped me develop my open field running. Over the years, I got by many a player by racing up to them and sidestepping, twirling, spinning, and away I'd go.

I played football all through high school, started before the war and played right through it. In my senior year I was elected captain and we had one of the best teams in the state that year. A lot of our players went on to be college stars at Illinois and Northwestern and one or two even went to Michigan, I think.

It was no picnic, though. In those days we had no headgear and obviously therefore no nose guards. I recall one time in high school, playing down in Champaign, I'd carried the ball and some guy swung around and totally flattened my nose. Another time in high school I played with a broken arm. I had my father, who was a pattern maker, fashion a couple of pieces of walnut to the shape of my arm. With those taped around my arm, I was able to play in the last game of the season. I generally just used the other arm, but I don't recommend that anyone should play with a broken arm.

Football was popular in Springfield in those days, throughout Illinois in fact. When we got our new field at the high school in 1916 or 1917, there might be as many as a thousand people who would come to one of our games. They had stands around it so they could sit, bleachers or benches, but there was no overhead covering. When we played in the rain, not too many came out to watch us. We played teams from all the neighboring cities, some not too close, either: Peoria, Decatur, Bloomington, Taylorville, Jacksonville, Pekin. I enjoyed traveling to those other cities because my family did very little traveling then and I got to see some different places.

Like my brother Dutch, I went to the University of Illinois. In 1919, I played on the football team, the freshman squad. We had about 225 fellows who tried out for it, and I was one of the fortunate ones to make it. You couldn't play on the varsity as a freshman. I also wrestled that year in the 135-pound class and I got all the way to the western intercollegiate finals. In my sophomore year, Bobby Fletcher was the quarterback and star of the varsity team, so I didn't get to play. But the next year, as a junior, I played a lot. We had been doing poorly, lost maybe the first four games of that season, when our coach, Bob Zuppke, decided to move me from halfback to quarterback and switch Laurie Walquist, who had been playing quarterback, to halfback. Well, that worked because Laurie was a fine halfback and I was much better suited to play quarterback. After that, we started to win some ballgames.

Zup was a fine coach. He had coached Dutch and George Halas earlier. He was also a fine man and he never wanted you to get cocky. And, of course, he disliked the pros. He was very outspoken about that, just like old Amos Alonzo Stagg up at Chicago. Zup never wanted anybody to play the game for money.

I remember playing against Stagg's team up in Chicago. They were very good in those days and I think we lost to them. Thousands of people would come to those games, the Illinois/Chicago rivalry. But the game I remember the most from my college days was that junior year against Ohio State. They were really something, supposed to be the best team in the country that year. We were really up for them. I ran about 80 yards with a punt return for a touchdown; it was called back, but then I scored on another run. And I kicked a couple of field goals that day and, by golly, we won, knocked off the number one team in the country. That day, all eleven of our starting players played the entire sixty minutes. After the game, Zuppke said, "A dead man would have been ashamed to be taken off that field."

That was also the year, though, that Doug Simpson came up after the season and said, "How would you like to play in a game and make fifty dollars, maybe a hundred dollars?" He said Carlinville was going to come over and play Taylorville—these were two football-crazy towns in central Illinois. A lot of money was being bet on the game and therefore the towns could afford to pay the players some good money for playing in the game. He said that Laurie Walquist and Oscar Knop, who had been in the backfield with me at Illinois that year, were going down; so were a lot of other players. I didn't think there was any chance of the people at the university finding out, so I said okay.

Well, that day, lo and behold, there were all kinds of players there in Taylorville: college, pros, semipros. I didn't play in the first half, Charlie Dressen of the old Decatur Staleys did for Taylorville. He later went on to become a well-known baseball manager with the Brooklyn Dodgers. Anyway, he got messed up somehow and so I went in for the second half at quarterback. We had some of the other Illinois boys in there, too, and Carlinville had most of the Notre Dame team playing for them. They had Hunk Anderson and Eddie Anderson and Chet Wynne, the whole dog-gone team. The score was 0–0 at halftime. I was able to move the ball down the field and then I drop-kicked a field goal. I got two more later and we won 9–0. And the story they told afterward was that they had to move the First National Bank of Carlinville over to Taylorville.

A while later, back at school one day, I got a call from George Huff. He wanted to see me. He said, "I understand you played down in that Taylorville game." He knew it and that was that. So we all got kicked out of athletics at Illinois. So did the Notre Dame players. It didn't matter so much for most of them because they were seniors anyway, but I still had a year of eligibility left and so it affected me a lot more. There's always been the story going around that I wore paint on my face and adhesive bandages to disguise who I was, but that wasn't really so. I don't see why I would have. We didn't think the schools would hear about it and, hell, everybody at the game knew who we were, where we came from. But I guess it made for a better story. As it turned out, those of us from Illinois who were there ended up on the Bears the next year and a lot of the Notre Dame boys were on the Chicago Cardinals.

The Bears team was the natural place for me to go. When the fellows came back from World War I, there was a lot of activity in pro and semipro football around the midwest. My brother Dutch came back from the army and went with the Staleys, this team that was sponsored by a corn products company in Decatur. He and George Halas went there and ran the football team and worked for Staley in his plant there. They became the big shots on the Staleys. The team didn't do all that well, I guess, or something went wrong down there, and Staley washed his hands of it. So then they incorporated it and Dutch and George brought it up to Chicago and it became the Chicago Bears. My brother and Halas shared everything then. They were co-owners, co-coaches, they both played, and they were always trying to recruit players from places like Illinois and Notre Dame.

A little while after, they brought in Chick Harley, an all-American from Ohio State, a big shot, one of the biggest names in the game then. Along with him was his brother Bill, a real egotistical fellow. Hell, he wanted to take over the whole thing but Dutch and George were not about to let him do that. "We're not going to take him in," Dutch told me. "That Bill is just too bossy."

So I went with the Bears when I couldn't play at Illinois any more—that was in 1922. Dutch talked me into it. It worked out well. I was able to beat out Pard Pearce for the starting job at quarterback, which he'd had since the Decatur days. I had myself a pretty good year, scored maybe four or five touchdowns, which was a good amount in those days. That year Dutch still did most of the kicking, field goals and extra points.

The game was rougher than college football, I found out, but it didn't bother me. The players were bigger, hell, they were *all* bigger than me. I was only 5 feet 6 inches and about 150 pounds. But I wasn't afraid of any of them.

And it sure was a simpler game than the one they play today. We didn't have a training camp or anything like that in 1922. We would just go out there maybe a week before the season and start practicing. We'd go over to a field at DePaul University in the early part of the season because the Cubs would still be playing at Wrigley Field. Then, when the baseball season was over, we'd go to Wrigley Field for practice and our games. In the off-season, I didn't work. Actually, I went back to Illinois and took courses to finish my schooling.

During the season, we would practice every day, but just in the afternoon. There were only 16 of us on the team then. The only way we'd put in a substitute was if one of the fellows got hurt. Usually he had to be

Joey Sternaman, pint-size (5-foot 6-inch, 150-pound) quarterback of the Chicago Bears, takes off around end in this game against the Chicago Cardinals at Cubs Park in 1924. "Little Joey," as he was known, played seven and a half seasons for the Bears, broken up by a half-year stint with the Duluth Kelleys and a year as owner/coach/quarterback of the Chicago Bulls of the American Football League (1926). (*Joey Sternaman*)

carried off the field before somebody would replace him. That's just the way we played the game in those days. I played quarterback on offense, called the plays and signals, returned punts, and played safety on defense. I started out making about $150 a game which was pretty high for a player back then, a little more than the others were making, except, of course, Halas and Dutch. The most I ever made playing football was $250 a game a few years down the road. They'd pay you at practice on Tuesday, after that week's game, give you a check, and it had to be signed by both of them, Dutch and George.

I didn't stay in Chicago the next year. I got an offer to go up to Duluth and play and I took it. The Kelleys was the name of the team. I'd only signed a one-year contract with the Bears so I was free to go. They always tried to get you to sign a long-term contract in those days, lock you in, but I wouldn't do it. I was the coach up there for the Kelleys too, that's partly why I went. We had a fair team, played about seven games, some in Duluth, but we also traveled a little to places like Akron and Hammond, towns that also had pro teams then.

Their season ended before the Bears' and so, when it was through, I left Duluth and came down and played for the Bears a few games. And in 1924 I was again the Bears' starting quarterback. We were a good team. The whole backfield was from Illinois. Besides myself, there was Dutch and Laurie Walquist and Oscar Knop. We really won the championship that year but there was some question about it and I don't think we were recognized as winners. There were a lot of teams claiming it. You see, we all didn't play the same number of games then. One team might play twelve or thirteen games and another only seven or eight. Some teams that had far fewer wins had better winning percentages maybe. So it wasn't always that easy to figure who really won the championship.

That was also the year when a play came off that I'll never forget. It was the time our fullback, Oscar Knop, intercepted a pass and took off for the goal line, only it was the wrong goal line he was racing toward. It was in a game against the Columbus Tigers. The ball bounced off the chest of the intended receiver and into the arms of Knop, who somehow got turned around on the play. The entire Tiger team just stood there and watched as he started running the wrong way. Most of them were laughing, I think. I took off after him, yelling, but I guess he couldn't hear me. Ed Healey was after him too, and he made a lunging tackle that stopped Knop just before he got to the goal. If it weren't for Healey, Knop would have had the distinction of being the first pro to score some points for the other team.

Before practice the next day, our trainer, Andy Lotshaw, came up to me as we were getting ready and started wrapping my index finger in a big white bandage. I asked him what the heck he was doing and told him there wasn't anything wrong with my finger. He said loud enough for everyone in the locker room to hear that he wanted to make it conspicuous in case I had to point out the right goal line to some of the other players.

The next year Red Grange came with us. He was a great open field runner. Red could sidestep anybody without losing speed, he had wonderful moves. He could wiggle and do this and that with his body and fake out most defenders, and he was very, very fast. I remember going over to Michigan to see him play in that famous game where Illinois whipped Michigan, who were supposed to be the best team in the country. I remember their coach, Fielding Yost, saying something about how he didn't think Red Grange was all that hot stuff. Then, on the kickoff, by golly, Red got the ball and started around toward the sideline. He had good interference, and he went all the way for a touchdown. A little later he went about 60 yards for another. Michigan players went for him, dived at him, grabbed air, and he just zipped around them or spun off them and raced on for a touchdown. I think he scored four or five that day. It was the greatest display of running I ever saw on a football field.

Well, when he came with the Bears, I was the play-caller, and I said to him, "Are you interested in doing well for yourself, or are you interested in winning ballgames?" After all, he'd been used to an offense down at Illinois that was built solely on opening a hole for him. Everything was geared to that. Well, we had a lot of different things and we needed them in the pros. We had a quick opener that would work well with Red, but we also had a lot of deceptive plays that we used. We were not just going to blow open a hole for Red Grange. Well, Red was honestly interested in winning games and, as I found out, he was one of the finest team players around. So what I did a lot after Red came with us was use him as a decoy. I'd fake handing the ball off to him and they would swarm after Red; why, they'd just clobber him, and, hell, I'd be bootlegging it around the other end or off on the other side passing it to one of our ends. We used a lot of deception and it worked well. And Red took a real beating, especially that first year, but he never complained, just played his best.

It wasn't just Red that year, either, we had a good team. In the line there was Ed Healey and George Trafton, Bill Fleckenstein and Jim McMillen. They were all fine ballplayers. Actually, Red didn't come with us until after the college season. He played his last game and then quit school. That's the year we went on tour after the season. In one twelve-day period we played *eight* games and they were in *eight* different cities, too. And, of course, most of us played sixty minutes of each game, and we got pretty banged up, I might add.

It was just before the Thanksgiving Day game with the Cardinals, which was always a big one in Chicago, that Red came with us. We didn't have a chance to practice much with him in the lineup. But we won the game and he wasn't that big a factor, that day anyway. Then, a week later, we got on the train to go to St. Louis, the first stop on our tour. We won there, got on another train and went to Philadelphia and beat the Frankford Yellow Jackets in a heckuva rainstorm on a Saturday afternoon. After the game, we didn't even have time to change out of those wet, muddy uniforms. We went right to the train, the last one out to New York, and changed on it. There wasn't enough time to get them cleaned, much less dry, by the time we played the New York Giants the next day. We got a day's rest in New York and then went down to Washington, D.C., and from there up to Boston to play the Providence Steam Rollers. Then it was on to Pittsburgh, Detroit, and finally back to Chicago, where we played one last game against the New York Giants. Those were eight games we played, all within two weeks [December 2–13]. We had a full house in practically every place we played. Red really pulled them in. In New York, at the Polo Grounds, we must have had seventy thousand people. There wasn't a square foot to be found in the standing room area. Red was the big attraction but he played hard for us, never let up, but he got hurt somewhere along the line on the tour and we couldn't use him all that much in the last few games.

We sure spent a lot of time on trains that year. The second tour took us all the way to California. We had a week or so rest after the first tour and then we got back on a train for Florida. We played some kind of an all-star team down in Coral Gables on Christmas Day. For that second tour, we were pretty hot stuff. C. C. Pyle, Grange's manager and the guy who put it all together, got us our own Pullman car and personal porter for the whole tour. Very fancy. Then we went to Tampa and over to Jacksonville for two more games. After that we headed west, played a game in New Orleans and then on to Los Angeles. That was the biggest crowd, at the Los Angeles Coliseum. They really pushed that game beforehand and there must have been eighty thousand people out for it.

From there we went down to San Diego and then up to San Francisco,

Portland, and finally Seattle. This second tour lasted five weeks, a lot easier than that first one of two weeks. I think through it all I got $200 a game. Red, of course, got much more, thousands, I believe, but he was the drawing card. It was quite something and we all enjoyed it, the second tour, that is. We saw all the nightlife of New Orleans and a lot of the stars in Hollywood and there was always something going on. Pyle saw to that. I had my first airplane ride while I was on it. Up in Portland, Oregon, there was this fellow, Oakley Kelley I believe his name was, and he took me up in an open cockpit plane. I was sitting on a parachute while we flew over the city. That was really something in 1925. That Kelley was the first man to fly across the country, coast to coast, from dawn to dusk.

In 1926, I left the Bears again to start the Chicago Bulls. Red Grange and Pyle went out to New York; Pyle had started a new league when he couldn't work things out with the Bears or with the NFL for Grange. It was called the American Football League, and Grange went with the Yankees, which was the name of the AFL franchise in New York, and I started up a team in Chicago. There were a number of teams in other cities. Well, I owned the Bulls, coached them, and played quarterback. It was a big gamble and I got talked into making it. It seemed like a real good thing at the time.

We actually had a pretty good team, though, and as I recall we even beat Red and his New York Yankees. But we didn't get the crowds. We played out at Comiskey Park on the South Side, not the best of neighborhoods in those days, and we just couldn't make it go. We sure tried. But everywhere in that league it was tough. We had plenty of big names and fellows who tried to make it work. Besides Red Grange and myself in the AFL, there was Eddie Tryon, Harry Stuhldreher of the old Four Horsemen of Notre Dame, Wildcat Wilson, Century Milstead, people like that. But it went under at the end of the year. I came out broke after it, it was a bum gamble.

I went back to the Bears again after that and played with them through the 1930 season. Grange came too after his knee injury, and we had Paddy Driscoll, but we didn't do as well as we should have in those years.

As I think back on it, it sure was a lot different in those days, not just in the fact that we made maybe $150 a game and some of the boys today may make a million a season. Take the quarterback, for example, because he sure is different today than he was when I played. I'd call each play, set the signals. We'd talk in the huddle. Somebody would tell me who was pulling out on defense or who might be hurt a little bit and maybe slowed down some or who he felt he could move out or beat. We'd talk things over. And often I'd just call a play like, "Left halfback around right end." No numbers, no code, just that, and everybody had the sense to know what to do. I always listened to the other players, then made up my own mind what was the best call. Today the quarterback is just there, hands the ball off and that's it. Sure, he's a good passer. But somebody runs out onto the field and tells him what play to call. And they've got coaches in the press box and radios and headsets and a dozen coaches on the sideline. Hell, our coaches, guys like Halas and Dutch, were on the field playing in the game, in the huddle with us. Today the quarterback wouldn't think of blocking somebody. And today a team loses ten percent of its interference because a quarterback doesn't block. That was natural to me, one of the best parts of the game, running interference.

I think everybody in those days felt that way. Running, blocking, tackling, it was all part of the game and you had to be good at each part. I played against all kinds in those days, mean and nasty ones, those who didn't care what happened to you or them. And there were some great ones to be sure. I never played against George Gipp although he played in some of those games for money while he was at Notre Dame, like the rest of us did, like that Taylorville-Carlinville game. But I ran up against many who you can never forget. There was Red Grange, of course, maybe the greatest runner ever, and then there was Harry Stuhldreyer and Johnny Mohardt of Notre Dame, and Jimmy Conzelman, and Ernie Nevers. I especially remember playing against Jim Thorpe and Pete Calac and Little Twig who all played for the Indian team. Thorpe was a marvelous athlete, could do anything: run, pass, kick, tackle like a steam roller. You had to be careful when you ran up against him because he was so powerful and big, around 6 feet 2 inches and over 200 pounds, especially if you were 150 pounds like I was. I wouldn't ever try to run head-to-head with him. I'd just go as low as I could, tumble, and try to trip him up. Another really good one was Benny Friedman, a fine quarterback. And there were some truly tough fellows. We had a bunch on the Bears: George Trafton and Hunk Anderson and Jim McMillen. And Ed Healey was one of the greatest linemen I ever saw.

I quit after the 1930 season. I was over thirty and some new people had come along. It wasn't the way it had been anymore and I knew it was time to get out. But it was great to be there then, to play the game like it was in those days. What a game it was.

## Let Old Jim Run

Knute Rockne, Notre Dame's legendary football coach, also played for the pros in the early days of the game. He knew better than most the monolithic reputation of Jim Thorpe. He learned the truth of it in his first encounter with Thorpe on the football field, and told the story many times afterward.

Rockne was playing defensive end for the Massillon Tigers and Thorpe was in the backfield for the Canton Bulldogs. On his first carry, Thorpe was met by Rockne at the line of scrimmage and brought down with a good tackle. When they got up, Thorpe said, "Rock, you shouldn't do that." He nodded over to the spectators on the sideline. "Those people, they come to see Old Jim run. Be a good boy and let Old Jim run."

A few plays later, Rockne broke through and tackled Thorpe for a loss of a couple yards. "Rock, you're not letting Old Jim run. Those people aren't going to be happy. You've got to let Old Jim run."

Like hell, Rockne thought, more than a little pleased with the way he was handling the game's most reputed player and a little dismayed at how overrated the mighty Indian was, or so it seemed to him.

On the next play, Rockne broke through again and lowered his head to take on Thorpe. This time Thorpe lowered his head and shoulder, too, and met Rockne full blast. The impact was shattering and Rockne went down in a heap, alone and stunned. Through the fog that enshrouded his brain, he heard the cheers of the crowd. When he finally got up, he saw Thorpe in the end zone, some 50 yards downfield, holding the ball high above his head. Then Thorpe trotted back upfield and patted the dazed Rockne on the shoulder pads. "That's the way, Rock," he said. "You let Old Jim run."

## Big Money

Curly Lambeau on the launching of the Green Bay Packers:

"I had gotten out of Notre Dame the year before and in 1919 I was in Green Bay working for the Indian Packing Company. I talked my boss, a man named Frank Peck, into backing a pro football team. I told him it would take five hundred dollars to equip a team and get it through a season. He agreed and put up the money and I went out and got the players from around the area up there. We had only a couple of substitutes and everybody played about fifty minutes a game. We didn't have a fence around the field so we couldn't charge admission, but we chiseled from the crowd, passed the hat. We put the take from each gate into a bag and stowed it in a safe. At the end of the season we split the pot. We each got sixteen dollars and fifty cents."

# 2

# *Red Grange*

Grantland Rice gave him the name the "Galloping Ghost." Damon Runyon said of him, "On the field he is the equal of three football players and a horse." Countless writers since have said he was to football what Babe Ruth was to baseball, Jack Dempsey to boxing. Certainly the name Harold "Red" Grange is a certified sports legend.

A three-time all-American at Illinois, Red Grange filled college football stadiums wherever he performed. Just how good the redhead was is forever preserved in the statistics of the 1924 Illinois-Michigan game. Before the game, Fielding Yost, Michigan's famed coach, whose team was ranked number one in the nation that year, shrugged off Grange's talent: "All Grange can do is run," he said. That was true: against Michigan Red ran for five touchdowns, four of them in the first quarter. By the end of the game, he had gained 402 yards on twenty-one carries. And to disprove Yost, he also threw six pass completions, one of them for a touchdown, as Illinois annihilated top-ranked Michigan 39–14.

Under the tutelage of the game's first agent and one of its all-time masterful entrepreneurs, C. C. Pyle, Grange became a pro in 1925, signing with the Chicago Bears. The biggest name in football had defied the college mentors like Amos Alonzo Stagg and his own coach Bob Zuppke, both of whom denounced with special vitriol the game that was played for money, and in so doing he gave it a boost in popularity and a sense of respectability that it never should have been denied in the first place.

Grange certainly reaped the spoils, splitting with Pyle gate receipts of about $250,000 from the 1925 Red Grange/Chicago Bears tour and pocketing perhaps another $100,000 from endorsements, personal appearances, and motion picture contracts—all in an age when his fellow ballplayers were earning between $50 and a top of $200 a game.

Pyle and Grange launched the first American Football League in 1926, with Red the drawing card for the New York Yankees. While with that team, he injured his knee and would never again be the dazzling runner who had brought so many millions of people to their feet in both college and pro football stadiums.

George Halas lured Grange back into the game in 1929, and he played with the Bears through the 1934 season. He was, in the words of Halas, "the game's greatest runner until he hurt his knee and after that the game's best defensive back."

Something of what Red Grange was to football can be gleaned from the headline in a Chicago newspaper when his kid brother, Gardie, an end for the Bears, caught a game-winning touchdown in 1931: "Red Grange's Brother Beats Giants on Pass."

I was in about the seventh grade when I first started to play football. It was in Wheaton, Illinois, a little town about twenty-five miles west of Chicago. Now it really wasn't football that we played, it was a game like it. We called it "Run, sheep, run." There would be two or three guys in the middle of a field, who were to be the tacklers, and a goal at either end; usually the goals were sidewalks. All the rest of us would line up at one goal and on a signal run to the other. If you were tackled, you would have to stay out in the middle and become a tackler. It would go on until the last player was tackled. I used to get my pants and socks torn up all the time, and, of course, my folks were not fond of the game, for legitimate reasons, but that was where I first got a taste of running and tackling and I found I really liked it.

I was six years old and my mother had just died when we moved to Wheaton. My dad had been foreman in a lumber camp in Pennsylvania with about thirty-five lumberjacks working for him. He was a fine athlete although he didn't participate in any organized sports back then. Still any of the old lumberjacks would tell you he was one of the most agile runners around and he was big by the standards of that time, 6 feet and 200 pounds. He didn't encourage me to play football, but after I got started in it he became quite interested. He became a policeman in Wheaton and later chief of police and supported me when I chose to play football and when I decided to become a pro, which was frowned upon in those days.

One of my first nicknames was the "Wheaton Iceman." The reason I got it was because every summer while I was in school I used to deliver ice. In those days, folks didn't have electric refrigerators. The ice truck would come by and deliver ice. Practically every day I'd carry these big blocks of ice in from the truck to people's houses. I started in my sophomore year of high school, mainly because I needed the money. Most of the kids around there worked in the summer. I carried blocks of ice up to maybe 100 pounds. What it did, without me knowing it, was to develop my leg muscles. I mean I'd make about fifty calls a day on an average, up and down stairs with these huge blocks of ice, and it built my legs up.

It was in high school that I played football in an organized way for the first time. In my first year, I played right end. The way it happened was pretty simple. I went out for the team as a freshman and on the first day our coach called all the new kids together and asked them what they played. He said to me, "Kid, what do you want to play?"

And I said, "Well, what do you need?"

"We've got ten men back from last year," he told me. "All we need is a right end."

"Well, I'm a right end," I said, and that was it. I made it as a starter at that position.

The next year we lost most of our backfield and the coach felt I could run so he moved me there. And I played halfback ever since.

I chose Illinois for two pretty basic reasons. Chiefly, I guess, was because it was the cheapest place I could go and get a college education. And secondly, most of the kids I knew around Wheaton were going to the state university. How I came to play football there is another story, however.

I was on the track team in high school as well as the football team, and I used to go down to Champaign to compete in track meets that were held at the university there. Bob Zuppke, the Illinois football coach, who was a very big name in those days, came over to me at one of those meets and asked my name. I was out in the field, in the broad jump I believe it was, and he told me he'd seen me run earlier that day. "I think if you come down to Illinois," he said, "you'd have a good chance at making the football team." That made a big impression on me.

Zup, in his own peculiar way, very easygoing, sold many people on coming to the university. He was a great man to play football for. Used to call me "Grench," that's the way it came out with his German accent. He never called me anything else except maybe when he'd get mad at me for some reason or other and then he'd call me "Red," which I guess is kind of ironic.

Zuppke was probably the best psychiatrist I ever met in my life. He knew how to handle young people and he knew how to get 150 percent out of his football players without being nasty or mean about it. I never knew anyone who played for him who didn't give his best. And, of course, Zup knew football.

We had a lot of great kids who played with me at Illinois, like Earl Britton who was in the backfield with me. But the others didn't get as much publicity as they deserved. It wasn't a one-man team, there were never any one-man teams. Everything was a team effort. I carried the ball, that's why I got so much publicity, but I wasn't any more important than the guys doing the blocking. Everybody was a cog, each important in his own way. That's the way Zup turned out a team, 11 guys, each doing his job.

It was Charlie Pyle, however, who got me to join the pros. His initials were C. C., which some writer later said stood for "Cash and Carry." But Charlie was the most impressive man I ever met in my life, and I've met millions of people, presidents and everything else.

Charlie Pyle stood about 6 feet 1 inch and weighed maybe 190 pounds. He had been an excellent boxer, had taken it up as a kid, and he could take care of himself, believe me. At the same time, he was a very dapper guy, sort of a peacock strutting in spats and carrying a cane, the most immaculate dresser I've ever seen. I don't think he ever wore anything twice, and he would go to the barber shop at least a couple of times a week. He was a real, true dandy.

Charlie was in the theater business. He owned three movie houses, two of them in Champaign and another over in Kokomo, Indiana. I met him at the Virginia Theater in Champaign one night in 1925 when I was a senior. An usher came to my seat and said, "Mr. Pyle would like to see you in his office." Well, I'd heard of him and I knew that he was the one who gave out free tickets to his theater to those of us on the football team, so I went up to his office with the usher. When I opened the door, the first thing he said to me, before I could even sit down, was, "Red, how'd you like to make a hundred thousand dollars?" I thought he was crazy. That was like saying a million today. But I said naturally I would— who wouldn't?

Then he said, "Well, I've got an idea. Sit down." And he explained it to me. He wanted me to join up with a pro team and we would make a tour of the country after the regular pro season. He said we would go to cities where they had pro teams and play them, as well as to others where they never got to see pro football. He thought the Chicago Bears would be the ideal team to go with and said if I were truly interested in the scheme he would work it out with them. He would be my personal manager, handle all the financial and promotional things for me. He was like the agents of today but he also was the promoter of the tour. Charlie ran the whole thing.

As it turned out, there were two tours. The first went out east to places like New York, Boston, and Washington; the second went from Florida to California.

It wasn't all that easy, though. Pro football was pretty questionable in those days. Most of the college coaches and a lot of the sportswriters were very down on it. Zup was opposed to my becoming a pro. Amos Stagg had been against it since it started, too. "Football isn't meant to be played for money," Zup said to me.

On the other hand nobody seemed to mind that baseball players made money by playing the game. So I told Zup, "You get paid for coaching it. Why should it be wrong for me to get paid for playing it?" No matter what, he was still opposed to it, and we didn't really talk to each other for a number of years after I agreed to play with the pros. That's just the way it was in those days. College football would draw seventy or eighty thousand to a game, but the pros might not get more than four or five thousand. It was a different time altogether.

Needless to say, I went with Charlie Pyle and the Bears. I played my last game in Columbus, Ohio, against Ohio State. It was kind of a madhouse because there were all these rumors that I was going to go pro right after it. I had to sneak out of the hotel there, down the fire escape, and I got a cab and went to the railroad station. Then I went to Chicago and checked into the Belmont Hotel under an assumed name. Charlie was over at another hotel setting up the deal with George Halas and Dutch Sternaman, the two owners of the Bears. The next day I signed the contract. I signed first with Charlie, making him my manager, and then we both signed the deal with the Bears. You see, I couldn't sign anything before that, not while I was playing college ball. A lot of people and a good number of newspaper writers said that I had signed a contract beforehand, but that just wasn't true. It made a good story, I guess. But that day in Chicago was the first time I met Halas or Sternaman. I'd known of them, of course, in fact they had gone to Illinois themselves, about five or six years ahead of me.

The first game I played for the Bears was on Thanksgiving Day in 1925, against the Chicago Cardinals. It wasn't part of the tours, just a regular season game. My first impression was how much bigger the pro players were. A college lineman ordinarily only weighed about 190 pounds back then. The pros were all 230 or 240. It was a big difference.

After that, a week or two later, we went on our first tour. Out in New York we played the Giants at the Polo Grounds and more than seventy thousand were in the stadium. There were hundreds of others up on Coogan's Bluff watching it, too. That was the biggest crowd ever to attend a professional football game up to that time. I believe the proceeds that the Giants got were enough to save the team. You see, the Giants had lost a lot of money that year. It was their first year in the NFL, and Tim Mara, who owned them, dropped plenty until that game.

I have another memory of that game in New York. We were staying at the Astor Hotel over on Times Square. Babe Ruth, who was at the height of his prestige and glory, called on me during the two or three days I was there. I was very flattered that he would take the time and effort. I remember he said to me, "Kid, I'll give you a little bit of advice. Don't believe anything they write about you, good or bad. And further, get the dough while the getting is good, but don't break your heart trying to get it. And don't pick up too many checks!" He told me that but he was a guy who would spend money right and left. What a guy to give that kind of advice.

We went to Washington after that. The senator from Illinois, McKinley I believe it was, arranged for us to meet the president, Calvin Coolidge. We were taken in and I was there with George Halas. The senator introduced me as, "Red Grange, who plays with the Bears." Coolidge shook my hand and said, "Nice to meet you, young man. I've always liked animal acts."

On the second tour we went out to California. That's the first time real pro football was ever played in the west. I don't think they'd ever gone west of Rock Island, Illinois, before that. We met all kinds of people out there: the Hearst family, the Wrigleys on Catalina Island, the Hollywood stars like Douglas Fairbanks and Harold Lloyd. They were all good football fans too.

Charlie Pyle arranged for me to make a couple of movies out there as well. The first was called *One Minute to Play*. It was about a halfback

Taking a breather on the Chicago Bears bench during his first professional football game, on Thanksgiving Day 1925, is Red Grange *(third from left)*. A record
crowd of more than thirty-six thousand showed up to watch the "Galloping
Ghost" make his debut. A week later, Grange and the Bears launched their his-
toric barnstorming tour of the nation. To the right of Grange is his flamboyant
and ever-present manager, C. C. ("Cash and Carry") Pyle; to the left, guard Bill
Fleckenstein and owner/coach/end George Halas. *(Dutch Sternaman Collection)*

who was declared ineligible to play in the big game of the year. Then, in the last few minutes it is learned that he really is eligible, that the other was just something cooked up by gamblers to keep him out of the game. And naturally, as Hollywood would have it, he goes out and wins the game in the last minute.

That was the movie where Charlie Pyle proved his showmanship. It was being made in June in Hollywood. For the major scene, they needed a crowd of about three thousand to fill the stadium to make the big game look realistic. And the game was supposed to be the last one of the season in the Midwest. Well, it was about a hundred degrees in Hollywood in June, hardly a typical November day in Michigan or such. Also they would have to pay extras fifteen or twenty dollars for a day's work— that's forty-five thousand or fifty thousand dollars in salaries just to produce a crowd. So Charlie came up with this scheme. He got hold of Wildcat Wilson, an all-American from out there and a very popular football player in California. Between the two they rounded up enough players for a football game. I was to captain one team and Wilson the other. Then Charlie took out an ad in the Los Angeles papers to announce this big exhibition game. In it he said that everyone who wore a coat and hat would be let in free. Well, more than three thousand showed up, and it was about a hundred degrees, but they were there in coats and hats and scarves perspiring through four quarters. Charlie got it all for the price of a couple of ads and I think he paid each of the players twenty-five dollars.

The other movies I made were *Racing Romeo*, that was in 1927, and two years later there was *The Galloping Ghost*. Pyle arranged for all of it, engineered the deals. He also handled all the premium deals, too. There was a Red Grange candy bar, autographed footballs, a Red Grange doll, clothes, even a ginger ale and a yeast foam malted milk.

Grantland Rice was with us for a while on the tours. He was a great writer, not just on football but on all sports in those days. He was known and read all over the country. I had a lot of respect for him as a sportswriter. Damon Runyon was there too. And Westbrook Pegler. I knew Pegler very well in those days. He was a great guy personally but he was brutal when he wrote. As he used to say, nobody would read him if he didn't tear things down. That was his style. He never wrote a good thing about anyone, I don't think. When somebody would complain about what he wrote about them, Pegler would just say, "Hell, don't worry about it, another million people know your name every time I tear you down." He did have a tremendous following around the country. Millions read him.

The Bears had a wonderful team at the time I joined them. Little Joey Sternaman was the quarterback, and there was never a better one than him. He could run with the ball, he was smart, he could pass, he could kick. Laurie Walquist was the other halfback and he had played at Illinois before, too, and was very good. But the best, the very best player I ever encountered, was one I played with later on the Bears, Bronko Nagurski. We played in the same backfield for about five years. Bronk was big, about 240 pounds, and fast. He could do everything on a football field. And he had respect for all his fellow players. If he gained some yards running, he'd pat his blockers on the back. Everybody liked to play with Bronk, on his side; I'm not sure they liked to play against him, though.

On the other side of the fence, there were players like Ernie Nevers, one of the finest I ever played against. Ernie came out of Stanford University and played with the Chicago Cardinals against us. Nevers was probably the first and best of the triple-threat backs. He could run, kick, and pass. He played out of the double wingback offense and he was a star through and through. Guys like Nevers and Nagurski would have played the game for nothing. They were insulted if they were taken out of a game, even if it was just for a few minutes or because of an injury.

Another great back of that time who should also be remembered was Paddy Driscoll. He played with the Cardinals and then with me at the Bears. Paddy was a runner, a passer, and a great dropkicker. He could drop-kick it through the uprights anywhere from the 50 yard line in. And he was a good defensive player as well.

All these guys, who were the big stars of the day, could also block and tackle. In my time they stressed blocking and tackling. It was the first line of business and you had to do it well if you were going to be any good at the game. Because you played sixty minutes you had to master both. You learned those things in high school then. And when I'm asked who were the hardest tacklers I ran up against, my answer is all of them because I can't remember anybody who stuck around the pros who wasn't a hard tackler. I've got the bumps and pains to prove it.

And certainly one of the most memorable characters of the time as well as one of the finest players was Johnny Blood. I ordinarily played against him but we played together and roomed together a couple of times, too. After the regular season was over we used to barnstorm in those days and Johnny and I did it together. Johnny was a great pass receiver and there never was any better runner in the open field than Johnny. Quick as a rabbit. He was a character, though, although a likable one. Money was never an objective for him. He didn't care about it and usually blew it as fast as he got it. I remember one time a girl asked him for an autograph after a game and he said, "Sure," then cut himself on the wrist, took her pencil, and signed her program in blood. It took a couple of stitches to close up his wrist afterwards. Johnny Blood was also one of the smartest persons I ever met. He could talk with anybody about literature and poetry and he could recite Shakespeare and practically every poet who ever lived. He liked that almost as much as he did raising a little hell.

George Halas was our player/coach and he was certainly a tough cookie. But if you wanted to play, wanted to work, he'd go to hell for you. There was no fooling around with George. If football was anybody's life it was his. You worked, gave your all, and he would give you anything he had; if you didn't, he didn't want you around. But he built the Bears. When I joined them, George would lug equipment around, write the press releases, sell tickets, then run across the road and buy tape and then help our trainer, Andy Lotshaw, tape the other players' ankles.

I remember an incident that happened in 1934 that George was a part of that kind of tells you what he was like. It involved Johnny Sisk, one of our backs who they called "Big Train." Sisk didn't like to practice and would complain about injuries in order to get out of it. But he was always ready to go on game days. Johnny came out this one day and told Halas he couldn't practice because he'd hurt his knee in the game the previous Sunday. He hobbled around to show Halas. Well, George watched him limp around for a little while and then told him to go sit in the stands until practice was over. An hour or two later, after the practice session, everyone went into the dressing room to shower. Except George. A little later, Sisk went out to get into his new car. Halas was out there watching him limp along. Well, when Johnny started up his car a smoke bomb exploded. Naturally it scared hell out of him and he jumped out of the car and came flying back to the clubhouse—he was a sprinter and he was really moving. George just looked at him and said, "Okay, John, six laps."

Originally I had signed with the Bears only for the two tours. I hadn't given much thought to playing for them after that. My destiny, so to speak, was in Charlie Pyle's hands in 1925. So when it was all over I went with the AFL, the new pro league. Charlie started that league himself, got it all organized. I signed with the team in New York, the Yankees, which played in Yankee Stadium. There were teams in many cities. Joey Sternaman left the Bears, too, and started a team in Chicago and called it the Bulls. The league actually drew pretty well, and in the beginning gave a scare to a lot of the NFL owners. But after a year it had gone downhill and Charlie wanted out and when that happened it sort of fell apart. What actually happened then was that the two leagues consolidated, or I guess I should say that what was worthwhile in the AFL was absorbed into the NFL.

It was while I was playing in New York that I hurt my knee. The Yankees became part of the NFL in 1927 and we were playing in a game against, of all teams, the Chicago Bears at Wrigley Field. I had my cleat dug into the ground and it was a kind of wet day and somebody fell over my knee. It was nothing deliberate, just one of those things. I was hit from the side by somebody and boom, out went the knee. Knees and shoulders, those are the two places a ballplayer got hurt the most seriously in those days. I got it in both places and have the aches to prove it. But the knee injury that day in Chicago, it was by far the worst.

After that injury, I came back, but I could never do again what I'd been able to before. I was just an ordinary back after that, the moves were gone forever. I wore a brace with steel hinges on both sides. The injury not only slowed me down but I couldn't make the turns anymore. In other words, I became a straight runner, one who doesn't try to get away from tacklers but instead just opts to run into them. And even if a player's knee gets well, he never gets well up in the head. He always protects it. I know I did. And as a result you are never the same runner again.

I was out of football for a year after the injury. I thought I'd never play again. But George Halas talked to me about it. "Why don't you get yourself up and in shape and give it a try again?" he asked. I decided I would and it worked out all right. I guess I was about seventy percent of the football player I'd been but I worked on playing defense and that became a strong point with me. The secret of offense is pulling the defense out of position and I worked hard so that never, or at least seldom, would happen to me. I stayed where I was supposed to, and I was a good tackler. I played for the Bears for six years after my knee went out, and we did pretty well, won a couple of championships.

In 1934, I decided it was finally time to get out of the game. Actually for a year I knew it was time. Every football player knows when his time is up. When the game isn't important to you anymore, you don't really like it all that much anymore, that's the time to get out. I got out when it started to be a drudge. I didn't like to practice anymore. It was a much bigger labor than it had been. The things I'd been able to do, I simply couldn't do anymore. It was during a game against the New York Giants that year when I took a handoff and there was a big hole. I got into the open field, but I was caught from behind by a lineman. I realized before I'd reached midfield that I was through. My legs kept getting heavier and heavier. I knew I'd never reach the end zone, but I knew I'd reached the end.

So, I went to George Halas and told him, "This is my last year," and that was it. I stayed around with the Bears for three years as an assistant coach, but I didn't really like that role and was glad to get out of it. George and I parted good friends, just like we'd always been since 1925 when we first met in that hotel in Chicago with Charlie Pyle.

I did stay with the game as an announcer and commentator for ten years, though, and I did enjoy that. I never lost my desire for watching the game. I worked with Bob Elson in Chicago for a long time on radio. And I was with Lindsay Nelson on national television. I had my own show after the Bear games in Chicago.

All in all it was a great sport to be involved with. I hope the players today get as much out of it as I did.

# *Running for His Life*

George Trafton, center for the Chicago Bears from 1920 through 1932 and notorious on-the-field ruffian, was less than popular in Rock Island, Illinois, when that city fielded an NFL team, the Independents, in the early 1920s. During one particular game in 1920, a number of the Rock Island players had to leave the game with assorted injuries after encounters with Trafton. The crowd, already angry, became enraged when Independent fullback Fred Chicken joined the casualty list as he tried to race around end and out of Trafton's reach.

"I tackled him right on the sideline," Trafton said. "There was a fence close to the field, and after I hit Chicken he spun up against a fence post and broke his leg. After that the fans were really on me." An understatement, to say the least. At the end of the game, they chased him out of the stadium and down the street under a shower of rocks, empty bottles, and other lethal objects at hand that were throwable. Dutch Sternaman, a halfback and half-owner of the Bears, tried to pick him up in a taxicab, but the pursuers were too close. Trafton finally managed to escape with the help of a passing motorist.

The next time that the Bears appeared in Rock Island, the game was again an especially physical one, and the crowd grew almost as ornery as it had the time before. When this game ended and George Halas was handed seven thousand dollars in cash—the Bears' share of the gate receipts—he gave the money over to Trafton for safekeeping. "I knew that if trouble came," Halas said, "I'd be running only for the seven thousand dollars. Trafton would be running for his life."

## *Debaucheries*

Amos Alonzo Stagg, legendary coach and athletic director at the University of Chicago, was not a big fan of professional football, as evidenced by this written statement he gave to the nation's press in 1923:

"It seems like a matter of little consequence for one to attend the Sunday professional football games—nothing more than attending any Sunday event—but it has a deeper meaning than you realize, possibly a vital meaning to college football. . . .

"For years, the colleges have been waging a bitter warfare against the insidious forces of the gambling public and alumni and against overzealous and shortsighted friends, inside and out, and also not infrequently against crooked coaches and managers, who have been anxious to win at any cost. . . . And now comes along another serious menace, possibly greater than all others, *viz.* Sunday professional football.

"Under the guise of fair play but countenancing rank dishonesty in playing men under assumed names, scores of professional teams have sprung up in the last two or three years, most of them on a salary basis of some kind. These teams are bidding hard for college players in order to capitalize not only on their ability but also and mostly on the name of the college they come from and in many cases the noised abroad mystery of their presence. The well-known Carlinville and Taylorville incident of 1921 is likely to be repeated in essence on different occasions this Fall. There is nothing that a bunch of gamblers will not do for their purpose and quite often they carry along with them the support of a thoughtless group of businessmen and well-meaning citizens.

"Cases of the debauching of high school boys not infrequently have come to notice. Also recently one of the well-known Sunday professional teams on which several men are said to be regularly playing under assumed names employed a well-known conference official who officiated under an assumed name. . . .

"To cooperate with Sunday professional football games is to cooperate with forces which are destructive of the finest elements of interscholastic and intercollegiate football and to add to the heavy burden of the schools and colleges in preserving it in its ennobling worth."

# 3

# *Johnny Blood*

Johnny Blood, *aka* McNally, seventy-nine years old in 1983, arrived at a brunch honoring the twentieth anniversary of the Pro Football Hall of Fame in Canton, Ohio, a coat-and-tie affair, wearing a T-shirt with the name Duluth Eskimos emblazoned across the front. He was an honored guest, having been inducted into the Hall as a charter member in 1963. He said he was wearing the T-shirt to honor his old pal Ernie Nevers, now deceased, with whom he had shared backfield duties at Duluth back in 1926 and 1927.

Besides Duluth, Johnny Blood played for such NFL teams as the Milwaukee Badgers, Pottsville Maroons, Green Bay Packers, and the Pittsburgh Pirates and Steelers. A fleet runner and free spirit, he was admired for his speed, elusiveness, and great pass-catching abilities. In his fifteen years as a pro, he scored thirty-seven touchdowns and accounted for 224 points, and he led the league in touchdown pass receptions in both 1930 and 1931.

His reputation off the field was even larger, and if there were a rogue's Hall of Fame he surely would be a charter member of that, too. One writer of the time referred to the mercurial Blood as "a Peter Pan who would never shed his eternal youth." Johnny Blood broke as many training rules as he did tackles, and ignored team curfews just as he did Prohibition. His carousals, antics, and insatiable appetite for life provided an endless stream of amusing and ribald stories throughout the NFL circuit from the mid-1920s through the 1930s.

But Johnny Blood was not merely a roisterer, he was also a highly intelligent, well-read young man and a world traveler. After packing in his football togs, he spent the war years in the Army Air Corps in the China-Burma-India theater of operations. Before settling down to a serious business career, he was a football coach, college instructor, and an unsuccessful candidate for sheriff in St. Croix County, Wisconsin, where, when asked what his chief reform would be, he answered, "Honest wrestling." During those years, he also worked as a typesetter, brickmaker, bartender, bouncer, cryptographer, hotel desk clerk, and seaman, among other things.

And Johnny Blood was as well-liked by the football players he ran with and continually entertained as he was by the chorus girls he dated and also entertained.

**M**y first lesson in playing football, my first experience was in an old child's game in Wisconsin called "Run, Run, Forward." We played it in the town of New Richmond up there where I was raised. There was a lot of tackling, that sort of thing. This was back around 1910. I was very young when I got into it.

Starting when I got to kindergarten, I went around with boys who were always two or three years older than I was, played with them and tried to compete in their kinds of games. I wasn't as physically developed as they were and consequently got knocked around a lot. No one ever considered that I would wind up being an athlete back then.

I got out of high school at the age of fourteen, my mother had kind of pushed me through it fast, and I never played a game of any kind in high school, no sport at all. I'd graduated but then I spent another year, sort of postgraduate high school, that was a first up there. After that, I went to a teacher's college called River Falls Normal. I don't know why they sent *me* to a normal school. The truth of it, I suppose, was because my mother had gone there in the 1890s. Anyway, I went there but I didn't last too long, went AWOL from this River Falls Normal, a dropout. I think I went on a little spree of some sort and just forgot to go back there. My father then took me to his school, where he had gone in 1895, called St. John's University. It was in Minnesota and there were only a couple hundred of us there but they called it a university anyway. I was only 16 when I went up to Collegeville, where St. John's was, out west a ways of Minneapolis. It was both a monastery and a school, very strict school. I'm not sure it was ready for me, but still I stayed there for three years, somewhat amazing when you think about it.

My father hadn't lasted that long. He'd gotten thrown out in 1895. It had to do with him being a master spitter, tobacco, that is. You see, he had come from a small farm in Wisconsin, and they were all Irish immigrants around there and there wasn't much for them to do, no organized games or sports. So he mastered the art of spitting accurately, and this you know leads to a well-known sport. Well, one day my father was sitting inside a classroom, it must have been in the spring, and was spitting out a window. He and another student were having a little contest. This is a fact, I wouldn't kid you, they were trying to spit at flies that were going by. They both missed, he later told me, but he claimed that he came the closest. Some consolation anyway. Well, as it turned out, a prefect was walking along outside, just below the window, unknown to them, and a big splat of this tobacco juice landed on the prefect. So the next day at lunch, in the lunch hall, the abbott got up and said, "We know who did this dastardly act yesterday and if he'll stand up and admit to it, we will consider his case." Nobody stood up, of course. And they did in fact know it was my father, something like it had happened before, I think. So they kicked him out, but he still brought me there.

At St. John's I played basketball and was on the track team, and that's also where I played my first game of football. It happened this way. One day I was standing at the bulletin board, I guess I was seventeen by then, and a guy came up and said he drew me in the draft. At the time, I didn't know what the hell he was talking about. What they had were different football teams on the campus and that's how each got their material, a draft. It was really a kind of intramural league. So I said, "Is that so? How did you happen to pick me?" This guy said he had seen me running around the track one day, thought I was fast, and that maybe I might be pretty good at running with a football. So I said all right, and, well, I was pretty much an immediate success on a very small football team. As I recall, our team's name was the Cat's Pajamas.

As I said, I was a runt as a kid, but by the time I got into St. John's I'd grown up to be a spike. I suppose I never got to be any heavier than 165 pounds while I was there, but I'd been toughened up by working on the farm there in Wisconsin. I still worked there in the summers while I was going to St. John's. And also I was about the fastest guy around. Later, when I got playing for the pros, I was up around 185 or 190, just about right for a guy 6 feet 1 inch.

After three years there, I left of my own accord again. I guess I wanted the bigger time, so I went down to Notre Dame and enrolled there. But I didn't last the year, got in some trouble around St. Patrick's Day, some pretty good celebrating for the saintly Irishman, and then went AWOL. They didn't take to it that well and, as I used to call it, I became a double-dipped dropout at Notre Dame. I'd tried out for the football team while I was there. Knute Rockne was coaching and they had the "Four Horsemen" on the varsity that year. I ended up on the freshman team because it was my first year of eligibility, but I didn't do anything there. I always like to say that my one contribution to Notre Dame football was that I used to write Harry Stuhldreyer's English poetry papers for him.

That kind of ended my career as a student. After it, I went to work for a newspaper in Minneapolis, and they put me in the printing end of it. It didn't pay very much and I was quick to find out it was not my kind of job. I'd also gotten one of my buddies from St. John's, Ralph Hanson, a job there. Around that time, I'd heard that there was a way to pick up some extra money by playing in a semipro city league in the Minneapolis/ St. Paul area. Ralph had played football with me at St. John's and so we thought we might be able to pick up a little extra dough by playing football, something we both liked anyway.

At the time, I was thinking that maybe one of those days I might be going back to Notre Dame, in the unlikely event they'd have me, but still it was a possibility. And if I did, I'd want to play football there. I also knew we might play some games out of state with that Minneapolis team. So I said to Ralph, "I still have some eligibility left and I don't want to lose it. So when we go out for this team, let's use some fake names and that way we can protect our amateur standing." He agreed.

I used to get around town on my own motorcycle then, and so we both hopped on it and headed out to where this team practiced, some playground in back of a factory. On the way there, we passed a movie theater on Hennepin Avenue and up on the marquee I saw the name of the movie that was playing, *Blood and Sand* with Rudolph Valentino. Ralph was behind me on the motorcycle and I turned my head and shouted, "That's it. I'll be Blood and you be Sand." And so we went to the practice, tried out, and made the team, Johnny Blood and Ralph Sand. And, of course, I kept it as a football name from that time on.

I got a nickname too, "the Vagabond Halfback," which came about in a rather amusing way. In my childhood, back in New Richmond, Wisconsin, I was enchanted by railroads. In the town, two sets of tracks crossed, one going north and south and the other east and west, so there were trains going through both ways all the time. Freight trains and passenger trains, that was the way you moved most things in those days. And I would hear this loooong whistle, very plaintive and compelling; it was very romantic to a child. Far away places, dreams, new worlds, all that kind of thing. Maybe I'm still childish, but I'm still enchanted with the sounds of railroads.

Anyway, in those days, we used to play all kinds of games with the railroads. Hop a freight train and ride it down to Hudson or to other towns and then catch another train back. It was just part of growing up in a small town in Wisconsin back then. Hitching rides on these trains was a sport to all of us. We got to know the engineers, we knew a lot of the conductors on the passenger trains, and the workers on the freight trains.

Much later, when I was playing football at Green Bay, I decided to use the talents I'd gained with the railroads as a child. We had won the championship three years running: 1929, '30, and '31. Still, it was the Depression and we didn't get much money from playing football so most of us worked in the offseason at whatever jobs we could find. I was lucky because we were pretty well off, the family, that is, and as a result were pretty strong in New Richmond. Therefore, I was able to get a job there at a mill in the offseason. Well, when I got ready to go back to Green Bay for the 1932 season, I thought I'd save myself a little money, everybody worried about it in those days. To get there, I had to take the train and so I decided to do it the way I had as a kid. We might have been the NFL champs and I had a decent job in the offseason but I never had any money then. I spent it as fast as I got it.

Well, the Soo Line Railroad took you over to a junction where you could get another train that would take you to Green Bay. You see, New Richmond is on the western side of the state and Green Bay is just about as far east as you can get in Wisconsin. The first train was cheap, so I rode as a passenger on it. But before boarding it, I had the stationmaster wire ahead to hold the second train, the Green Bay & Western it was, for a passenger. The junction was in Chippewa Falls, as I recall, about thirty miles away. Anyway, the telegram was sent to hold the train for a passenger, which you could do in those days. When somebody needed to make a connection, they would hold a train if the wait wouldn't be too long.

So I rode the Soo to Chippewa Falls, got off, and sure enough there was the Green Bay & Western waiting for its passenger. I ran hippity-clippity down the siding and jumped on it, in the baggage car, that is. Well, they waited for their customer who'd sent the telegram but, of course, he never showed up, and so they finally went on. After a couple of stations, the door to the baggage car was slid open and a guy was staring at me, one of the railroad men. He did a kind of double take and then said, "Hey, aren't you Johnny Blood?" We were pretty well known in the state because practically everyone in all those towns were great Green Bay fans and we'd been the champs three years running.

"Yeah, sure am," I said.

"Well, come on down," he said. "Come on up front."

The upshot is that he took me up with the engineer and gave me a cup of coffee and a ham sandwich, shared his stuff with me. They treated me royally and I got to Green Bay for nothing.

I had a good friend down in Milwaukee, a writer for the newspaper there, who came up to Green Bay for all the ballgames. I told him the story and he said he wanted to write about it for his paper. "That's great," he said. "We'll call it 'The Hobo Halfback, Riding the Rails.'"

I said, "I don't know about that, 'hobo' is not really my style." I thought about it for a minute, then said, "Why don't we say 'The Vaga-bond Halfback.' It has a little more class." He agreed, and so he started referring to me in his columns as the Vagabond Halfback. Other writers picked it up and it stuck for a long time.

I didn't go directly to Green Bay as a pro, however. After that semi-pro team in Minneapolis, I'd built myself a little reputation as a good runner. One day, while I was working at the newspaper in Minneapolis, these two pro football players—I didn't know them—came in and asked for me. They said they were with a team in Ironwood, Michigan, which is up north on the border line between Wisconsin and the Michigan penin-sula, way north. They said they'd pay me sixty dollars a game if I played halfback which sounded all right to me at the time. So I went. We played a few games up there. But one of the guys who had talked to me had played some games for the pro team in Milwaukee the year before. The team was named the Badgers and they were in the NFL, a big step above what we were playing in. Well, I did quite well up in Ironwood in those few games and the next thing I knew I got an offer to come down and play for Milwaukee, in fact the other two guys did, too. There was more money in it as well, so, of course, we went down there and played the 1925 season with the Badgers.

That was the same year that Red Grange came into the pros, at the end of it, that is. I played against him for the first time after the season, on that tour he and C. C. Pyle put together with the Chicago Bears. It was an exhibition game out in California. I got myself out there. It was the beginning of a lot of travel for me.

With the Milwaukee Badgers, we didn't travel all that much, not far anyway. I played five or six games that first year for them and I think we

Volatile both on and off the field, great runner and receiver and classic roisterer Johnny Blood was one of early football's most memorable players and personalities. During his fifteen-year NFL career (1925–39), the itinerant Blood played for the Milwaukee Badgers, Duluth Eskimos, Pottsville Maroons, Green Bay Packers, and Pittsburgh Pirates and Steelers. He served as head coach as well during the last three years of his career at Pittsburgh. *(Pro Football Hall of Fame)*

went to Steubenville, Ohio, Green Bay, Rock Island in Illinois, and that was about it. I played wingback that year and our team was pretty awful. We lost all the games that we played. There were twenty teams in the league that year, a lot of them from small towns like Hammond, Indiana and Duluth, Minnesota and Canton, Ohio. The big teams were from Chicago, the Bears and the Cardinals.

The next year, 1926, I was twenty-one years old and I signed with the Duluth Eskimos. It is one of my great memories because it was there that I got to play with Ernie Nevers, who was the star. No, he was the *team*. Ernie was a fine man, just out of college that year. He'd starred out at Stanford and he brought to Duluth the offense that Pop Warner had used so successfully out there, the double wingback with a blocking back and a fullback. The fullback was everything in that offense, and the fullback was Ernie Nevers. It was an offense especially designed for him. He received the ball from the center and he called the plays, and Ernie was also the coach. I admired and respected him. He was a fiery kind of guy, a different specimen really, and we had a pretty good football team up there, considering it was Duluth and not Chicago or New York. The "Iron Men from the North" is what Grantland Rice called us.

The Eskimos were actually run by a little Norwegian guy who had inherited the team from his father. I guess the guy had gone to high school with Ernie Nevers and looked on him as his hero. His father, who died, had a little money, too, and the guy inherited it which enabled him to sign up Ernie. The Duluth team he'd inherited had been a volunteer team prior to that, made up of guys who lived and worked in the iron range up there. Just like Pottsville, Pennsylvania, they had an iron industry and these guys who played worked there. They weren't necessarily very good football players, but they were rugged and strong, a different breed.

The Duluth club folded up after 1927 and a lot of us went over to the Pottsville Maroons, myself and Walt Kiesling among them. Walt was a great lineman. Nevers dropped out of football for a year. I think he went back to help Pop Warner coach out at Stanford. But then he came back to play with the Chicago Cardinals and was all-Pro, and, of course, scored that forty points all by himself in one game. No one has ever broken that record—single-handed he scored forty points in a game, that's hard to beat.

It was a game of running and tackling at that point, in the 1920s. In those days, the passing game hadn't been developed. I was a legitimate halfback, running back, and I played both right and left halfback, according to the way we shifted. We used alternating halfbacks most of the time. By that I mean the halfback would line up to the left on one play and the right the next. I played sixty minutes of every game and it was tough. You had to pace yourself. It was a primitive game, anybody who played it then will tell you that. The equipment, what there was of it, wasn't too good. The pay was worse. In Duluth I think I got $70 or $75 a game, less if we lost. Nevers, though, got $15,000 for the season, which was very big money in 1926. He and Red Grange were the big attractions then and they were the only two who got big money out of it.

I only played on the Pottsville team for one year, 1928. The great Pete Henry was our coach there and the mainstay of our line. He was just a huge butterball but, my, how he could play football. But as a team we were a pretty sorry group. Lost most of our games, but we did surprise Green Bay and clobbered them and they were one of the top teams in the league that year.

It was the next year that I went with the Packers. The Vagabond Halfback: it was my fourth team in five years. We had a wonderful team, though, won the title the first three years I was in Green Bay. We had Cal Hubbard and Mike Michalske in the line and Red Dunn and Verne Lewellen in the backfield with me. After them came Clarke Hinkle and Arnie Herber. Curly Lambeau, of course, was our coach, had been since they first got a pro team up there. I got along pretty well with Curly, for a while anyway. I was one of the only ones who did, most didn't like him at all. But for the first three or four years he put up with me and my antics. I think I was one of the few who could get the best of him, he had a hard time keeping up with me.

Actually, in the long run, I guess I didn't get along so well because he finally fired me. On paper I was sold to the Pittsburgh team but he really fired me. It came after several of us had been out one night, myself and a couple of other players. We were out all night as a matter of fact. Well, I went directly to practice in the morning, got all suited up. Lambeau was looking at me kind of funny as I remember. Anyway, I tried to punt the ball, missed it, and fell flat on my ass. Lambeau told me to get the hell off the field and after practice was over he told me he was getting rid of me.

I came back to Green Bay a year later and Lambeau took me back but we never got along very well after that.

There were a lot of good times in Green Bay, it was a swell town in those days. We were kind of riding on top of the world, champs, well-known. I have a lot of memories from up there. One in particular I'll always remember. I was known to kid around a lot, do the unexpected, so to speak. It was back around 1930, one of the years we won a championship. Well, we were all celebrating on the train on our way back to Green Bay. And I was a notorious celebrator.

After a while, we began horsing around and I started throwing some wet napkins at Lavie Dilweg. He was one of our ends, a big, tall, strong boy. He didn't like it a real lot and told me to stop. Of course, I didn't and he finally got up after me. Well, I took off down the aisle and he was chugging along trying to get his big hands on me. We'd been up near the front of the train, in the club car, and we just went racing through car after car, the people looking up wondering what the hell was going on.

I kept razzing him all the way. And he kept coming. Well, when we got to the last car, he thought he had me, but I went out onto the rear platform. He kind of yelled in triumph as he came through the door. But I stepped up on the back railing and pulled myself up onto the roof of the train. I looked back down and you should have seen the look on his face. He just stared up in disbelief. Then I said, "So long," and ran on back up the train, on the roof, jumping from car to car as I went.

Dilweg didn't follow me, of course. He had better sense than that. I went on past the club car, all the way to the engineer's cab. I surprised the hell out of him and the fireman when I climbed down from the roof—we were moving pretty fast at the time. I rode with them into town, it was only about another 15 miles, and they were nice, kind of got a kick out of it, I think. As I said, I've always had this thing for trains. They bring something out in me.

Another season in Green Bay I held out. That was kind of unheard of in those days. I was underpaid for the work I was doing, I felt. After all, I had made all-Pro and I was still making less than many of the other guys on our team. Lambeau, I knew, always felt that I was a soft touch, that money didn't mean all that much to me. He thought I wouldn't protest, maybe I was too easygoing. So this one year I decided to hold out. The Packers lost the first two games of the season and then they called me back. I went to the board of directors of the Packers, however, not Lambeau, and said, "I made all-Pro last year and I'm underpaid here." They knew all that, I found out, and so they told Curly to hire me back. Well, he had to, but I knew he'd be watching me all the time after that.

Lambeau had used me as a signal-caller before and he put me back in to do that after I held out. I got results for him. And he told somebody how much it surprised him because he could not believe that a character like me, who seemed to be so reckless, could call signals and get good results on the field for him.

In Don Hutson's second year with the Packers, 1936, he established himself as a fabulous receiver. We were now a good passing team, the best in the league. With Hutson and myself as receivers and Arnie Herber throwing, we were a real scoring threat. And, of course, we had Clarke Hinkle running, one of the very best in the game then. We came down to a very important game against the Detroit Lions late in the season, a truly crucial one. I was still calling the plays and signals then and Lambeau came up to me before the game. "We're going to surprise them," he said.

"Good," I said. I always believed in surprises on the football field. Trick plays, surprises, they can turn a game around.

But this wasn't that at all. Remember, we had the best passing attack in football at that time. It was our old ace in the hole. At the same time, the Lions had the best running attack. They had Dutch Clark and Ace Gutowsky and Glenn Presnell, all great threats. Dutch was one of the best ever. I remember one time when he was trying to run the ball out of the end zone and it looked for sure like we were going to tackle him for a safety. The entire left side of our line was surging in on him and he ran right at them, hooked his arm around the goalpost, swung himself around and headed off to the other side and made maybe 10 or 15 yards instead of being caught behind the goal line.

Lambeau's surprise wasn't anything tricky. "The surprise plan is," he said, "we're going to run the ball at them all day." I couldn't believe it. Before the game, he told the rest of the team. No one said anything; he was the coach, after all. But we all thought it was crazy. "Run it. Run them to death," he said. And that was that.

We had this play which worked well for us so often. It was a kind of option where we would fake a handoff to Hinkle and draw the defenders because he was such a threat, and then Herber would throw a pass to myself or Hutson. I brought it up to Lambeau and he said, "Fine, but don't pass. Just give it to Hinkle and let him run it at them."

Well, we got out there and after about five minutes I knew we were not going to win that ballgame. There was no way we were going to beat Detroit by running the ball. So I called a pass, called two or three passes in a row. Lambeau pulled me out of the game and I sat on the bench. Meanwhile, Detroit was doing what they always could do so well against us: marching, marching, marching. Dutch Clark was having a fine day for himself. They'd move the ball and we couldn't. After a while, Lambeau came over to me on the bench and said, "If we lose this game, you are responsible."

I didn't say anything but I was burned up over it. We were actually leading by a point when he pulled me out even though they had been controlling the game. I said to myself, "How could I lose the ballgame sitting on the bench. We're ahead and I'm out of the game, but if we lose it's my fault. Crazy!"

When Curly finally put me back in the game we were losing by a couple of points. There was about five minutes to go and we had the ball. He looked at me on the bench and said, "Get in there." He didn't tell me not to pass, but he didn't rescind the no-passing order either. From his look I knew he still wanted to run the ball.

The ball was on our 40 yard line or thereabouts. Well, I ran out there, took a look at their defense and knew they were laying for a run. After all, that's what we'd been doing all afternoon. I said, "By God I'm going to try it." I called the option play but told Arnie Herber, our passer, to zoom it. That meant to fake it to Hinkle and let it fly to Hutson or myself. Arnie looked at me kind of funny, "Zoom it?" he said. I shook my head and when I did I knew my job was really on the line. Anyway, Hutson lined up on one flank and I was spread out on the other. When the ball was snapped we took off for the goal line like a pair of rabbits. I was well covered. That surprised me. There were two Detroit defenders hounding me. I thought, oh boy, this is it, especially when I saw the ball coming toward us. All three of us went up for it and somehow I got my hands on it and they bounced off each other and fell down. I scampered off for the end zone. I thought as I stepped across the goal line that if I didn't have the ball I wouldn't have had a job either. Well, it worked and we won the ballgame. That was in 1936 and we won the championship that year but if we hadn't won that game—it was the next to last of the season—we might not have won the title. After the game, Curly never mentioned the pass. I didn't mention it to him either.

I was reckless, they said, on the football field. Reckless in a lot of things, I guess. I liked to have a good time back then: women, travel, a little drinking, loved to spend money. I had a lot of experiences. I was very uninhibited, that way all my life, even as a little kid. I was kind of split between my father and mother. They were a loving couple and treated me very well. But they were very different personalities, each had different goals. And I was usually caught in the middle. One time, when I was about three or four, and I got this from people who remembered it, my parents had a little game they played with me. They had three daughters who were older and now they had a son, which they had both wanted. I happened to be a responsive type of little kid, so they tell me.

Anyway, they had this game. We had a pretty good size living room and parlor and one of my parents would get at one end and the other at the other end, maybe twenty-five or thirty feet apart. They would put me in the middle and say, "Which one do you love the most? Come to the one you love best." Well, I didn't know which one I loved the most. I had an aunt, who was older than my parents and she was there watching this one day and she said to them, I learned later, "You ought not to play that game. You're shaking the kid up." I'd start toward one, you see, and then I'd start back toward the other. This was my fear. I had an emotional loyalty to both of them, but it was separate because each was different. My mother was a culture vulture, she believed in civilization and people and poetry. Whereas my father was a witty Irishman and interested in things more close to the earth. My mother would teach me Shakespeare and my father taught me sports. So all the time I was in the middle. Sometimes I would try to go with my mother, other times I would go with my father, and sometimes one would work on me and sometimes the other. I was a semisplit personality.

I guess we're all that way a little. Even Curly Lambeau. I remember back in 1963 when we were both elected to the Hall of Fame. I was out in California at the time, when we heard about it, down in Palm Springs, I believe it was. Curly had a home in California, too, and so I went up to see him in Los Angeles. I took him to a place for dinner and we wound up at the Palmer Hotel. Well, Curly was out with me and so I kind of guided things. In this place, in the Palmer, Chubby Checker was entertaining. He was there doing the twist, when it first came out. Chubby put on a demonstration and then the nightclubbers got to do it. I didn't get up, but out there on the floor was Curly, doing the twist. What a spectacle. Here was the guy who used to frown on me doing all that kind of stuff, and here I was watching him from the sideline.

I guess Curly was a human guy after all. He was not perfect, not an angel. But there weren't many angels in the pro league back then. I met a lot of good men there who had an angelic side and a devilish side. I'm sure a lot of them would say the same about me.

## Dealing with Fats Henry

Arthur Daley once told this story when writing about players who had earned their way into the Pro Football Hall of Fame, which is located today in Canton, Ohio. It gives a pretty good idea of what Wilbur

Pete "Fats" Henry, the six-foot, 250-plus-pound tackle who played for the Canton Bulldogs, New York Giants, and Pottsville Maroons in the 1920s, was like on the football field:

The Pottsville Maroons pleaded with Charlie Berry [who later became a famous American League umpire] to join them as soon as the baseball season ended. He did. In the first pro game of his career he had to face the Canton Bulldogs in general and Fats Henry in particular. As an end, Berry had to block Henry.

"It was like bouncing off a rubber ball," he later described it. "I never budged him once. After five minutes I felt as though I'd just finished a full sixty-minute game."

Pottsville took command early. At quarterback for the Maroons was Jack Ernst, once a Berry teammate at Lafayette College. He suddenly remembered that Berry had been an expert field goal kicker and might welcome some practice.

"Like to try a field goal, Charlie?" he asked.

"I sure would," said the weary Charlie. "I'll be thankful for anything that will get me away from Henry for even one play."

The field goal try never got higher than a table.

"Like to try another?" asked Ernst later on.

"Just keep me away from Henry," said Charlie.

Again he barely got it off the ground. . . . [Meanwhile] Henry continued to teach Berry the considerable difference between college and pro ball. Charlie was not enjoying it. And Ernst had ceased to be cooperative in offering respites. They got in a huddle.

"Hey, Jack," said Berry, "let me try once more. This time I'll try a drop kick."

The teams lined up. Berry took position and found himself looking into the eyes of his tormentor, Henry. The jolly Pete smiled at him and then spoke to his Canton teammates.

"Duck fellows," he shouted, "he's kicking again."

## *On Thorpe*

George Halas: To have Jim Thorpe tackle you from behind was an experience you couldn't forget. He wouldn't actually tackle you. With his great speed he'd run you down and then throw his huge body crosswise into your back. It was like having a redwood tree fall on you.

Steve Owen: I was playing for the Oklahoma All-Stars in 1923, fresh out

"Old Jim" is how he referred to himself during his pro football days, but anyone who encountered Jim Thorpe on the gridiron quickly learned that age had neither slowed nor weakened the legendary Indian. A member of the Sac and Fox tribe and a product of Carlisle Institute, Thorpe was named titular president of the NFL when it was founded in 1920. Between that date and 1928, he played for six different NFL teams: the Canton Bulldogs, Cleveland Indians, Oorang Indians, Rock Island Independents, New York Giants, and Chicago Cardinals. *(Pro Football Hall of Fame)*

of college, and we went up against a team that had Thorpe. He had lost some of his speed and power by that time, I'd been told. On the first play that I was on defense, I broke through into the backfield and charged into Thorpe, who was blocking. I shoved a hand into his face and knocked him down. On the next play I did the same thing and thought, Old Jim really has slowed down. Then on the next play I kind of ignored him and went straight for the ball carrier. Suddenly I thought the whole grandstand had fallen on me. I went down, stunned and shaken. When I finally got back up, I realized Thorpe had blocked me. He patted me on the back and said, "Always keep an eye on an old Indian!"

# 4

# Red Badgro

Morris "Red" Badgro was an exceptional athlete, lettering in football, baseball, and basketball in each of his four years at the University of Southern California. He was an all–Pacific Coast Conference selection in both football and basketball his senior year. After graduation, Badgro signed contracts in 1927 with both the New York Yankees football team, which had just been absorbed into the NFL, and the St. Louis Browns baseball team of the American League.

Football, however, is where he made his professional mark. Red Badgro was the perfectly balanced end in that age where a player was required to do more than one thing on a football field. "He could block, tackle, and catch passes equally well," his coach at the New York Giants, Steve Owen, said. "And he could do each with the best of them."

The bulk of his career, six of nine years, was spent with the Giants, a team that participated in the first three NFL championship games. With Badgro and Ray Flaherty at ends and Benny Friedman and later Harry Newman passing the ball to them, the Giants had one of the first truly effective passing games in NFL history. Red was named to three of the first four all-Pro teams ever selected (1931, 1933, 1934), and his sixteen receptions in 1934 was the league high.

Another redhead by the name of Grange said of Badgro, "Playing offense and defense equally well, he was one of the best half-dozen ends I ever saw." And Johnny Blood remembered him as "a tireless competitor, big, strong, fast, and injury-proof."

In 1981, at the age of seventy-eight, Red Badgro was formally inducted into the Pro Football Hall of Fame, with the distinction of being the oldest person ever elected to it. In the Hall, he joined teammates Steve Owen, Mel Hein, Ken Strong, and Ray Flaherty.

As a youngster I played a lot of baseball and basketball, and a few of us kids had a go at football on occasion. We played out in a cow pasture on the farm where I lived up in Washington. I always liked it as a sport but when I got to high school—I went to a pretty good size school just outside Seattle—I played mostly baseball and basketball as organized sports. I think I played maybe three games of football in the four years I was there.

I was a pretty good basketball player and for that I won a scholarship to Southern California. But I thought at the time that I was going to go somewhere and try to play football, too, whether they liked it or not. Well, in those days, it didn't really matter all that much. You could play several sports if you wanted to, and there was no problem when I talked to them at USC.

Howard Jones was the coach of the USC Trojans then and they had a wonderful football program. At the time, they and Notre Dame were two of the greatest teams in the country. This was in the mid-1920s. We played some very good football out there on the Coast. California had a good team. So did Stanford. They had Ernie Nevers then, and he was one of the all-time greats.

I have a particular memory of him out there. One year we would have gone to the Rose Bowl if it weren't for him. Nevers was punting out of his own end zone. We were losing, 13–12, late in the game and a safety would win it for us. Well, we put on quite a rush and Jeff Cravath, our center, blocked Ernie's kick. I was right alongside him and crazily the ball bounced back up into Nevers' hands. If either Jeff or I had come up with the ball we would have gone to the Rose Bowl. But Ernie had it and ran the ball out for a first down.

Another wonderful player out there at that time was Mort Kaer, who was the first all-American from Southern California. He was our quarterback and I was at end. We got some attention because we had such a good team. Care was the best-known of our players, and as a result a number of pro scouts came out to talk with us.

I was thinking mostly about playing professional baseball when my college days would be over. And I had a couple of offers. I still had a couple of units to go at USC when one day I bumped into a fraternity brother of mine who had also been a starter on our football team. He was leaving the frat house with a suitcase and told me he was going out east to join Red Grange's New York Yankees. He asked me if I wanted to play pro football. I told him I hadn't really thought about it, baseball was what I had in mind. I also said I probably wouldn't mind playing it, however. Well, he said when he got to New York he would make a pitch for me. "You'll hear from me in a couple of days," he said. "That is, if they haven't signed up all their ends yet." And I got the call in a couple of days and pretty soon I was on the train going from L.A. to New York.

The Yankees were owned by C. C. Pyle and I think Grange had part of it as well. They had been in the league Pyle started, the first American Football League the year before, 1926. When that league went broke and folded up, the Yankees were brought into the NFL. We were a road team for the most part. I believe we played thirteen games away and only three in New York City. The Giants were there, already well-established and playing at the Polo Grounds. When we did stay at home, we played in Yankee Stadium. We had a pretty good team. We had Grange, of course, but he got his knee pretty badly hurt after about four games. We also had Eddie Tryon, who was a good running back. He had been an all-American at Colgate. I got to start at one end and Ray Flaherty was at the other. We also had Mike Michalske, a great lineman, and Wild Bill Kelly, who was our passer.

The Yankees broke up after the 1928 season. When they did, many of the fellows went to Green Bay, some went to the Bears, and a few to the Giants. I was playing baseball at the time, too, with the St. Louis Browns in the American League, and I thought maybe I'd just concentrate on that. I felt if I could hit pretty well and really make it in baseball, well that would take care of it. But I didn't hit the ball as well as I thought I would. I wasn't on the starting lineup. So after two years I decided that I'd go back to football. I qualified as a free agent and Steve Owen, who was the head coach of the New York Giants then, came down to Houston where I was playing in the Texas League at the time, and asked if I'd like to come to the Giants. I said sure. And so I spent the next six years in New York, actually seven because I spent one year with the Brooklyn Dodgers—the football team, not the baseball Dodgers—after being with the Giants. What happened was that when I quit in 1936 the Giant management didn't think I'd ever play again so they didn't keep their ownership of me. I'd left them to go up and coach and play for a team in Syracuse, New York, in the American Football League. I got up there and played in two games and then the guy who owned it went broke and couldn't even pay me a week's salary. So I said to heck with it and left and went back to New York City. I found out that the Brooklyn

Dodgers, Dan Topping's team, had picked up my option, and so I went over there and played one more year.

Tim Mara signed me to my first contract with the Giants. He was a good owner, I never had any trouble with him or any owner for that matter. I signed up to play for just so much and that was it. At that time, we didn't consider what the other fellow got. If he made five hundred dollars a game or a thousand or only two, we didn't care. It was a job, you signed for so much and were happy you were employed. But the money sure wasn't very good in those days. I got a hundred and fifty a game when I first signed with the Giants. I didn't exactly get rich on that salary.

In that time of the Depression, a player needed to work in the off-season, too, and I did as much as I could, but it was hard to pick up a job. Times were tough for everybody.

Dr. Harry March, a grand old fellow, was running the Giants for Tim Mara when I came to them in 1930. One thing I'll never forget about him. I got my chin cut open in practice one day and I needed eleven stitches to close it up. I just went by his office and he didn't have any of his medical equipment with him, so he got a plain needle and sewing thread out of his drawer and sewed up my chin. He liked football more than the practice of medicine, I believe.

We only had about twenty or twenty-two players on the team in those days. You had to play offense and defense, and the schedule wasn't always like it is today. Sometimes we would play as many as four games in eight days, what with the barnstorming and exhibitions and that sort of thing.

I was fortunate to latch onto a very good team. In 1930, we had Benny Friedman at tailback. We also had Steve Owen in the line; he didn't take over full duties as head coach until the following year. We ran second to the Green Bay Packers, as I recall. They had Johnny Blood in his prime and Red Dunn and Cal Hubbard and Lavie Dilweg. That was also the year we played the special exhibition game at the end of the season against Knute Rockne's all-star team of former Notre Dame players. They had the Four Horsemen there and Hunk Anderson and a raft of others. We walloped them pretty good, though. There was a huge crowd for it and the game earned over $100,000 for charity.

We played in the first NFL championship game in 1933. That year we had Ken Strong, probably one of the best fullbacks and kickers ever to play the game. And there was Harry Newman, a fine passer. Ray Flaherty and I were at the ends, and in the line we had Mel Hein and the

One of the game's finest all-around ends in the late 1920s and early '30s, Red Badgro could tackle and block as well as he could snare passes. The redhead played two years for the New York Yankees, six for the New York Giants, and one for the Brooklyn Dodgers. *(Pro Football Hall of Fame)*

Owens, Steve and Bill, although Steve was pretty well along in years as a player by then. I thought we were going to win that game. We were really up for the Bears. I caught a touchdown pass from Newman kind of early, and in the fourth quarter we were ahead by four or five points. But then Bronko Nagurski threw a pass to Bill Hewitt and he lateralled off to their other end, Bill Karr, and he ran it in for a touchdown.

Even after that we still had a shot at it. On the last play of the game, I caught a pass and the only person between me and the goal line was Red Grange. I planned to lateral to a teammate who was running along just behind me—it was Hein or Dale Burnett—but Grange grabbed me around the arms and upper body and I couldn't. Had I been able to, we would have won the championship. We got to the championship again the next year, but I didn't play in it because of an injury. Neither did Harry Newman. But we won it anyway, that was the game where our fellows wore sneakers in the second half. They were able to run much better on the frozen field. The Bears were a real rival.

We had some good games against the Packers in those years too. I remember a couple of incidents. One involved Clarke Hinkle, their fullback, a great runner. Well, we were playing at Green Bay and leading, 10–7. It was late in the game and we had kicked off to them. Hinkle got the ball, broke out to the side with it and had a blocker in front of him. I don't know where the rest of our team was but suddenly there was only me between him and his blocker and the end zone. I figured I had to get him some way or they would win the ballgame. The odds sure weren't with me because Hinkle was such a powerful runner. He didn't even need that blocker probably. But he had the goal line in his eyes. I don't know exactly how it happened but I held off the blocker and Hinkle ran right into him, bounced off and hurtled into my arms. We both went down and the blocker ended up on top of us. I know Clarke would love to have had that play over because probably ninety-nine times out of a hundred he would have scored. He was more surprised than I was when he found himself on the ground. Afterwards he told me he thought his blocker had tackled him.

Another situation involved Johnny Blood. This time we were playing Green Bay in New York and we were leading, 13–7. They were down on our goal line and they ran the ball three times but didn't make it. There were just seconds left and I sensed they wouldn't run at us on fourth down, the last play of the game for them. They had a play they relied on a lot in those days. It was a quick pass to Johnny Blood out in the flat, a fake to the fullback first and then out to Johnny. It would work in this instance, they thought, because there was only a yard to go and we'd be bunched up to stop Hinkle if he tried to bull it in. I still didn't think they would run it and so I kept my eye on Blood and sure enough I saw him take off for the flat. I said, "To hell with it," and I just ran across the line of scrimmage and tackled him in the backfield. When the quarterback looked up from his fake to throw the ball, all he saw was Johnny and myself on the ground. He was left standing there with the ball and no one to throw it to. Then our fellows smothered him. The referee didn't call anything and we won the game. Things like that you remember.

The Giants were a fine team all the years I was with them. The team I was with my last year, the Dodgers, weren't much of a team, however. The best memory of that season was when we played my old team, the Giants, and we were a heavy underdog. It was late in the game and we were losing, 10–7. I caught a long pass—I think it was from Bobby Wilson—30 or 35 yards and it set up a field goal which Ralph Kercheval kicked and we ended up in a 10–10 tie to everybody's surprise.

After Brooklyn, I went back to Southern Cal to get the couple of units I still needed to graduate. After that I went to Ventura Junior College and coached football, baseball, and basketball. While I was there, I was contacted by Lou Little, who used to come down from Columbia and watch the pro games when I was with the Giants. He gave me a call and wanted to know if I would like to come back east to Columbia and be his assistant football coach. I went back there and stayed in that capacity for five years. After that, it was back across the country to the west coast where I coached football at the University of Washington as an assistant for eight years. Then I went to work for the Department of Agriculture in the state of Washington. Between playing and coaching, I guess I spent about twenty-two years in football. I hold a lot of fine memories from it.

## Kicking to Grange

Red Grange made his pro football debut on Thanksgiving Day 1925, playing for the Chicago Bears against their crosstown rival, the Cardinals. The game ended in a scoreless tie. Grange not only was held to 36 yards rushing but he was unable to exercise one of his other notorious threats, returning punts.

The Cardinals' triple-threat tailback Paddy Driscoll punted many times that day, but he always kept it away from Grange, kicking either to Joey Sternaman or out of bounds. "Kicking to Grange," Driscoll said, "is like grooving one to Babe Ruth."

After the game was over, and Grange had made his uneventful debut, Driscoll stopped at the seats behind the Cardinal bench to talk to his wife. As the other players headed for the locker room, there was a lot of booing. "I hate to hear the fans boo a young man like Grange," Driscoll said. "It wasn't his fault he couldn't break one today."

"Don't feel sorry for Grange," his wife said. "It's you they're booing."

## *Show Biz*

Jimmy Conzelman, Hall of Fame halfback and heralded raconteur, often liked to recount how he had obtained the franchise of the old Detroit Panthers and tell of his somewhat unorthodox plan to promote the ballclub:

"In 1925, Joe Carr, the head of the NFL, asked me to bring pro football to Detroit. He said the franchise fee was a thousand dollars, but he'd let me have Detroit for fifty dollars. I said fine, and suddenly I was the owner, coach, and only player for the Panthers. But I got together a team and uncorked a plan to make them well known.

"My plan was to get Notre Dame's fabled Four Horsemen for the team. Not only would they play football for us, but I would work out a vaudeville act and the four of them and myself would take it on the road before and after the season. I talked to them and they were for it so I lined up some theatrical agents to work out the details.

"I was to be the piano player. Harry Stuhldreher was a pretty good singer and he was going to sing a song called "She's a Mean Job." Jim Crowley planned to do a clog dance and had a routine for a comic monologue. The problem was that Elmer Layden and Don Miller didn't have an act, so we took some time to see if we could get them to do a song or some kind of routine. Time went by and finally Layden called me up and told me he had agreed to take a job with some recreation department and to count him out. I didn't think we could make it as 'The Three Horsemen and Conzelman,' neither did the theatrical agents, and so the whole deal fell apart."

# 5

# Mel Hein

People who witnessed Mel Hein's efforts on behalf of the New York Giants in the 1930s and early 1940s knew they were watching the best center, on offense and defense, in the game. And those who knew him swore there was not a finer gentleman associated with the sport. He could never be accused of playing dirty football, like so many others who inhabited the scrimmage-line trenches along with him, nor was he a brawler; he was simply a big, fast, and incredibly talented football player.

At 6 feet 2 inches and 225 pounds, he was an especially mobile lineman, so mobile in fact that Don Hutson, the game's greatest and most elusive end of that era, claimed Hein made his life more difficult than any other player in the league. Bronko Nagurski said Hein was perhaps the surest, cleanest, and most effective tackler he ever encountered.

Mel Hein joined the Giants in 1931 and remained through the 1945 season. Extraordinarily durable, he played sixty minutes in practically every game, more than two hundred of them, and it is said that in fifteen years he never missed a game because of an injury. He has the unique distinction of being named all-Pro in *eight* consecutive seasons (1933–40). He was the team captain for ten years, during which time the Giants won seven divisional crowns and two NFL titles.

When it was rumored that Mel would retire after the 1940 season, the Giants staged a Mel Hein Day at the Polo Grounds late in the season. Mayor Fiorello LaGuardia gave a speech, and the team gave him an automobile. However, the Mara family, the team owners, talked him into coming back for a few more years. When he finally left the game as a player in 1945, the Giants retired his number, 7.

Hein did not leave football, however, and coached for the Los Angeles

Dons and the New York Yankees of the old All-American Football Conference and for the Los Angeles Rams of the NFL. After that, he spent twelve years at the University of Southern California. Later, he served as supervisor of officials for the American Football League, a post for which he was sponsored by Al Davis, with whom he had been associated at Southern Cal before Davis became general manager of the then-Oakland Raiders.

Mel Hein is a charter member of the Pro Football Hall of Fame.

I was raised in the town of Bellingham, up in northwestern Washington. It was a town that was only about fifteen miles from the Canadian border. And that's where I first played football. I played two years in grammar school there, then four years in high school.

I remember getting going in it at Lowell Grammar School, that had to be about 1920. We had uniforms and a league. It was well-organized, surprising as it might seem back then. I think we had five schools in that grammar school league. But we did not have turf fields back in those days. We played on dirt fields, with rocks and gravel. It would tear up our shoes, socks, pants, and kind of drive our parents crazy, but we all loved football anyway. It was painful playing on fields like that.

It was the same in high school. The league was organized but the fields were rough. Even when I was in college at Washington State some were that way. Why, I remember we would play the University of Oregon at a stadium in Portland and that field was nothing but dirt and sawdust. It was like a circus ring. Without grass it got pretty sloppy and we would all get scratched up pretty bad from the sand and the stones. Nobody wore face masks in those days, so our faces took quite a beating. In fact, all our equipment was quite different from what they wear today. The helmets were leather, and you could sure feel it if you got rapped pretty hard on the head. Our shoulder pads weren't built like they are now either. They were leather and strapped against a player's shoulders. They didn't have the cushion that those of today have. The hip pads were just about like they are now. And we all wore high-top shoes instead of the low-top shoes they wear today. When I think about it, I was lucky. Playing without a face mask and no teeth guards for about twenty-five years, from grammar school through my years with the Giants, I came out of it without losing a single tooth. A dentist told me sometime after all that, when he was going to pull one of my teeth, that I had the deepest rooted teeth he had ever seen, so maybe that's why I didn't lose any. But I remember a lot of people tried to make me lose a few back then.

When I was getting out of high school, football was not exactly the foremost thing on my mind. My ambition was to go to the University of Washington, not Washington State. The University is over in Seattle, and at that time, in the 1920s, they had good crew teams. Rowing is what I was most interested in then. The coach of the crew team gave a speech at our high school banquet and I was very impressed. I made up my mind to go to the University of Washington then and there and to try out for crew. I lived right on the bay on Puget Sound and we had a row boat and from then on I'd go out every day and row. I wanted to build up my back so I could make crew at Washington. They did not give scholarships and so I decided to stay out of school for a year after high school and earn the money to go to Washington.

I had an older brother over at Washington State, however, who was on the football team, and he told the coach, Babe Hollingberry, about me and that I was a pretty good football player. Well, they looked up my records, and the coach made some long distance calls to us in Bellingham. I told him I didn't want to go to Washington State. But finally he talked my father into it, and my father talked me into going there. After I got there, I was very happy that I'd chosen it because we had a championship freshman team and most of the freshmen went on the next year to start on the varsity.

We had a good season as juniors, only lost two games. And as seniors, we went to the Rose Bowl. That was the last time Washington State played in a Rose Bowl game—1931—and we played Alabama. In those days, they selected teams from different parts of the country, not just the Pac-10 and Big-10, like they do today.

There's one thing I'll always remember from that game. Our coach, a fine man, Babe Hollingberry, was somewhat of a showman and he was superstitious. In the showman role he bought a lot of new uniforms for our appearance in the Rose Bowl: bright crimson red, the headgear was red, the shoes were red, the stockings were red, everything was red. I think it scared us more than Alabama because we didn't play too good a ballgame. They walloped us 24–0. They simply had a better team than we had. In fact, that was the first time all year that we ran up against a team that passed the ball. They had a fine passer and good receivers and we couldn't defend against them. They scored all their touchdowns on pass plays.

The superstitious part of Babe Hollingberry came out when we got back to Pullman, the city where Washington State's campus was located, after the game. No one ever saw those uniforms again, and the story is that Babe had a big bonfire and burned them all. He didn't want any of his teams ever to wear those uniforms again.

I went from Washington State to the New York Giants but I almost went with another team. Portsmouth, out in Ohio, was in the league then. That was before the team moved the franchise to Detroit and became the Lions. They wanted me, and I had a contract offer from them. I had another contract offer from the Providence Steam Rollers out of New England, who were also in the league at that time, and it was better than the one from Portsmouth. I hadn't received anything from the Giants, although I'd heard they were planning to make me an offer. Well, Jimmy Conzelman was the Steam Roller coach, and he was pushing me, so I signed with Providence for a hundred and twenty-five dollars a game, which was a pretty good salary for a lineman in those days. A lot of the linemen when I started in 1931 were only making maybe eighty or eighty-five dollars a game. After I signed the contract, I went down to Spokane for a basketball game, another sport I played at Washington State. We were playing Gonzaga and Ray Flaherty, the captain of the Giants at that time, was coaching there during the offseason. He came down to the dressing room after the game and asked me if I'd received a contract from the Giants yet.

"No, I haven't," I said. "But if one is on the way, it's too late now." Ray didn't know what I was talking about, so I told him. "I signed one with the Providence Steam Rollers and mailed it back to them yesterday."

Ray said, "Oh, no. How much are they paying you?"

I told him, and he said, "The Giant contract is a better offer, one hundred and fifty dollars a game. I know that's the figure and I know the contract's on its way to you. Damn!" A little later he came back to me and said, "Why don't you go down to the postmaster when you get home and see if he won't send a telegram to the postmaster in Providence to see if he would intercept the letter?"

The next morning I did. I went down there but the postmaster said he wouldn't do it. He said that I could try myself but that he truly doubted I'd get the letter back. So I sent a telegram myself and, sure enough, the letter with the contract came back and in the meantime the contract from the Giants for one hundred and fifty dollars a game had arrived. I signed with the Giants and tore up the other contract with Providence. I think at that time one hundred and fifty dollars was probably the highest pay of any lineman in the league. It was pretty good money, even though it would not sound that way now in the 1980s, but you could buy a loaf of bread for a nickel and get a full meal for thirty-five cents in the Automat back then. And you had no income tax.

Tim Mara was the owner of the Giants at that time, Jack Mara, his son, hadn't gotten involved yet. I believe my first year with the Giants was Jack's last at Fordham. He became vice president of the team after he graduated from Fordham; he had been studying law and was a lawyer when he came on the Giant payroll. Tim Mara was easier to deal with as far as a contract was concerned. Jack, being a lawyer, was a bit tougher to get anything out of. I think Tim was a little more generous and, needless to say, I preferred to deal with him if I wanted to get a raise or anything like that. He would listen to me longer.

Tim was a terrific fellow in many ways. He used to travel with the team but he was a New Yorker through and through. In 1934, we won the world championship, we beat the Chicago Bears in the famous "Sneakers Game." In those days, the league champion always went to the west coast and played two or three postseason exhibition games against an all-star team made up of different players from the National Football League. So we went out there, the Giants, and we stayed at Pacific Palisades in a nice hotel overlooking a golf course. It was very beautiful and very quiet, and away from the busyness of Los Angeles. Tim had come out with us too. Well, after two days in that hotel, he went home. He said he had to get back to New York City. Why? Because it was too quiet in California. He said the birds would wake him up in the morning about six o'clock. Tim said he had to get back to New York, where he was raised on the East Side, and where he could hear the subway and the fire engines and all the racket. He couldn't sleep unless he heard all the noises of New York. So he never did see the game. After two days he was all worn out from the quiet and had to get back so he could get some rest.

Steve Owen was the Giant coach when I joined the team in 1931. It was his first full year as head coach. Actually, Steve was player/coach that year but he only suited up for about three games. He was about thirty-three or thirty-four then. Steve was a very good coach, though, and all the players respected him. He made it harder on some of the rookies. That was just his way, his method. I didn't agree with that philosophy. As a result, even the players wouldn't have much to do with the rookies. A couple of years later, when I was captain of the Giants, some of the rookies complained to me about the way Steve was treating them, a lot rougher, they said, than the way he handled the veterans. I told them that Steve was basically a very good-hearted, fair fellow, and the reason that maybe he was tougher on the rookies was because he wanted them to know that pro football was a very tough game and that they had to work hard to make the team. After awhile, I assured them, they'd get into the spirit of the thing and everything would work itself out. Then I talked to Steve myself and we went back and forth some, but from that time on, I believe, the Giant rookies were treated much more fairly and felt more like they were part of the team.

The closeness of the Giant team in the 1930s was one of the reasons we did so well. There was a lot of team spirit and togetherness. Most of the players lived in the same area—between 100th and 103rd Streets around Broadway. We stayed in about three different hotels up there. I stayed the longest at the old Whitehall Hotel at 100th and Broadway, and a number of others did, too. It was a small hotel and each room had its own kitchenette. Steve Owen lived there all year round with his wife. He had the penthouse. He liked to have his players nearby and usually tried to talk them all into staying at the Whitehall. After the season, of course, all the ballplayers went back to their hometowns. There were a few of the players who didn't want to live in a hotel, and they got apartments of their own, but still they were within two or three blocks of us. That worked out quite well in bringing us all kind of close, and we got to know each other personally and to know each other's families. It unified us in a way that a lot of other teams were not able to accomplish. That and the winning attitude that Steve gave to us was what made us a winning football team.

As a rookie, though, I wasn't all that sure I was going to make the team. If I didn't, I wasn't going to get that $150 a game, and I was a long way from the state of Washington. I was married and had my responsibilities.

There were two veteran centers on the team, and teams only carried twenty-five players then. Two of them would be centers, certainly no more. Well, I made the team and played behind Mickey Murtaugh, who had been there since 1926. He was out of Georgetown. But he got hurt in the second game of the season and I went in and I guess I did okay because from that time on I was the Giants' starting center.

You learned about the pro game pretty quick in those days. It was very rough in the line, a lot of punching and elbowing and forearms and that sort of stuff. You had to stand up for yourself or you would be walked all over. A good example is the little encounter I had with George Musso of the Chicago Bears. He was a rookie in 1933 and played nose guard on defense. George was about 260 pounds and as strong as they come. I was about 50 pounds lighter than him. I was centering to the tailback on the single wing, who was about four yards behind me. Centering that way, I had to keep my head down, looking back at the tailback. Well, the first time George lined up opposite me and I snapped the ball, he popped me one right in the face. We didn't have faceguards, of course, and I said to him after the play that he'd better never do that to me again. Coming from me, about 200 or 210 pounds, it didn't make that much of an impression on big George. On the next play, he let me have it again. So, on the following play, I was ready. I snapped the ball with one hand this time and at the exact same time delivered one heck of an uppercut with the other hand and got George square in the face. He really felt it, I could tell. He shook it off in a dazed kind of way and then smiled and said something like that was a helluva good shot. He never tried it on me again, and we became good friends. George was not a dirty player, and I never heard of him doing that kind of thing to anybody later. He was just massive and strong. We played against each other for more than ten years and I, for one, can say he surely deserved to be inducted into the Hall of Fame.

One of our more colorful players in the early years was Shipwreck Kelly. He came from Kentucky and had this slow, southern drawl. He came up with us in 1932, I believe it was. I remember well the first time I saw Shipwreck. We trained in Magnetic Springs, Ohio, that year. It was a kind of health resort, with big hotels where elderly people went for the spas. Anyway, we were all there and Shipwreck Kelly drove up to training camp his first day in this huge Cadillac. I guess his family had a lot of money, and we thought, gee, is this guy crazy, joining the team to play for peanuts, to get his head knocked around when he could travel in such style? He was not your ordinary ballplayer in those days, like those of us who lived for our little paychecks. But he was truly colorful, a man about town. Still he was a fine football player when he wanted to be. Steve Owen and Shipwreck clashed a few times, I remember. For example, Shipwreck would be back to punt—he was a pretty good punter. It would be fourth down and maybe two to go and he wouldn't punt. He'd just

Mel Hein Day at the Polo Grounds, December 1, 1940. Helping to honor the great New York Giants center are *(left to right)* Mayor Fiorello LaGuardia, New York Democratic kingpin James A. Farley, and Herman Berjassi, who organized the celebration. An eight-time all-Pro, Hein played fifteen years with the Giants and was as adroit a linebacker on defense as he was a bulldozing blocker on offense. *(Pro Football Hall of Fame)*

take off and run. I'm going to make that first down, he'd say to himself. And Steve would fume on the sideline. Once in a while he didn't make it. Steve would yank him out of the game and they would have a big argument on the sideline. He was an erratic ballplayer, but a good one, and he sure could run.

Ken Strong was one of the finest players in the early days. Ken graduated from New York University and played first for the Staten Island Stapletons, which we used to call "Stapes" for short. We always played them on Thanksgiving Day. The Giants would take the ferryboat over to Staten Island. They had a little field over there and people would stand along the sidelines to watch the game. We never did draw too many people, that's why Staten Island had to give up football. Ken Strong was their whole team in those days. He carried the ball ninety percent of the time and handled the passing, the punting, the place kicking, and most of the tackling as I recall; it was all Ken Strong. Then, when they broke up, he came to the Giants. In his later years, he didn't play as much but he stayed with the Giants to do all the kicking.

We also had two of the best ends in the game during that time, both are in the Hall of Fame: Ray Flaherty and Red Badgro. The only other two who would rank with them were Don Hutson, the great pass catcher with Green Bay, and Bill Hewitt of the Bears, who was as tough on defense as he was agile on offense.

Then there was Bronko Nagurski. I learned that if you hit him by yourself, you were in trouble. If you hit him low, he'd trample you to death; if you hit him high, he'd take you about 10 yards. The best way to tackle Bronko was to have your teammates hit him about the same time—one or two low, one or two high. He was the most powerful fullback that I ever played against in all my career. Bronko had a knack of running fairly low. He had a big body and he could get that body, that trunk, down and be able to throw his shoulder into you. If you didn't get under his shoulder, he just knocked you butt over tea kettles. Another thing about Bronko was his blocking. The Bears had this little scatback in those days by the name of Beattie Feathers. Well, Bronko could open up the whole defensive line for him. He would burst it open and Feathers would be right on his butt, following him through and then he'd break one way or the other. It gave Feathers an advantage no other running back had, and he set a rushing record, over 1,000 yards, in 1934, I believe it was. After that we worked at special defenses to go up against that and we were able to stop Feathers pretty well in later years.

Probably the greatest tackle I ever played against was Cal Hubbard of the Packers. We were playing up at Green Bay one time and the score was 0–0 at the end of the half. Hubbard was the left defensive tackle and he stopped everything. We used to like to run to our right from the single wing, running to the strong side of the line. That was our normal tactic out of that formation. But against the Packers that meant we would be running into Cal Hubbard's side of the line. So we just changed it and were running everything to the left that day. Well, we were making yardage because we were running away from Hubbard. Between halves they decided to move Cal to middle linebacker. They had a seven-man line and they set him up right behind them as a solo linebacker. From that position, the son of a gun made tackles all over the field and they finally beat us, 6–0.

I've often been asked to select an all-Pro team from the players I actually played against, which is not an easy thing to do because there were an awful lot of excellent football players on the field in the 1930s. But if I were to do it, I'd have to have Iron Mike Michalske of Green Bay at one guard and Danny Fortmann of the Bears at the other. My tackles would include Cal Hubbard, of course, and either Turk Edwards or Joe Stydahar. Center, I guess would be Bulldog Turner. At ends, Don Hutson, everybody's all-Pro, and Bill Hewitt. That takes care of the line. In the backfield, I would rate Sammy Baugh the best quarterback of that time and maybe any other time as well. Bronko Nagurski would be the fullback. And I think I would want Cliff Battles and George McAfee as my halfbacks. Ace Parker, who played with the Brooklyn Dodgers, was so good a back that he deserves mention in that same class of ballplayers. So was Dutch Clark.

I played in seven championship games over fifteen years in the NFL while I was with the Giants. The most famous, I guess, was the "Sneakers Game" of 1934, when we came back in the second half. We were losing 10–3 to the Bears at the half. Everybody was slipping and sliding all over the place and Chicago was winning simply because they were bigger and stronger than us. They were actually a better team than us but that didn't matter that day, not with those field conditions. Their size gave them an advantage in the first half but the advantage we got from the traction provided by the sneakers in the second half was much greater and that's why we were able to outscore them 27–3 in that period. Our passer was Ed Danowski and he was able to stay on his feet and set up or to scramble if he had to, and our receivers were able to get free. And Ken Strong was able to gain a lot of yardage running. George Halas, their coach, shook his head throughout the whole second half. It was especially nice because we'd lost to the Bears in the championship game the year before. It was only by a couple of points and the Bears won it in the last minutes, so it was nice to get revenge. The winner's share of that 1934 championship was $621 per player, a far cry from all the money a Super Bowl winner takes home today. But we thought it was a lot of money, that we were suddenly wealthy.

We got to the championship again the next year, in fact we have the distinction of having made it to the first three NFL championship games. In 1935, it was against the Detroit Lions and they had Dutch Clark and Ace Gutowsky and Glenn Presnell, a wonderful backfield. It was an awful day, mud and snow and terrible winds. We could never get going in it. They beat us pretty soundly.

We played Green Bay for the title in 1938 and 1939, beat them in the first and lost to them in the second. Ed Danowski threw a pass to Hank Soar, who, incidentally, later became a well-known major league umpire, to win the '38 championship for us. But they clobbered us the next year, 26–0. They had Don Hutson and Cecil Isbell and Arnie Herber. Clarke Hinkle was their fullback and I've got a number of aches and pains to remind me what tackling him was like.

We were actually pretty lucky to have gotten into that championship in '39. We beat the Redskins out of the Eastern Division championship when Bo Russell kicked a last-minute field goal that could have won the game for them, which was ruled no good. We were winning 9–7 at the time. I was backing up the line and the Redskins had worked the ball down to about our 25 yard line. There was only about forty-five seconds to go. Russell lined up and kicked the ball. It looked like it was good to a lot of people. But the referee, Bill Halloran, gave the signal that it was no good. Ray Flaherty, who was coaching the Redskins, and practically their entire bench came running out onto that field and raised the dickens about it. But Halloran paid no attention to them and we won the game. I had a pretty good angle to see it and it looked to me like he missed it. The Redskins sure didn't think so, however. The next year Halloran didn't come back as a referee. I think George Preston Marshall, the Redskins owner, saw that he was fired. I don't know how he did it but George Marshall had a lot of influence in the National Football League.

I retired after the 1945 season. But I'd almost gotten out earlier, in 1943. That was after twelve years in the league. I'd taken a job as head football coach up at Union College in Schenectady, New York. I also taught physical education there and it was a fairly good-paying job because they made me an associate professor. They had to give me that title in order to pay the money I wanted. Well, the war, of course, was under way and many of the students, the athletes, were leaving the campus for military service. We started with thirty young men on the football team and were down to about eighteen so I called the president of the university and told him with that few players I didn't feel we could field a football team. Others would certainly be going too. He said that I was undoubtedly right and agreed that we should disband the football team for the duration of the war.

Steve Owen saw the announcement in the *New York Times* sports section about Union dropping football so he called me up and asked me to come back and play again for the Giants. I said, "No, they're keeping me here to work with the civilian population in physical education and we're getting some of the military trainees. The government is going to pay half my salary and the university the other half. It's going to be a year-round job."

Steve said, "That's too bad. I was hoping you'd come back because we're losing a lot of our men too." Then he said, "What do you think about just coming down to New York City on Sundays. You could stay in condition up there and just come for the games."

I told him that I did play touch football during the week and I was working out in the phys. ed. courses that I was running. And, of course, I did miss playing the game. "Let's give it a try," I said. So I would go down on Friday nights after my last class, work out with the team on Saturday, get the new plays, the defenses, and things like that, and then play on Sunday. For three years, I played sixty minutes of each game— no preseason games, just the league games for '43, '44, and '45—under those conditions, and then catch the train back to Schenectady after the ballgame each Sunday evening. One of the sportswriters dubbed me the "Sunday center." But it wasn't all that easy. I was getting up in my thirties at the time. In fact, I remember very well my first game. I went into it without any physical contact at all before it that year. We were up in Boston and our other center, who had worked out with the team in the preseason, was supposed to start until I'd gotten myself into decent shape. But he had gotten hurt in the last preseason game against the Chicago Bears. So I had to start. I played sixty minutes, and I think it was the hottest day Boston ever had. I tell you it really took a toll on me.

I could hardly get on the train to get back to Schenectady that night. It took me about three weeks to get rid of all that soreness and begin to get well. Still, the next week, I had to go the full sixty minutes again. It was a pretty tough time.

I stayed with the Giants all those years because I wanted to. I was satisfied with New York. The Maras treated me very well, but as far as salary went, well, I remember we went back and forth a few times. One year in particular, 1939 I guess it was, after we had won the NFL title, I asked for a certain amount of money, like three hundred dollars a ball-game. I asked Jack Mara for it and I got a telegram back from him. He offered me a contract but the amount did not come up to exactly what I'd asked for. I said no. Then he offered me a season contract, flat sum for the year, but it also turned out to be less than what I'd wanted. So finally I got teed off and started looking around for something else. Well, there was the Los Angeles Bulldogs out on the west coast at that time, which was a pro team but not an NFL team, and the owner offered to get me a year-round job at a tire and rubber company out there if I played for the Bulldogs. Financially it looked pretty good. Well, after about five different telegrams from Jack Mara with offers, all of which I turned down, I finally sent a telegram to him that said, "Don't send anymore telegrams or call me, my mind is definitely made up. I'm going to stay out on the Pacific coast." Right away, boom, I got another telegram from Jack with the salary I wanted.

Another time, I decided I wanted to get into coaching, perhaps on the college level. So I talked to Lou Little who was head coach then at Columbia, which wasn't far from where we were staying in New York, up around 150th Street. Lou had been president of the coaches' association that year and they were having their national meeting out in Los Angeles. I asked him if I could come out there and hang around the hotel and maybe meet some of the head coaches. He said, "Sure, Mel, darn right, you come on out and hang around and I'll find out if there are any positions that are open. I'm sure we can help you."

This all took place right there near the end of our season. Well, the Giants had a breakfast at our hotel after the last game of the season, before all the players started heading back for their homes. Tim Mara, who knew I was thinking about going from a player to a coach, said to me, "Mel, see me after breakfast."

After it, he handed me a check for five hundred dollars, a bonus. Then he said, "Mel, I want you to sign a three-year contract with us for five thousand dollars a season." That was real big money in those days. I couldn't believe it. I said, "Sure, glad to!" I lived on the seventh floor of that hotel, and I ran up the stairs, didn't even wait for the elevator, and showed my wife the check for five hundred dollars and told her about the five thousand dollar contract. Then I called Lou Little and told him I wouldn't be seeing him out in Los Angeles. That's how you got your raises in those days; it's a little different from the way they do business these days!

# On Tour

Red Grange and the Chicago Bears went on their famous nationwide exhibition tour after the 1925 season. One day, as the tour was coming to an end, C. C. ("Cash and Carry") Pyle, Grange's manager and the man who put the tour together, cornered sportswriter Westbrook Pegler, who, never known to treat anyone gently in his writings, had been traveling with the team.

"I don't understand it, Pegler," Pyle said. "Through this whole tour, you drink all my booze and then write all those bad things about me in your column."

"Look, Pyle," Pegler said. "You don't have to worry about anything I write about you until I stop referring to your name in the singular."

# The Guarantee

Barry Gottehrer, a well-known writer and editor, wrote in his book *The Giants of New York* of this benevolent confrontation between Tim Mara, owner of the New York Giants, and George Halas, player/coach/owner of the Chicago Bears. Their two teams were scheduled to meet at the Polo Grounds in December 1926:

By game time, the temperature was 18 degrees, the wind was blowing 25 miles an hour, and two-foot snowbanks covered the entire field . . . except for a few photographers, reporters, and members of Mara's family, the stands were deserted. . . . Mara crossed over from the Giants' dressing room to tell the Bears the field was in unplayable condition. Halas, who with the rest of his players was still dressed in street clothes, listened while Mara talked and then nodded his head. 'That's fine with us,' he said, 'but where's our $3,000 guarantee?'

" 'What guarantee?' shouted Mara. 'There aren't a dozen paying customers in the house.'

" 'That's your problem, Tim,' said Halas. 'We've got a $3,000 guarantee, rain or shine, and we're not leaving without it.'

" 'Okay, if that's the way you want it,' said Mara. 'You boys better get into your uniforms. If you think you're going to get that $3,000, you're going to play that game even if there are only two people in the stands.' Mara slammed the door and stormed out.

"The Bears cursed, grumbled, started undressing, and cursed again. Ten minutes later, someone opened the Bear dressing room door a few inches and, without coming into view, said, 'How about $2,000?' Halas looked at his players, who wanted to play even less than Mara, and answered, 'We'll take the two.'"

# 6

# Glenn Presnell

Glenn Presnell could play tailback, quarterback, wingback, or fullback. A chunky firebrand of a ballplayer at 5 feet 10 inches and about 190 pounds, he was both a strong runner and a deadly accurate passer, but he had the misfortune of playing mostly in the shadow of Dutch Clark during his six-year career with the Portsmouth Spartans and the Detroit Lions (1931–36).

The one year that Clark did not play in the same backfield, 1933, Presnell took over at tailback, led the league in scoring with sixty-three points, ranked second in passing to Harry Newman of the Giants and third in rushing, was tops with five field goals, and was named all-Pro. The next year, Glenn kicked a 54-yard field goal to set an NFL record which stood for nineteen years, until Bert Rechichar booted one two yards longer in 1953. It is still a Detroit Lion standard, although it was equalled by Eddie Murray in 1983.

In his senior year at the University of Nebraska, Presnell led the nation in total yards gained and earned all-American honors. After World War II, he returned to Nebraska to serve as head coach for the Cornhuskers.

In his six years in the NFL, Presnell rushed for eighteen touchdowns, passed for fifteen, and accounted for 217 points. He was the starting quarterback on the Detroit Lions NFL championship team of 1935, working in a dream backfield that included Dutch Clark, Ace Gutowsky, and Ernie Caddel.

After coaching for a year at his alma mater, Presnell moved to Eastern Kentucky in 1947 as head coach, eventually became that school's first full-time athletic director, and remained there until retiring in 1974.

In 1922, I was a sophomore in high school in DeWitt, Nebraska, which was a pretty small town, and that's when I played my first game of football. I was a running back. In 1924, I went to the University of Nebraska and played on the freshman team there, then on the varsity the next three years. I chose Nebraska because I only lived about forty miles from Lincoln and besides all my friends were going there.

Nebraska didn't give scholarships in those days, so I had to get a job. The coaches found me different jobs in Lincoln. I waited tables, racked billiard balls in a pool hall, read meters for the Iowa and Nebraska Power & Light Company. I had more jobs than I knew what to do with. I never got a bit of aid from the university, but my credit was pretty good and I could borrow against it if I had to. It was a long time before they gave scholarships at Nebraska. I went back there to coach after I quit playing pro ball in 1937 and they still weren't giving them like they do today. They had what they call "workships," a scholarship and a job that lasted through the entire year.

As a sophomore, I played against Red Grange. We opened the 1925 season against Illinois in Champaign. Red was a senior and, of course, everyone had heard of him. But we beat them that year. I think the score was 14–7. I was a substitute then and all I played was the last four or five minutes of the game. We had Red pretty well bottled up that day. Ed Weir was the big wheel for Nebraska that year. He was an all-American tackle and later played for the Frankford Yellow Jackets. He keyed on Grange all day and was able to stop him. The next day the Chicago *Tribune* had the headline in their sports section, "Weir 14, Illinois 7."

We played some very good teams in those years besides Illinois. One of them was New York University when Ken Strong was their star player. We played Pittsburgh when Gibby Welch was there—he was an all-American tailback. Gibby played a couple of years in the pros, too, with the New York Yankees and the Providence Steam Rollers, I think it was. We played Syracuse, who had a great quarterback named Skinny Baysinger. My senior year we lost only two games, one to the University of Missouri, 7–6, and the other to Pittsburgh, 20–13.

One of the games I remember most, one I hate to remember in fact, was that game against Missouri down in Columbia during my senior year. It was the most one-sided game I ever played in, even though the final score was 7–6. We made twenty-two first downs and they made two. We were ahead 6–0 all the way. I gained something like 256 yards in about forty carries, but we could only get across the goal line once. We got stopped just about every time. But we totally dominated the game. Then, on the last play of the game, they threw what had to be a 50-yard pass into the end zone that their receiver bobbled around and finally got hold of for a touchdown. They kicked the extra point and won the game. That actually cost us the conference championship. We were then in what was called the Missouri Valley Conference, which later became the Big Six and now is the Big Eight.

After graduating, I went to Ironton, Ohio, to play with a team called the Ironton Tanks. The manager of the team in Ironton had contacted me while I was at Nebraska. He told me the way they operated the team was that they also got the players jobs in the town. They tried to get players who had earned teaching certificates in college who could then teach in the local school system. We only had a squad of about twenty-two players, and about sixteen of us taught in the school system in the country there. The reason I took them up on it was because they insured me a job teaching science at Ironton High School and another playing for the football team, the Tanks. The two jobs combined offered me more money than I would have gotten if I played with one of the NFL teams. The New York Giants had offered me a contract, so did the Providence Steam Rollers and the Kansas City Cowboys and several others, but none came near the amount of money I could make in Ironton with the two jobs. Actually the money I could make just teaching school was about equal to what the pros were offering me. There was also some security because if I didn't make it as a football player or got hurt bad and couldn't play anymore, I'd still have the teaching job to fall back on.

We were very successful as a team at Ironton. In fact we played several National Football League teams. In our own league, there was a team from Ashland, Kentucky; American Rolling Mill Company sponsored a team from Middletown, Ohio; and there were other Ohio teams from Akron, Cincinnati, Columbus, and Portsmouth. We played about ten or eleven games a season. We practiced at night after work, had floodlights on the stadium, and we played our games on Sunday afternoons. A few of our players had regular eight to five o'clock jobs in the mills or the factories.

When I played with the Tanks, we beat the New York Giants 13–12 in 1930. We played them in Cincinnati because a group down there wanted to get involved in pro football and so they scheduled the game, brought the Giants in on an off-date to show the Cincinnatians what real professional football was like. We also played the Chicago Bears there. The idea was to get the people behind it so they could start their own professional team.

The Giants had a fine team that year. Benny Friedman was their quarterback and he was the best passer in the NFL. They also had Steve

Owen in the line and his brother Bill and they had Red Badgro at an end. They were beating us 12–6 with only a short time to go in the game. I was playing safety at the time and we held them back in their own territory and forced them to punt. I caught the punt, it was a short one, and ran it out of bounds to stop the clock. I asked the timekeeper, the referee, how much time there was left to play. They kept the time on the field in those days, the referee had a stopwatch, no electric scoreboards. Anyway, he looked at his watch and said, "Looks like you got about three seconds left." I went back to the huddle and called a forward pass play. The Giants rushed me real hard and I was trapped in the backfield, but somehow I was able to sprint out of it. I ran across the field with Giants everywhere chasing me. Well, their backs on defense thought at this point that I was running the ball so they relaxed their pass coverage and came up to tackle me. I spotted this little halfback we had by the name of Gene Alford standing down in the end zone frantically waving his arms and so I just flipped the ball to him, about 30 or 40 yards, and he caught it. We kicked the extra point and beat them 13–12. And this was the New York Giants team that had gone 13–4 in the NFL that year.

We played the Bears shortly after and they had Red Grange and Bronko Nagurski. I remember it was the first day Joe Savoldi joined the Bears. He suited up, but he didn't play. Savoldi was the guy who got kicked out of Notre Dame for getting married. George Halas signed him up immediately. There was a big flap about it in the NFL. The thing was about tampering with college players, but Halas said it didn't apply here because Joe Savoldi had been booted out and wasn't a student anymore. Joe Carr, the NFL commissioner, intervened later and told Halas he still couldn't do it and, I think, fined the Bears. But Savoldi was there that day in Cincinnati, in uniform, and everybody was talking about the controversy around him.

Anyway, as good as the Bears were, and they were very good, we beat them, too, 26–13. Everything seemed to go right for me that day. I remember breaking off-tackle on one run and going 88 yards for a touchdown, and I got in two TD passes that day as well. The reason we played so hard in that game, I truly believe, is because we were very scared, especially of Nagurski, who everyone had heard all the war stories about. We didn't want to go down to Cincinnati and get annihilated, and as a result we really got keyed up for the game. On the other hand, the Bears figured this little team from Ironton would be a real soft touch and they consequently didn't get up for the game.

Even though they lost, we all learned that what everybody had been

saying about Nagurski was in fact very true. He was a magnificent specimen of a football player—he ran his own interference. I remember one
game up at Wrigley Field in Chicago a few years later. We were playing
the Bears and the field was frozen. It was near the end of the game and
they needed a touchdown to win, a field goal wouldn't do it. So they sent
Bronko out on an end run and I moved up from safety to tackle him. I
met him at about the 10 yard line and he just lowered his shoulder and
brought his forearm up at the same time. I was just hoping to knock him
out of bounds but when he plowed into me he knocked me all the way
into the end zone and just charged on in himself and skidded into the
Cubs dugout behind the end zone. He practically knocked himself out.
No telling what damage he did to the dugout.

Greasy Neale was the coach of the Tanks the year we beat the Giants
and the Bears. He was about forty years old then. And he devised the
defense that enabled us to contain Nagurski that day. I think we threw a
seven-man defensive line against the Bears and it worked.

Nagurski was big, about 240 pounds and solid as a mountain, but most
of the rest of us were small compared to the players today. I was only 5
feet 10 inches and maybe 190 pounds. Our tackles went about 220 or 230
and they were the giants on the field. We were all at a disadvantage going
up against Nagurski.

In 1930, the Depression got pretty rough and Ironton, which was an
industrial city, was hit pretty hard; the town just couldn't support the
team anymore. I still had my teaching job, but I was looking for a little
bit more. Fortunately for me, the Portsmouth Spartans had joined the
National Football League in 1929. Well, we had played against them and
beaten them and somebody must have noticed me because in 1931 they
offered me a no-cut contract after the Tanks folded up. It was too good
to turn down. I went over there and played three years for Portsmouth.

Potsy Clark ran the show. We called him the "Little Colonel." He was
a tough taskmaster, one who believed in perfect conditioning, and that
was the secret to our success, I believe, during those Portsmouth years.
We maybe didn't have as many big-name stars as some of the other teams
in the league but we were always in superb condition, top form. Potsy
had a way of instilling confidence in you and he created a good esprit de
corps among the players and an intense desire to win. We were like one
big family, which was a lot easier in those days, with the smaller squads,
and also Portsmouth was a small town, only about thirty thousand people, and there weren't a lot of distractions there. We socialized a lot
together.

One of the key ingredients in the success of the Portsmouth Spartans and the Detroit Lions in the early 1930s was halfback/tailback/place kicker Glenn Presnell. Playing all of his pro career in the shadow of Lion legend Dutch Clark, Presnell took advantage of the one year that Clark did not play, taking over the position of tailback, making all-Pro, and leading the league in scoring. He played three years with Portsmouth and three with Detroit. *(Pro Football Hall of Fame)*

There's one thing I'll always remember about Potsy. He would some-times signal a play from the sidelines, although it was illegal in those days. He'd do it with elaborate hand gestures. It never worked very well and it sure wasn't subtle. I remember one game in Chicago. Before a play I looked over at the sideline and just caught the end of his gesturing and couldn't figure out what play he was signaling. Then one of the Bear players came up to me and said Potsy wants you to call a particular play and then told me which one it was.

The years in Portsmouth were good ones. We had a fine team. Dutch Clark was the tailback and he was one of the best ever to play the game. He was a great shifty runner, what I call a "rabbitback." He wasn't an exceptional passer or kicker, he was just a terrific open-field runner. Ace Gutowsky was also in our backfield, and he was my roommate for five years, two at Portsmouth and then three in Detroit. Ace was a wonderful fullback, weighed only about 195 pounds, but he had the fastest start of any back in the game then. We had a lot of spinner plays and he could spin and hit back into the line as fast as anybody I've ever seen. Ace was from a little town in Oklahoma called Kingfisher and he played his col-lege ball at Oklahoma City University.

Father Lumpkin also played with us in Portsmouth. He was a great blocker, a big man for a back in those days. He went maybe 210 or 220 pounds and was at least 6 feet 2 inches. He was also a fine defensive player, played safety some of the time and linebacker at other times. Father Lumpkin came from Georgia Tech, I believe.

Ox Emerson was another memorable one. He was an all-Pro guard but he weighed only around 190 or 200 pounds and he stood less than six feet tall. George Christensen was a good tackle, he weighed about 230 and was the biggest man on the team.

In my first year with Portsmouth we ran a close second to Green Bay, ended up only a game behind them at the end of the season. We won eleven of fourteen games that year, in fact we had winning seasons all three years at Portsmouth.

In 1933, Dutch Clark didn't come back to Portsmouth. He stayed out at the Colorado School of Mines where he was coaching. So Potsy moved me to tailback. I'd been playing mostly at wingback before that. It was a good year for me. I led the league in scoring and I was runner-up in passing to Harry Newman of the Giants. I was fourth in rushing. And I played sixty minutes of practically every game. We ended up in second place in the NFL West behind the Chicago Bears, who went on to win the first NFL championship game ever that year.

We were called the "Iron Men" during that time. The nickname came about after a game we played up in Green Bay in 1932. They were the defending league champions and had players like Clarke Hinkle and Johnny Blood and Arnie Herber. They'd beaten us earlier in the season, and Potsy Clark, old "Never-Say-Die" Potsy, said after that game to Curly Lambeau, their coach, "We'll take care of you when you come down to Portsmouth." Well, they came down at the end of the season and the game was very important for them. As it turned out it would knock them out of the race for the title that year. Before the game, Potsy Clark gave us one of his most impassioned pep talks. Then he named the starting lineup and he said, "You people, you *eleven* men, are going to stay in this game. The only way any one of you is going to come out is by being carried off on a stretcher." And sure enough, we played that game with eleven men, didn't make a single substitution all afternoon. It was some game, but we beat the Packers, 19–0. After the game, some writer referred to us as the "Iron Men" and it stuck for quite some time. Another writer called us "Potsy's Army," but that didn't last too long. That was also the year we played a kind of championship game indoors against the Chicago Bears. It was at the Chicago Stadium and there was dirt on the floor which was left over from a circus that had performed there the week before. It didn't smell all that great, and the field was only 80 yards long and the sidelines were right on the railings.

But the Spartans were doomed. Like at Ironton, things were getting pretty desperate in the early '30s. People just couldn't afford to pay to see a ballgame, so many were out of work. The team had a heckuva time of it. They weren't able to pay the players because they didn't make enough money. I didn't get paid at all for the last four games of the season. That was 1933. There were promises. I remember we had a team meeting and decided we might as well play, we really didn't have anything more to lose. The owners promised they would sell more stock in the team after the season and make up our back pay. The team had a number of stockholders, unlike some of the other NFL teams then that had individual owners. So I played the last games, but still I never did get paid. I don't know whatever happened to the stock sale. And the Portsmouth Spartans went out of business after the season. When it was over, I decided to quit the game and I found a coaching job at the University of West Virginia.

In the meantime, the Portsmouth franchise was sold to some businessmen in Detroit, and they bought the players' contracts as well. What came of it, of course, was the Detroit Lions. The new owners got Potsy

Clark to come to Detroit as their head coach. By that time, I was living in Morgantown, West Virginia. Well, Potsy and the new owners insisted I come back and join the team. The reason was that I'd had such a good year in 1933 with the Spartans, leading the league in scoring and making all-Pro. That, incidentally, was the same year I tied Jack Manders of the Chicago Bears for the most field goals in a season. It wasn't all that many in those days, nothing like the number a kicker would kick today—I believe we each kicked five that year. A kicker today might do that in a single game.

The Lions made me such an attractive offer I agreed to come back to football. I stayed at West Virginia through the spring practice sessions and then I went up to Detroit. I played three years there with the Lions, and we had some great teams. Many of the other boys from Portsmouth did like I did and signed up.

In 1934, the Lions' first year in the league, we got nosed out for the championship by the Bears. That was the year they went undefeated. They had, of course, Bronko Nagurski and that little running back Beattie Feathers, who broke the rushing record that year. They were an extraordinary team. They had a slew of good linemen too, fellows like George Musso, Bill Hewitt, Link Lyman, and Joe Kopcha.

On the other hand, our 1934 team in Detroit was probably the greatest defensive team ever. We weren't scored upon in the first *seven* games of the season. It wasn't until the eighth game of the year before a team scored *a point* against us. That was the Pittsburgh Steelers and they got only one touchdown that day. We beat them 40–7. That year we outscored our opponents 238–59. Our opponents didn't even average a touchdown a game. That's really unheard of in football. It's a record that will never be broken.

In 1935, we won the NFL West, beating out the Green Bay Packers, and the New York Giants won the NFL East. We met them for the championship in Detroit. The Giants had beaten the hell out of the other teams in their division, but we handled them in the title game. It was an awful day, I remember. The field was muddy, and it was bitingly cold and windy. Then there was a snowstorm. They had the field covered before the game but by the time it was half over the mud was frozen and there were about three inches of snow on top of it. I think only about fifteen thousand people showed up for the game. We won it easily, the score was 26–7, and they were never really in the game. Our winner's share of that championship game was around three hundred dollars each, and I think the Giants maybe got two hundred dollars apiece.

I played one year after that, 1936, my ninth season in professional football, and then I retired. I went into coaching on the college level, first as an assistant at Kansas and Nebraska. I was head coach for a year at Nebraska, then I moved to Eastern Kentucky.

The biggest differences I see in the game that I played and the one that is being played in the NFL today is the size and the speed of the players. That's equally true on the college level. When I was coaching at Nebraska in 1940, for example, we had a very good team and played Stanford in the Rose Bowl that year. One of our tackles weighed 200 pounds, and we had an all-American guard in Warren Allison and he weighed in at about 185. The other guard was 175, and our center wasn't over 190. There were no weight-training programs for the ballplayers in those days.

Another big difference in those days was that so many of the professional teams used different formations: Green Bay used the Notre Dame box, the New York Giants used the A formation when Steve Owen was coaching there, we were a single wing team, the Boston Redskins under Lone Star Dietz used the double wing, and the Bears mixed it up with the single wing and a little bit of the T formation when Ralph Jones was their head coach. The Bears didn't really adopt the T formation with a man in motion until later, around 1940, when Clark Shaughnessy brought it in for Halas and Sid Luckman carried it off, and that, of course, changed football forever.

I loved playing the game of football when I did, but I certainly wouldn't mind playing it in the 1980s, especially when I see what some of the salaries are. As far as finances go, I'd be in pretty good shape, especially if I made all-Pro now like I did then. I was a good rusher, played defense at safety all the time, and was a kicker. The field goal I kicked against Green Bay, 54 yards, was a record in the NFL for about twenty years. Maybe I could have named my own price.

Back then, however, the pay was poor. And you got very little exposure, especially if you played in towns like Ironton and Portsmouth. We made the newspapers in those towns, but hardly anybody else read or heard about us in New York or Chicago or Cleveland for that matter. The only time they would learn about you was when you went to one of those cities to play. There would be a write-up after the Sunday game and maybe a little hype before it, but once you left town it was over. Today, of course, it's very different. Every time one of those players turns around, his name is in the paper or he's on national television. It's big business nowadays.

The topless Detroit Lions of 1936, then the defending NFL champions, at their summer camp. (*Top row, left to right*) George Christensen, John Schneller, Bill McKalip, Ace Gutowsky, Clare Randolph, Ox Emerson; (*bottom row*) Harry Ebding, Ernie Caddel, Glenn Presnell, Dutch Clark, and coach Potsy Clark. Potsy Clark would leave after the 1936 season, having served as head coach since the club's inception as the Portsmouth Spartans in 1930 and having compiled a won–lost record of 53–26–9. Ace tailback Dutch Clark would take over the coaching duties in 1937. (*Pro Football Hall of Fame*)

Back in the 1930s, there was a heckuva lot of camaraderie among the players. It was more like the college game then. That was one of the nicest parts of it.

### Smart Indian

George Halas told this story many times. In 1927, an aging Joe Guyon, then thirty-four years old, was in the backfield for the New York Giants. As he faded back for a pass, Halas, the Bears' right defensive end, burst through. Guyon's back was to Halas, a perfect set-up for a blind-side hit, maybe a fumble, but if nothing else a reminder that the game of football was a rough one. At the last second, however, Guyon unloaded the pass and wheeled around to greet the charging Halas with his knee. It broke several of Halas' ribs. Guyon shook his head at the grimacing Chicago Bear on the ground.

"Come on, Halas," he said. "You should know better than to try and sneak up on an Indian."

# 7

# Shipwreck Kelly

John Sims "Shipwreck" Kelly arrived in New York City in 1932 and soon after engraved a truly inimitable imprint everywhere from Ebbets Field to the Stork Club. He came from the rolling hills of central Kentucky, from a wealthy family, owners of a 3,000-acre dairy farm among other things, and he was unawed by Manhattan and its sophistications.

An all-American halfback at the University of Kentucky who was dubbed in his college yearbook as "the fastest man in the South" because he ran the hundred-yard dash in 9:8, Shipwreck was equally adroit, he quickly proved, at moving through New York's cafe society. He was a fine football player—he led the NFL in pass receptions in 1933, in fact—but his name was found more often in the social columns than on the sports pages of the 1930s.

Shipwreck signed first with the New York Giants and played a season with them. The following year, in partnership with Chris Cagle, the all-American from Army who had also played in the Giants backfield in 1932, Shipwreck, at age twenty-three, bought the Brooklyn Dodgers NFL franchise.

When Shipwreck was not in a locker room or on a football field, he could usually be found in places like El Morocco or "21" or perhaps out in the Hamptons or up in Newport. His closest friends included people like Dan Topping, Jock Whitney, and Bing Crosby. He dated Tallulah Bankhead and various Broadway starlets, and he married New York's most glamorous debutante, Brenda Frazier.

The setting for the interview which follows here gives some idea of how Shipwreck Kelly's lifestyle was quite a bit different from those of the other young men with whom he played the game of football. It was conducted in the trophy room of Shipwreck's home, "a little place I have on the water," as he referred to it, which was in actuality an eighteen-room mansion on the shore of Long Island Sound which F. Scott Fitzgerald surely had in mind when writing *The Great Gatsby*.

The trophy room was not one to house mementos from his successful careers in football and track, however. Instead, it was an enormous room, a hall, perhaps from some Adventurers' Club, filled with relics of an incredible life. The trophies were the mounted heads of animals he had hunted and killed: lion, tiger, caribou, elk, impala, moose, puma, practically every form of big game. Draped across chairs and tables, everywhere, were skins of leopard, cheetah, bear, jaguar; on the floor was a huge polar bearskin rug and the skin of an enormous maned lion, both with mouths gaped open in fierce snarls. On one wall was an original Grandma Moses painting and in one corner was a poker table covered in leopardskin instead of the traditional green felt where, according to Shipwreck, Jock Whitney once staged a game of poker in which each chip was worth ten thousand dollars.

And throughout the room were framed photographs, on the walls, on tables, of Shipwreck and his friends. Here was Shipwreck golfing with the Duke of Windsor, there he was in the south of France with Aristotle Onassis and Maria Callas, at a bullfight in Spain with Pablo Picasso, hunting with Ernest Hemingway in Africa, crouched over a freshly slain mountain lion in Idaho with Clark Gable. Many others posed with Shipwreck, making a kind of scrapbook of the celebrity register of the mid-twentieth century: Irving Berlin, J. Edgar Hoover, Richard Nixon, Bob Hope, Bill Paley, Casey Stengel, Fred Astaire, and on and on.

Unframed is a letter from J. Edgar Hoover attesting to and thanking Shipwreck for his service as an undercover agent for the FBI during World War II.

His football career was somewhat less lustrous: a year with the Giants and three with the Dodgers. But when Shipwreck played he was good and he was respected. As an owner, he was instrumental in bringing stars like kicker Ralph Kercheval and tailback Ace Parker to the Dodgers, and he tried feverishly if unsuccessfully to lure Don Hutson to Brooklyn. Shipwreck Kelly was surely one of the most colorful men ever to be associated with professional football.

M y football career started at Springfield High School in Kentucky.

After that I went to St. Mary's College, a little Catholic college, for a year and then came back to Springfield. From there I went to the University of Kentucky, and I thought I was hot shit, but they didn't. I knew I could play football, and that I could run like hell. But the coaches there hardly ever let me play.

Finally they put me in during the last freshman game of the season against Centre, which was a smaller school in Kentucky. Centre was beating us, 21–0 at the time. I made three touchdowns after they let me in the game that day, and from that time on they knew I could play.

It was while I was at Kentucky that I got the nickname "Shipwreck." Around that time there was a man who was known as Shipwreck Kelly, an old sailor, who went around sitting on flagpoles. He came to Lexington one day and climbed up and stood on a flagpole and people thought that was very funny. I guess I was a junior or senior then and a pretty big hot shot. Well, after we won a big game, somebody said something like, "You sure can play football, but you can't sit on a flagpole like Shipwreck Kelly."

I said, "Bullshit." And I climbed up on a flagpole and stood there on top for a few minutes. Then I started down and somebody yelled, "What are you coming down for?"

"I have to piss," I said.

By the time I got to New York, after I graduated, I was known mostly as Shipwreck because I climbed that flagpole. The nickname just stuck.

It was Percy Johnson who wanted me to move to New York. He was from Kentucky and was like a father to me. He was chairman of the board of the Chemical Bank, a guy like J. P. Morgan, wealthy as hell. When I was in school he used to come down to Kentucky and watch me play football. He had a son who was my age and in the same class and we were great friends. I used to go up to New York every summer and stay with them. Then, after I graduated from Kentucky, Percy Johnson said, "Come on to New York."

So, in the summer of 1932, I came and he gave me a job at the Chemical Bank. I worked there two weeks, I think it was. I saw what it was like and decided I wanted to play pro football. I went to see the people at the Giants and they offered me a contract, a shitty contract like they all were in those days, but I played. Tim Mara was the man I talked to there, the owner. There was also Jack Mara, his son, and a little kid called Wellington Mara, but Tim Mara was the whole thing. Steve Owen was the coach, a nice friendly sort of guy, too friendly in fact and a lot of the players used to bullshit him a lot because he was too nice sometimes. His brother Bill played on the team and was pretty good.

I didn't get to play until the second game of the season. It was against Green Bay, and we weren't doing a thing. The Giants hadn't scored a single point in their first game that year, and against Green Bay we hadn't scored one either. So Owen sent me in. I broke a couple of runs, one was about 30 yards, and I caught six or seven passes that day, but we still didn't score a point. But I became a starter after that.

I played about six or seven games with the Giants that year, but then I quit because the doctor told me I wasn't in shape for it. I had a small touch of rheumatic fever and I didn't feel very good and they weren't paying me very much money anyway. I had some money myself and so I went back to Kentucky.

After the season, Chris Cagle, who had been the Giants' best back that year, called me up on the phone and told me there was a football franchise for sale, the Brooklyn Dodgers. Bill Dwyer owned them and he wanted to sell out, Cagle told me. So I called up Percy Johnson and asked him what he thought about it. I told him I might want to buy the team. He said, "Well, if you think you can make it go, come on up and I'll help you."

So I went back to New York and I bought the Brooklyn Dodgers with Cagle. We turned out a pretty good team that first year, won more than we lost. We had some pretty good players. Of course, Cagle, and we had big old Herman Hickman in the line. He was all-Pro. And I'd gone out and hired Benny Friedman, supposed to be the best passer in pro football then.

I paid Friedman a helluva lot of money to play for us. He was a nice fellow. But let me tell you what happened to him in the first game he played for us that year. We were playing against the Bears and on the first play Friedman went back to pass. Well, they had this end who used to play without a helmet, Bill Hewitt. Tough son of a bitch. If you could have seen what he did to Friedman. Knocked him on his ass and Fried-man left the game. He sat on the bench and after a while I went over and asked, "What the hell are you doing?"

Friedman said, "I'm tired, I'm weak today."

I was paying him thirty-two hundred dollars a game, and this was his first game. I said, "What's the matter with you. I'm paying you to play, not to rest your ass on the bench."

"I took a laxative last night," he said.

Shipwreck Kelly *(left),* co-owner and fleet halfback of the Brooklyn Dodgers, poses here in 1933 with his tailback and the finest passer of the early 1930s, Benny Friedman *(right).* Kelly, who was among the game's most colorful personalities, played only three seasons with the Dodgers but maintained his part-ownership into the late 1930s. Friedman, one of the biggest attractions in football during the late '20s and early '30s, directed the Dodger offense for three years before retiring in 1934. Before that, he had starred for the Cleveland Bulldogs, Detroit Wolverines, and New York Giants. *(Pro Football Hall of Fame)*

I said, "You took a thirty-two hundred dollar shit on us, that's what you did."

I didn't talk to him anymore that day and he stayed out of the game and the Bears beat us, 10–0. But he did play after that, and he was there for the Giants game, that was the big draw in New York back then, when Brooklyn played the Giants. He was a great passer though and with he and Cagle throwing the ball I caught the most passes in the league that year, twenty-two I think it was.

We didn't do as well in 1934. Early in the season Cagle wanted out. He needed the money, I guess. And Friedman left, too. I think he went to coach some college team. Anyway, in the meantime, I had gotten to be friends with Dan Topping, who was a playboy and big shot around New York. On account of my playing football and he liking sports I got to know him pretty well. So Dan and I got together and talked about it and Dan bought Cagle out. Dan and I owned the Dodgers for a number of years. I moved in with Dan, we shared an apartment in New York for a number of years, until he got married. Then I got my own apartment. Then he divorced that first wife and married Sonja Henie, the famous ice skater. When he married Sonja Henie, she decided that she wanted to get into sports, besides the skating. So she bought half of Dan's ownership in the Dodgers.

It was around that time that I got Ralph Kercheval to come to Brooklyn. He'd played at Kentucky just like I had. He was a halfback, but his real greatness was in kicking the football. He could punt, he could placekick. He was the best kicker ever to play the game. Hell, he could fart the football farther than these guys can kick it today.

New York was a great place to be back then. I had a helluva life. I really was a protégé of Percy Johnson when I came up to New York and if you're a protégé of someone like that you can tell everybody to kiss your ass, and everybody's nice to you because he was so powerful and had so many influential friends. I met all kinds of people through him, the socialites, the big people on Wall Street, a lot of very important people. I would be invited out to Southhampton and East Hampton and the place where I met most of the hot shit was Newport, up in Rhode Island. I nearly married Bill Woodworth's daughter around then. Bill Woodworth, he was one of the biggest bankers in the world then, had houses in three or four places.

I was having a great time around then. Topping and I were all over Broadway and shit like that. He loved the showgirls. There was another guy, another multimillionaire, that I was good friends with, too: Ed Madden. He bought me a LaSalle so I could get around New York easier. After a while I shit him around. I said, "You mean you want me driving around in a car like this?" So he took it back and got me a Cadillac instead. Madden also got me to run for the New York Athletic Club. I ran the 100 and the 220 in a lot of those big relays, in New York, Philadelphia, Pittsburgh, quite a few places. I ran the 100 in 9:8 then and I tried out for the 1936 Olympics, but I lost out to Jesse Owens and Ralph Metcalf in the sprints.

We used to go to the nightclubs around New York all the time, too, but not during the times I was playing football, at least not a lot. I was serious about football. The one that was my favorite was the Stork Club because Sherman Billingsley liked me. He owned it and he had piles of money. I used to go in there and if I wanted any money he'd give it to me and say, "Pay me back when you get ready." He was a wonderful guy. He did the same thing for Walter Winchell and a lot of people that went in there. He'd give it to you and you'd pay him back when you wanted to.

The hot shit place of them all, though, was El Morocco. I knew John Perona, the owner there, and he was very nice to me. The big thing was to get into the nightclub and even then only if you were a hot shit would you be sitting where the hot shits were. If you were not, they'd put you in the back or in a corner somewhere out of the way.

I remember one night in the El Morocco when I was with four or five people at one table. In walked a big guy with a beard—there weren't many beards in those days—and John Perona came over and said to me, "Do you know who that guy is?"

I said I didn't. "It's Orson Welles, the actor." On second thought, I said, I thought I'd seen a picture of him somewhere. So Perona brought Orson Welles over to the table and introduced me to him. I tried to be a smart aleck, like I did a lot of times in those days. I said, "Gee, Mr. Welles, it's nice meeting someone like you." He didn't know who I was or that I played football or anything about me. But he was very pleasant. Then I said something like, "Why do you cultivate something on your face that grows wild on your ass?"

"Mr. Kelly," he said, "you are fresh in New York, and if I were you I wouldn't tell my friends how much you know about my ass."

I felt like shit and got up and left.

Another time I remember was at the Stork Club. I took Tallulah Bankhead there. I used to date her a lot around that time. In walked this beautiful young girl, Brenda Frazier, one of the richest, most famous debutantes of the time, with three young men and they sat down on the floor near the table Bankhead and I were at.

Well, the waiters were giving out balloons and one of them was supposed to have a hundred-dollar bill inside it. It was something Billingsley used to do every once in a while. I think this time it had probably been fixed because Bankhead got the balloon with the hundred dollars in it. She got up and walked over to where Brenda Frazier was sitting on the floor and handed it to her. "Here, my dear," she said. "I think you'll need it. I've been reading in the papers lately how broke you are all the time."

"Thank you, I can use it," Brenda said. "I don't get my money until I'm twenty-one."

I didn't let that crap interfere with my football playing, however. I kept the two apart. You had to because it was a rugged game, much tougher than college ball. The sons of bitches in the pros were bigger and stronger, and all of them were pretty damn good, whereas in college only two or three players on a team might be worth a shit.

Two of the toughest I remember were Bill Hewitt of the Bears and Father Lumpkin, who played for Portsmouth and Detroit and then came with the Dodgers. They both played without headgear. Harry Newman of the Giants was a helluva ballplayer, too. He was very small but tough and good. Probably the greatest was Dutch Clark. I played against him. The greatest I saw after I left the sport was Sid Luckman. I ran into him on the street one day in New York and he came up to me and we talked a little and he told me I had been his hero when he was a kid growing up in Brooklyn. That was very nice. I really appreciated it, him remembering me for playing football. I get tired of all those people remembering me because I married a rich girl and was in the café society thing all the time. Football was important to me. One thing I'm especially proud of is that I never made a fair catch of a punt. Never. I'd take it on the run no matter what.

I quit playing after the 1934 season. But then the coaches asked me to come back in 1937. One of their backs got hurt or something and the team was doing shitty. I guess they thought I could run like I used to be able to. Potsy Clark was the coach that year. Anyway, they had to persuade me to come back, but I wasn't the player I was before. I wasn't in shape. I couldn't help them on the field. But I did help them in another way. I got them to go after Ace Parker. I had read about him and seen him play for Duke. I thought he would be just what they needed, and, of course, he turned into a fantastic pro back.

After that I got out of football for good. Then I married Brenda Frazier. And after that I did that work for the FBI. Not many people know about that, but I did it all the way through the war, and then when it was over J. Edgar Hoover wrote me this letter, thanking me for what I'd done. I traveled everywhere for them. You see, I could because of the society that I hung around in. I mean I went to Europe, to Cuba, then to Mexico, to Peru, to Chile, and when we got in the war I spent a lot of time in Argentina. I could meet people at parties and things, the big shots there because of my connections. An ordinary person didn't have access to them. But I did. There were loads of rich Germans in Argentina and high-ranking officers, all in that same international society. I would try to find out about the ships, the submarines, things like that, that were off our coasts. And there were a lot of them. A lot of these people knew where they were, when they were around, that kind of thing. I kissed everybody's ass in Argentina to find out things like that, and I found out a lot. I also found out who the others who were sympathetic to the Germans were, others in that society. I worked at it all the way through the war for Hoover. Then I got out of that part of it and he and I were good friends, did things together many times in the years after the war.

But football was great. It helped me in a lot of ways. And I tried to do my job right in the years I played. And it's nice to be remembered for that part of my life.

## Mental Block

Benny Friedman, the game's first great passing quarterback who hurled the pigskin for a variety of pro teams from 1927 through 1934, told many stories about the men who played the game with him. One of his favorites was about Joe Westoupal from West Point, Nebraska, who was the center on the New York Giants in 1929 and 1930 while Friedman was their quarterback

"Westoupal was a rugged youngster, tough as a whipcord. He was a Bohemian and a good center, but every so often he would develop a mental block.

"In those days I lined up as the tailback and called the signals from the line of scrimmage—not just the signals but the plays as well. I'd look at the

According to Shipwreck Kelly, Ralph Kercheval, here delivering a rather unorthodox place kick, "could fart a ball farther than these guys can kick it today." His 1939 Brooklyn Dodger teammates, Beattie Feathers (holding) and Boyd Brumbaugh (providing his head as a tee), must have had as much faith in Kercheval's kicking precision as Kelly had in his power. Kercheval handled virtually all the Dodgers' punting and place kicking from 1934 through 1940. Feathers, as a Chicago Bear in 1934, set an NFL record when he rushed for 1,004 yards, the first back to break the 1,000-yard mark.*(Pro Football Hall of Fame)*

defense, how they were lined up, and then call off a series of numbers which would tell the players what play to execute. Then I'd give another series of numbers which would tell them what number the ball would be snapped on. And then the numbers up to the one where the ball was to be snapped.

"Sometimes, maybe once a game, maybe two or three times, I'd call the signals and, at the right one, nine of our players would leap into action, everyone except Westoupal, who would be hunched over the ball, frozen, and myself, standing back there waiting for the center snap. He would just have a mental block and do nothing. I'd go up and tap him and we'd go back to the huddle. I'd look him in the eye and say, 'Come on now, Joe, when I call the signal, center the ball.' Sometimes he'd just shake his head and I'd have to plead, 'Joe, we can't run the ball unless you center the ball.' Then finally he'd nod or say, 'Okay,' and everything would be fine, at least until his next mental block would come along."

## Devoted Fans

Ken Strong made his pro football debut with the Staten Island Stapletons in 1929 and played with them for four seasons before moving across New York Bay to join the Giants. He told this story from those days to author Bob Curran for his book *Pro Football's Rag Days*:

"I'll give you an idea of what those Stape fans were like. During those years I developed a rivalry with Ray Flaherty, the Giants' captain. One day, when we were playing at Thompson Field, I went around his end and he grabbed me in a headlock. Right near one side of the field we had a small wire fence that was right against the sidelines. Now Flaherty started to force me towards the wire fence. And something was getting him real mad. When the whistle blew, he looked up and saw this little old lady leaning over the fence waving an umbrella. She'd been hitting him on the head while he was pulling me towards the sidelines and he thought that I had been reaching up and punching him."

# 8

# Clarke Hinkle

Clarke Hinkle has the unique if painful distinction of being the only man ever to knock Bronko Nagurski out of a game. It happened as a result of one of their frequent bone-shattering collisions, and in that particular one the Bronk came out of it with a broken nose and a broken rib.

An Ohioan both before and after his pro football career, Hinkle played for ten years with the Green Bay Packers, a team that participated in three NFL championship games, won two of them, and never ended up lower than third in league or division standings. Four times he was named the all-Pro fullback, which is one more time than Bronko Nagurski was able to lay claim to that honor.

Hinkle was not especially big for a power back and linebacker—5 feet 11 inches and 200 pounds—but he was one of the most bruising hitters, either rushing or tackling, that played the game in the 1930s. "When he hit you," Ken Strong, legendary New York Giant back, once said, "you knew you were hit. Bells rang and you felt it all the way down to your toes." His quarterback at Green Bay, Cecil Isbell, observed, "Before a game, Clarke would get so fired up he'd be glassy-eyed. And if we lost, he wept."

Hinkle's running was the perfect counterpart to Curly Lambeau's passing attack at Green Bay. When Arnie Herber or Cecil Isbell were not tossing the ball to Don Hutson or Johnny Blood, Hinkle was hitting the line to grind out a few yards rushing. Over the years he carried the ball 1,171 times for the Packers and averaged 3.2 yards a carry. When he retired after the 1941 season, he was the NFL's all-time leading rusher with 3,860 yards. He scored a total of 358 points on forty-two touchdowns, twenty-six field goals, and twenty-eight extra points, and he maintained a 43.4-yard punting average. Clarke led the league in scoring in 1938 with fifty-eight points and headed the list of field goal kickers in both 1940 and 1941.

In only the second year of selections, 1964, Clarke Hinkle was inducted into the Pro Football Hall of Fame.

**M**y first experience with playing football was as a kid in Boomtown in Toronto, Ohio, on the banks of the Ohio River, when I was about seven or eight years old. My father was always interested in athletics and he had baseball bats and footballs around the house. When I was about seven years old, I played with my brothers. They liked sports, especially football, and I naturally followed them. My mother was also very supportive of we boys playing athletics. In those days, we used to play on a back lot near our house. We had to learn all parts of the game: running, passing, kicking, tackling. We'd pick sides; we didn't have organized sports, supervised like they are now for children. So we were pick-ups and we just kind of taught ourselves how to do it. When I went into high school, I could kick a football pretty good and I just kept after it from then on. I wanted to be a back and a kicker, so I really worked at both.

I played four years of high school football and I also played basketball and baseball. When I went to Bucknell University in 1928, I played on the freshman football team and then played three years of varsity ball. I played fullback at Bucknell in the single wing, and I did a lot of passing and punting as well. I played cornerback on defense. In my senior year, I played in the East-West game and was voted the most valuable player.

When I was with Bucknell we played some pretty good teams: Penn State, Temple, Georgetown, Villanova, and Fordham. There were some excellent players on those teams. Ed Danowski of Fordham was a great ballplayer. I remember him distinctly. They had a fellow at Temple by the name of Swede Hanson, a fine back, who later played with the Philadelphia Eagles. My last year we were coached by Carl Snavely and we were undefeated. We were tied three times, but we never lost that year and we were rated right up there with Pittsburgh at that time. Carl Snavely coached the single wing and was the foremost exponent of it. A couple of years later he went to North Carolina and made himself quite a reputation.

When I was a senior at Bucknell, that was in 1931, we played Fordham in New York on a November afternoon. Before that game, I had received a letter from the New York Giants to be a guest the following day when they were playing the Green Bay Packers. So after our game, I stayed over and, with the Bucknell line coach, went to the Polo Grounds and watched the Packer-Giant game.

I was more impressed with the Green Bay Packers than I was with the New York Giants, so during the second half we went over and sat on their bench. My line coach said, "Maybe we can get more money from the Packers." Of course, Curly Lambeau, the founder of the Packers, who happened to be losing at the moment, wasn't about to be interested in a guy from a small college like me. So I never got to meet him that day. One thing I do remember about that game was that I was impressed by a fellow that they had on their club by the name of Cal Hubbard. He stood about 6 feet 5 inches and weighed maybe 250 pounds. I thought I might be better off playing on his side than playing against him.

Later I was selected for the East-West game and, as I mentioned, I had a pretty good day and got the award after the game. Well, lo and behold, it wasn't an hour after the game and we were back in our hotel; Jim McMurray, who was an all-American player from Pitt, was my room-mate, and we were there, having a little drink. There was a knock on the door and there was Curly Lambeau with a contract in his hands. He scouted those games every year and he often picked up players from the East-West game. So I signed a contract, a hundred and twenty-five dollars a game. They didn't have the draft system in those days. The Chicago Bears had sent me a letter earlier, but it hadn't sounded too promising. They wanted to know if I wanted to try out for the team. Lambeau's offer was the only firm offer that I had. Bill Hewitt who was from Michigan, played in that same East-West game. He wanted to play for the Packers, too, and said, "How about me coming up there and playing," and he said he'd do it for ninety dollars a game. But Lambeau wasn't interested in him, and, of course, Hewitt went with the Bears and was one of the greatest ends of his time. He was their last selection, I think, last guy signed, and he sure came back to haunt Lambeau.

I also liked the idea of playing in a small town. I figured with a small town like that, everybody knowing everybody, they would have pretty good spirit, like a college. And besides that, they'd been the NFL champions for three years straight: '29, '30, and '31. When I went to Green Bay I found we were accepted right into the social life of the town and became part of the community. It was the first time I had ever had a chance to make any money. We were the children of the Depression. When I went to Bucknell the stock market had crashed and things were tough. But in Green Bay I had a livelihood, and I was living high on the hog. One hundred and twenty-five dollars a game and it was easy, just for playing football, which was something I loved to do. It was a real good experience for me, knowing everybody in town, and aware that you were playing with the best, it helped my ego. I thought, if I could play with them, I could play with anybody. And if it hadn't been for World War II, I would have played till my legs dropped off. I loved the game and I loved Green Bay.

The players we had in those years were remarkable. There was Johnny Blood, for one. Johnny had as great and colorful a career off the field as he did on it. He was a little eccentric, a little weird, particularly if he got a little giggle juice in him, then he could do some odd things. I tell this story all the time. One time we were playing the Giants in New York City. We dressed in the hotels at that time, instead of the dressing rooms at the stadiums where we played. They weren't too clean, and Lambeau was very particular about that. So, we dressed in the Victoria Hotel in New York, went on a bus to the game, got beat, came back with our suits on, and went through the lobby of the hotel up to our rooms to change out of our uniforms.

Some of the guys had a few bottles with them for after the game. Johnny Blood was one of them and he decided to have a drink while he was taking his uniform off, but he wanted some ice. So he called the desk and asked them to bring some ice up for his drinks. It never came. I don't know, the hotel was busy or something, or they didn't have any bellhops. In the meantime, Johnny got about half-stoned, and he got mad, took a shower, and got dressed. We were all sitting in the lobby by this time and Johnny Blood comes down, goes past us and out onto 57th Street, and that's the last we saw of him for about an hour. We were still sitting there when in comes Johnny Blood, with a 100-pound cake of ice on his shoulder. Right through the lobby of the Victoria Hotel he went with it— everybody stopping to stare at him—right into the elevator and up to his room. He put the 100-pound cake of ice into the bathtub, turned the water on, and then called everybody in the hotel and told them to come and have a glass of ice water in his room. Hell, we'd all get drunk after a game in those days. Lambeau would say, "The lid's off, boys, but stay out of jail."

Johnny also bought out whorehouses. He'd pay the madam for *all* the girls and have all the girls to himself. Now I'm sure he couldn't service all of them, but that's just the kind of guy he was. They all liked him, too, wanted to talk to him and have fun with him. He also had a knack for missing trains. One time he missed a train right after Lambeau told us anybody who missed a train would be fined. I think it was one hundred dollars, which was a lot then. Anyway, Johnny didn't show. Well, the train moves out and about a half-hour later comes to a screeching halt. On the tracks in front of it, in De Pere, Wisconsin, is a taxicab with Johnny sitting on the fender. He climbed aboard, waved to us, and said to Lambeau, "See, I didn't miss the train."

At the same time, Johnny was a very intelligent man. He was brilliant. When he was sober, he'd read Shakespeare, and he was going to write a book on money. I don't know whether he ever did, but he was always interested in economics and knew a lot about it. When he would get a few drinks, though, he'd buy the worst porno books he could find. He was a true Jekyll and Hyde. And Johnny wasn't the type of football player who would knock you down and hurt you, he was more the Don Hutson type. He had good speed and he'd go up in the air and come down with the ball with some great catches. And he was a clutch player, he'd do it when you needed it. But he never disciplined himself, was always broke. Johnny was always after Lambeau for money. But he always paid his debts.

Don Hutson weighed about 178 pounds and was about 6 feet 2 inches when he came to us in 1935. He didn't have the size for a pro football player. But then we saw his speed and the way he just glided—when he ran he didn't put his knees up to his chin, just kind of flowed. The best way I can describe Hutson is if you could picture a gazelle, running through a defensive secondary in the National Football League. He had a deceptive stride, and he did the hundred in something like 9:7. And what great moves he had. One day I saw him fake Beattie Feathers of the Bears out of his shoes, literally fake him out of his shoes. They had to call time out so he could put them back on. Hutson was the greatest offensive end who ever lived, even by today's standards.

He played defense, too, and he used to block these enormous tackles we used to play against. He could do a pretty good job blocking, even though he was awfully small for that aspect of the game. He did it well partly because he could get to whoever he was blocking so quickly. I remember running through many holes that he helped to open.

Lambeau played Don as a halfback on defense, and it worked out perfectly. He was a great pass defender by his very nature. He could use his hands and jumping ability as well on defense as on offense.

But most of all, he made life easy for our passers. He would run the basic patterns and all Arnie Herber and Cecil Isbell had to do was throw to a spot. Hutson might be ten yards away from the spot, but he would get there and catch the ball.

Then there was Curly Lambeau himself. He was the one who gave Green Bay the Packers. The drama of that franchise is spectacular: how a town of 45,000 could get a franchise in the National Football League and maintain it when all the other teams later represented much larger cities. It's an institution now. Curly Lambeau was the founder, the creator, and the coach. But I never liked him. Not really respected him either, but he was paying me and I gave him a thousand percent every time I played football for him. Lambeau was the first coach to use the forward pass as a basic offense. His running game was a threat, but he introduced passing as a major part of offensive strategy. He's one of the first who would pass from behind his own goal line on a first down, for example. He himself had been a forward passer in high school and then when he went to Notre Dame for one year.

There is one thing I do respect about Curly Lambeau. We were fighting the college football game back in the '30s. We hadn't gained the popularity the game has today. But Lambeau, whenever we went out on the road, he'd make us wear suits, coats, and ties. If we were in Green Bay, he wouldn't let us smoke in public because the people might think less of us. When we would leave Green Bay on the train, we had two Pullmans and a dining car. We'd stay in the finest hotels on the road, and he'd sign the check so we could eat at the hotel. He wanted us to get the proper food, and he was trying to project the image that we were educated people who happened to be playing sports.

Lambeau learned his football from the players who played for him. Back in the early years, when he had Cal Hubbard, Mike Michalske, and Jug Earpe and those guys up there, he would put a play up on the board and some of his blocking assignments were impossible. Of course, the players would pick the play apart and get him straightened out on it. Down through the years with this happening to him, he became a good football coach. He won six world championships. And he's the only one who built that franchise, and he should get credit for that. What happened to Lambeau in later years, around 1948 and '49, he went Hollywood for some reason or another. He was never the same after that. Before that he used to beat the bushes for good players, really go after them in the off-season, but then around '48 and '49 he didn't do that anymore and so his material became very mediocre. He was not beating the bushes, and I think the reason was because he had attained financial success he didn't have the desire anymore.

A savage runner and fierce competitor, Clarke Hinkle was *the* running attack for the Green Bay Packers in the 1930s. Here he roars out against the Chicago Bears in typical fashion. Hinkle was also a bruising linebacker as well as the team's punter and place kicker. All ten of his NFL seasons were spent in Green Bay. No. 76 on the Bears is center Oakie Miller. (*Pro Football Hall of Fame*)

Bronko Nagurski was probably the greatest player I ever went up against. I'd read about Bronko Nagurski, of course. He had been at Minnesota while I was at Bucknell but we never met in college. He was tough, everybody said, and very good. I think it was in 1929 that they named only a ten-man all-American team. Grantland Rice and *Collier's* magazine both did, because they had Bronko Nagurski at two positions: tackle and fullback. I don't think that ever happened before or since.

I remember in the first game I didn't know what to expect from Nagurski, hearing all those things, but I knew I was going to have to play for my life anyway. In the first series of downs, that first game I played against him, which was in 1932 in Green Bay, the Bears had the ball. The ball was handed off to Nagurski and he came through the line. I was backing up the line on the strong side and I waited for him to come to me. Well, he darn near killed me. He knocked me on my back and I ended up with four stitches on my face. I thought to myself, you either better start moving or go after him or get out of the way because otherwise you are going to get killed. So, from that day on, I figured I'd either go at him or away from him, but I knew that if I went at him I had to get there first because he had me by about twenty pounds.

People have asked me since, Were you at each other's throats? We weren't. There was no animosity between the two of us. Bronko Nagurski was a hell of a football player and he was a clean ballplayer. He was simply the most bruising back that I ever played against. I believe he felt the same way about me

When we met on the football field, everybody knew it. I guess the time I remember best was in 1935. I got the call for me to run with the ball and I got past the line of scrimmage and headed up the field. I saw Nagurski coming over to really nail me to the cross, but I had the ball and knew what I was going to do. So, before I went out of bounds at the sideline, I cut back in on him and caught him square with my shoulder and head. He knocked me back pretty near five yards. I sat there for a few seconds, because it really shook me up. Then I looked over at old Bronk and his nose was all over his face and he was in a helluva shape. Nagurski had a broken nose and later they found he had a broken rib too. George Halas was really mad about it, and he said I played Bronk dirty. I don't know how he got that. I was carrying the ball. I couldn't be doing anything dirty. Anyway, I think it was two weeks later, and we were going to play the Bears in Chicago. The headlines of the Chicago *Tribune* said: "Nagurski to Get Hinkle." I was a little concerned about it. Anyway, about five to ten minutes into the game, we had the ball and we shifted right—we used the Notre Dame shift then—and Cecil Isbell took the ball, handed it off to me. There was a nice hole over left guard. We had George Svendsen and Buckets Goldenberg at center and guard, and they moved George Musso, who was playing noseguard in a five-man line for the Bears, out of the way. But as I got through the hole, Nagurski hit me and boy he knocked me right back where I started from, back into our backfield. It was a clean hit. We hit that way all the time. Nagurski wasn't out to get me, even though that's what some of the sportswriters seemed to think.

Nagurski was a great guy and we have become real good friends. He was my presenter when I was inducted into the Hall of Fame.

I played about six years against Bronko altogether. I was able to tackle him and handle him pretty good, but I've got a lot of scars to show for it. I had to concentrate on getting there first, otherwise, as I mentioned, if I had waited for him, I would have gotten killed. I played him from the waist up. When he bowed, I bowed. I tried to get to him as much as he got to me, and I might have surprised him with my attack because he wasn't expecting it. I had this determination to survive, and I think he knew it. And I managed to survive. Not all the players who went up against him can say that.

One time, they say, when he was playing against the Pittsburgh Steelers, he took the kickoff and by the time he got through carrying that ball back up the field he had knocked out four Pittsburgh players. One day he hit me in Chicago when I was carrying the ball and they took me out of the game and over to a Chicago hospital. They put three stitches in my chin, and then I came back and played the second half. He could hit you just as hard on defense as he could pulverize you when he was carrying the ball. Nagurski wasn't a fast starter, but he had good speed once he got up momentum, and once he got that momentum up and you had to take him in an open field, well, it was like you were asking for suicide.

There were a lot of tough players in those days though. Some of them were downright mean. Others were just rugged. Butch Gibson, for one. He was one of the early guards with the New York Giants and came from Canton, Ohio. One game, I faked to the halfback and then went into the line myself. Well, Gibson hit me smack on the chin and I really saw stars. He was one I'll always remember. Ace Gutowsky of the Detroit Lions was pretty rough, too. He could hit hard. Tuffy Leemans of the Giants was another. He had legs like posts, when you tackled him you felt like you were tackling a pair of posts. Another was Bill Shepherd of the Detroit Lions. He didn't last too long, but he was a tough one.

George McAfee was the most dazzling runner I ever saw. They can talk about Gale Sayers, but if I had to choose between the two of them, I'd take George McAfee. He was a helluva runner, he could jump sideways as fast as he was going forward. He was also a very good defensive back. I had head-on collisions with him and he jolted me pretty good.

After Nagurski, the most powerful was Bulldog Turner. He came along in 1940, I believe. He used to rattle my ribs a lot, too. I lit into him to protect myself, as I had to do against Nagurski. Ah, that Bulldog, he weighed about 245 and had a twenty-one-inch collar, was a great blocker on offense and on defense was as fine a linebacker as ever played the game. They talk about Dick Butkus, but I'm not sure Butkus could carry Bulldog's shoes.

We always played tough games with the Bears, feuded continually. I especially remember one game in 1941. We beat the Bears that year, and that was the same team that had destroyed the Redskins 73–0 for the championship the year before. In fact, the game we whipped them in 1941 was the only one they lost that whole year.

It was a time when the T formation had just come into use. Old Clark Shaughnessy was helping out Halas with it. He got Halas to put the man in motion which eventually revolutionized offensive play in the National Football League. We'd seen it developing over the years, and we'd seen Halas put a little more T formation into his game plans each year. He used the single wing and the T, but by '41 it was mostly all T formation.

To combat it, Lambeau went to the library one day in Green Bay to look for a defense in one of the old books on early football. You see, the T formation was actually one of the oldest in football history. Anyway, Lambeau found one that was used back about 1890, a seven-spear defense, I think they called it. They lined up with seven linemen, then a fullback, like a linebacker, two halfbacks, and a safety. We used it against the Bears that day in 1941. We never charged our linemen across the line of scrimmage because the Bears were doing a lot of trap blocking. Our linemen followed the ball and they had a field day. I played fifty-eight minutes of that game and had the pleasure of kicking the winning field goal in the fourth quarter. We beat the Bears, 16–14. I would have played sixty minutes but on one play in the early part of the game Bill Osmanski, the Bears powerful fullback, cut me on the leg with his cleats. It was not on purpose, but it put about a four-inch gash along my shin and it went clear down to the bone. I called time out, and Lambeau gave me hell for it when I came to the sideline. I said I wanted to put a pad over it, that I didn't like to look at the bone. I missed only about two minutes, then went back in the game. When we went into the dressing room after the game, nobody would dress my wound. They were all so elated over beating the Bears in Wrigley Field, the NFL champs, that they were all celebrating and I couldn't find anybody to bandage me up. Then I had to walk fifteen blocks back to our hotel because I couldn't get a cab. Let me tell you I was really tired by the time I got there.

In the 1937 All-Star game in Chicago, which they played in August back then, it was 100 degrees. We played that night and got beat— Sammy Baugh was the all-star tailback—the score was something like 6–0. When the game was over I found I'd lost twenty-five pounds. In 1938 we went down to the Cotton Bowl in Dallas to play an exhibition game and it was the same kind of steamy night and that time I lost thirty pounds. Men bigger than me sometimes lost even more. We had a guy by the name of Tiny Engebretsen, who was from Northwestern and weighed about two hundred and fifty pounds. He lost fifty pounds during one game. As soon as that game was over, Tiny went into the dressing room and grabbed a full bucket of water. He just tilted it up and drank the whole thing. Then he got himself dressed and started downtown in a taxicab. But he passed out, clear out of the picture, and the cabby had to stop and get the fire department to bring him around. He damn near died.

The most memorable seasons, my best years, were 1936, '37, '38, and '41, I guess. I led the league a couple of those years in field goals and I was the leading scorer one year, 1938 I think it was. And 1941, I was very proud of the fact that after ten years in the league, in my last year as a player, I was able to make all-Pro, and I had to beat out a mighty good fullback, Norm Standlee, out of Stanford, who was with the Bears.

I left the game after that year. Now when people ask me how long I played, I tell them twenty years—ten years on offense and ten on defense. That's a lot of football.

Green Bay was a good place to play football and a nice place to live in those years. It was a different kind of time. I didn't work in the off-season, just lived off the money I earned from playing football. Then I got married. It was in 1936 and then I had to find work in the off-season. I really wasn't equipped for anything, though. I had had a very liberal education at Bucknell University. Someone asked, what did you major in? I said, "Coeds and football." I should have been doing something in the off-season the years before, but it wasn't easy then, what with the Depression and all. Nobody was going to take you for just eight months, knowing that you were going to leave for four months—at least I convinced myself of that back then. And in truth there weren't that many opportunities in Green Bay, just a couple of cheese processing plants and paper mills.

In New York, the sportscaster Ted Husing called me up one night— we were there getting ready to play the Giants—and he had a little radio program. He said, "I'll give you one hundred dollars for saying, 'I smoke Camels or Chesterfields,'" or something like that. In Green Bay there just weren't opportunities like that to make extra money.

I was thirty-two years old when I quit football. We were in the war and I went into the Coast Guard and was sent to the merchant marine training station they were building at Sheepshead Bay on Long Island. Then I got transferred to the Coast Guard Academy and was there for almost two years. After that I asked for sea duty and got it. I ended up with my own command. I spent four years in the service and when I got back Lambeau asked me to come back with the Packers as a place kicker. There was a two-way system by that time, but I said, "No way, because once I get on that field, you'll start using me to carry the ball and my legs are gone."

Football provided me with many opportunities, opened many doors for me, but it caused me a helluva lot of crises, too. I couldn't adjust to a normal life after it and the service because I had never punched a clock or carried a lunch basket. So I got to drinking pretty heavily. I couldn't face the reality that my football days were over and I wasn't up on that pedestal anymore. As a result of it I lost my wife, a very lovely girl from New York, who divorced me. I lost a lot of good jobs. I hurt my family and I hurt a lot of good friends and I was going straight to hell. One day I got up and my leg was paralyzed and I thought this is all from drinking. I had always been very proud of my physical condition, and I thought, "Gee, the Lord gave me this good body and here I am punishing it." But I finally came to my senses.

I had a talk with myself and through prayer and faith in God and practicing His teachings and reading the Bible, I quit drinking. That was twenty-three years ago and I haven't had a drink since. And the day I quit drinking everything turned good for me. But it wasn't easy. It took me about six weeks and during that time the nerves just came out on top of my skin. I couldn't sleep, couldn't do anything right, but I mastered it with the help of prayer.

Today pro football is a big business. These guys are making a lot of money, but they still have a tremendous responsibility to all the kids out

Some of the men who made the Green Bay Packers the potent force they were in the 1930s strike an impromptu pose here. (*Bottom, left to right*) guard Buckets Goldenberg, halfback George Sauer, guard Iron Mike Michalske, end Don Hutson; (*top*) tailback Arnie Herber, fullback Clarke Hinkle, and halfback Verne Lewellen. From 1932, when Herber and Hinkle became starters in the Packers backfield, through 1941, when both retired, Green Bay won eighty games, lost thirty-five, tied four, and won two world championships and three divisional titles. (*Pro Football Hall of Fame*)

there who look up to them. They owe them something. They owe the parents of them something. We always knew that when we played.

## Creative Refereeing

Red Grange remembers that refereeing was a little looser in the 1920s and early '30s than it is today, open, so to speak, to improvisation.

"They had a referee in the 1920s, Jim Durfee, who was a character. He and George Halas were pretty good friends. But Durfee loved to penalize the Bears right in front of the bench. When Halas was riding him pretty hard in a game one day, Jim began marching off a 5-yard penalty. Halas got really hot. 'What's that for?' he hollered.

" 'Coaching from the sidelines,' Jim yelled back. (It was in fact illegal in those days.)

" 'Well,' said George, 'that just proves how dumb you are. That's fifteen yards, not five yards!'

" 'Yeah,' said Jim, 'but the penalty for your kind of coaching is only five yards.'

"Another day Jim was penalizing the Bears 15 yards and Halas cupped his hands and yelled, 'You stink!' Jim just marched off another 15 yards, then turned and shouted, 'How do I smell from here?'

"After the game, however, they'd probably have a drink together."

## Shinguards

Benny Friedman remembered his introduction to shinguards and often told this story.

It seems in one game in 1930, he banged up a shin rather badly. Doc Alexander, who had coached the Giants a few years earlier and later was a kind of adviser in residence, told him afterwards that the best way to protect his shins was to wrap a copy of *Liberty* magazine over each and tape it tight. Friedman never did it but subsequently passed the advice on to a lady with whom he was talking at a cocktail party in New York. The woman had explained that she hated violent sports such as football but had agreed to let her son play soccer. Now she regretted it because he had been continually getting kicked in the shins.

"Don't worry," Friedman told her. "Tell him to do like the pro football players do. Tape copies of *Liberty* magazine over them to act as shin-guards."

"All right," the woman said, then looked at him quizzically. "Mr. Friedman," she said, "we don't subscribe to *Liberty*. Do you think *The New Yorker* would do?"

# 9

# Harry Newman

In 1933, with the NFL adopting new rules that would encourage the passing game, the New York Giants were in critical need of someone to replace Benny Friedman at quarterback after he defected to the Brooklyn Dodgers. So they went after the youngster reputed to be the best passer coming out of college football, an all-American from the University of Michigan, Harry Newman, and, in those times before the NFL draft, landed him with a most unusual contract. He was guaranteed a percentage of the gate receipts, perhaps the most potentially generous offering since C. C. Pyle worked out the deal for Red Grange with the Chicago Bears in 1925.

Newman proved his worth that rookie year by guiding the Giants to a divisional title and to the first official NFL championship game. He led the league in three key passing categories with fifty-three completions, 973 yards gained, and nine touchdowns, and was named the all-Pro quarterback.

Harry Newman was one of the smallest players in the game in those days at 5 feet 8 inches and 175 pounds, but he played a rugged game on defense as well as offense. After his impressive rookie year, he was touted as the best passing quarterback to come along since Benny Friedman. But Newman was also an accomplished runner, a fine complement to Ken Strong in the staging of the Giant running attack, and a fearsome kickoff return specialist.

Newman stayed with the Giants only two more years, however, but in both they emerged victorious in the NFL East. But his deal with the Giants had gotten out of hand, management felt, and Newman and the Mara family could not come to terms. So, along with Ken Strong and a few others, he founded what became the second American Football League. It only lasted

two years, and Harry then retired from the game to begin a long and successful business career in the automobile industry.

W hen I was a boy in the 1920s, we lived in Detroit in a middle-class,
actually fairly well-to-do neighborhood. I went to the local public school
and, I remember, we generally played baseball, football, and soccer,
mostly makeup games. After that I went to Northern High School there,
a pretty big one. I didn't play football my first two years there but I went
out and made the team as a junior. I played quarterback and tailback,
but I wasn't really the passer in those days. Our halfback was. I was
chiefly a running back and sometimes a receiver.

In high school, we normally played other teams from Detroit but we
did meet some from out of town, in fact a couple were from Ohio. We
had a fair team, won more than we lost. The highlight, I guess, was in my
senior year when in the final game of the year we tied the team that won
the state championship. There were a lot of very good football players in
Detroit then, and most of them went on to the University of Michigan.

That's the school I always had wanted to go to. I think they wanted
me too. I had been all-city and all-state my senior year. They didn't really
recruit me though. It was made clear I'd be welcome, but they didn't talk
scholarship or anything like that because in those days they didn't offer
you one if your family had money and we did have some.

It was actually Benny Friedman who was most instrumental in getting
me to go there and play football. He had been a great quarterback there
in the 1920s and when I was a senior he was already established as the
best passer in the NFL. Benny had a summer camp out in New Hampshire and a lot of kids from Detroit and Cleveland went to it. I was one of
them. It wasn't a football camp like they have these days, just an ordinary summer camp. Benny was the head counselor. He was a very nice
guy and took an interest in me. He thought I would have a good college
football career and told me I would be better off at Michigan than anywhere else. And it was Benny who taught me how to pass. We worked on
it a lot. I think I may have thrown two passes in high school and that was
all. Benny felt if I was going to make it to the top in college I needed to
be a good passer as well as a runner. And, of course, he was right. Later

on, Benny stopped working at that summer camp in New Hampshire and I got the job as head counselor.

So I enrolled at Michigan and I began playing football there my freshman year. We had some mighty good football players the years that I was at Michigan, quite a number of all-Americans. We had the first of the Wistert brothers, but he didn't go on to play pro football like his brother Al did later on. Bill Hewitt was a fine end and, of course, he had a terrific pro career with the Chicago Bears and the Philadelphia Eagles and was put in the Pro Football Hall of Fame. Ivy Williamson played and he went on to become a coach and athletic director at Wisconsin. My sophomore year there, there was a center and linebacker by the name of Doc Morrison, who made all-American; he played a couple of years with the Brooklyn Dodgers. In my junior and senior years our center was Chuck Bernard and he was an all-American, too, and played for the Detroit Lions.

It was all very organized at Michigan. We had spring practice, summer workouts, that kind of thing. It was a very important thing there, the football team. Even though it was the Depression years, we still attracted enormous crowds to our home games. They had the same big stadium back then that they do now.

I had been what they called a "junior all-American" in my sophomore year at Michigan, had a real fine year. But as a junior I broke an ankle, a bone in the ankle anyway, and I played most of the year with it until we found out it was in fact broken. It slowed me down a lot that year.

In my senior year, we earned a share of the national championship, I believe. We won eight straight games that year over many of the toughest teams in the country. We also won the Big Ten title that year, we beat Northwestern who used to have great teams around that time. They had Pug Rentner, an all-American running back, and he was very good in the pros, too, with the Boston Redskins.

I actually hadn't started the first game of the season my senior year. We were playing Purdue and at the end of the first quarter were losing 13-0. Harry Kipke, our coach, put me in at tailback—we played the short punt formation and I would call the signals and take the center. We got on the move and scored two touchdowns. I kicked the two extra points and we won the game 14–13. I did all our place kicking at Michigan. From that time on, I started every game. We didn't lose a game all that year. But we weren't invited to the Rose Bowl. Pittsburgh went instead and were killed by Southern Cal. It would have been interesting if we'd played USC—they were undefeated, too, that year. I think we would have won.

It was fine my senior year, though, and I had a great season. A lot of our games were close, but we came out on top in each. The last one was really a tough one. It was up in Minnesota and the temperature was six degrees below zero. They had Biggy Munn then who would become a great coach and they had Jack Manders who was a fine back and kicker for the Bears—"Automatic Jack" they used to call him because he was such a consistently good kicker. We just barely got by them to save our perfect record. I kicked a field goal and that was the only score of the game.

I was named to the all-American team and that meant an awful lot to me. I also won the Douglas Fairbanks Trophy that year, which was sort of like the Heisman Trophy. The Heisman didn't come along until a few years later. And I was given the Chicago *Tribune* Trophy for most valuable player in the Big Ten.

Actually, we lost only one game in the three years I played at Michigan. In my sophomore year, we won eight games and were tied once. Then in my junior year, that was the year I had the bad ankle, we lost once to Ohio State. They had Sid Gillman that year and Wes Fesler, I remember. The only reason we lost it, too, was because Jack Heston, one of our key running backs, got hammered on the opening kickoff. Jack was the son of Willie Heston, one of the all-time great football players at Michigan who played for Fielding Yost back in the early 1900s. Anyway, Jack was totally stunned, he was really unconscious, but he functioned and we didn't know it until later. So he stayed in the game. But he fumbled the ball three times, each somewhere around our 20 yard line. On two of them they scored afterwards. That's really why they beat us. I wasn't able to play the entire game either that day because my ankle was bothering me too much. But that was really something, only one loss in three years, and we played many of the very best teams in the nation.

Michigan was also a very tough school scholastically in those days. You had to work to maintain a good average. School work took up a lot of your time and you really had to keep up. I played a lot of tennis in those days but I didn't go out for the team at Michigan. I had enough with football and school work to keep me occupied. We played some baseball, too.

After I got out of college, I had several offers to go with the pros. I wasn't very big and that was a drawback, I was only about 176 pounds in

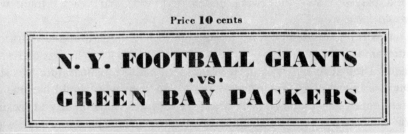

Price **10** cents

# N. Y. FOOTBALL GIANTS
### · VS ·
# GREEN BAY PACKERS

HARRY NEWMAN
All-League Quarterback
New York Football Giants

## POLO GROUNDS
### Sunday, November 11, 1934

Gracing the cover of a New York Giants program from 1934 is tailback Harry Newman, an all-Pro in his first year in the NFL. Wellington Mara, present-day owner of the Giants, refers to him as "a clone of Benny Friedman" because both were such similar passing and running threats, one succeeding the other. Newman played only three years for the Giants before leaving to help launch the American Football League in 1936. *(Pro Football Hall of Fame)* college and I was only 5 feet 8 inches. But George Halas of the Chicago Bears came up with an offer. It wasn't a very good one. The New York Giants came up with a better one. I talked with Tim Mara and I got the feeling they really wanted a passer and that I'd fit in with them right away. You see, that year, 1933, there were some new rules put in and one of them, that you could now pass from anywhere behind the line of scrimmage, really opened up the passing game. Mara wanted to take advantage of that.

The contract deal he came up with was that I was actually to receive a percentage of the gate. That was a very good deal in those days. As I remember it, the first year I was supposed to get ten percent of the gate after eleven thousand dollars had been deducted for expenses. The second year I was to get twenty percent.

It was kind of a foregone conclusion, I guess, that I was to be the starting quarterback, or tailback I think you'd call it. So I really wasn't treated like a rookie when I showed up there. We had our training camp at Pompton Lakes over in New Jersey back then. And from the time I got there I was starting. We had two sessions each day at camp, and I think that was the first time they started that, but it was turning into a different kind of game with all the passing we were going to do, a lot of new plays and all that.

I roomed with Kink Richards when I first joined the Giants. He was a helluva blocking back for us. Ken Strong came to the Giants that year, too; he'd been playing with the Staten Island Stapes before that. Ken, of course, was a magnificent football player and a fine guy. I used to pal around with him, too, quite a bit. Some others who were good friends then were Mel Hein and Ray Flaherty and Red Badgro. Mel was an all-Pro at center, and Flaherty and Badgro were two of the best ends in the league.

When training camp was over I lived in New York at a place called the Broadway View Hotel. Then I moved to the Terrace Hotel which was over on 96th Street and Riverside Drive. We didn't do too much carousing in those days. Some maybe, but during the season we were all pretty dedicated. We wanted to win and we knew we had a good enough team to win.

And we did win that year, at least we won the eastern division. We only lost three of fourteen games. And in one we set a record when we beat the Philadelphia Eagles 56–0. We split with the Chicago Bears during the regular season, lost to them once and beat them once. They won the NFL West and we played them in what was the first official championship game in the NFL. They had Bronko Nagurski and Red Grange and Jack Manders, a really fine team.

That game was really something. I think the lead changed hands six different times. There was one play in it that Bob Considine, the New York sportswriter, said was the greatest play he had ever seen. It wasn't a planned one, though. It was just an ordinary play, a handoff by me to Ken Strong who would then buck into the line. Well, the hole was all plugged up, just nowhere to go, so Ken spun out of the line. As he did, he saw me standing back there in the backfield and so he lateralled the ball back to me. I was surprised and suddenly all the Bears were coming after me. They chased me over to the right side of the field. I was hoping to get around end for some yardage but there was no way to do it, too many Bears in front of me. Then in just a flash I saw Ken down the field. After lateralling to me, he had raced down the field and was now in the end zone with no one near him. I threw it back to him and we had a touchdown. I believe that play put us ahead 21–16.

There was another famous play from that game. I got it from watching two of my nieces playing football, of all places. It was a little touch game and one of them was the quarterback and the other the center on this one team. One centered the ball to the other in a kind of T formation setup and then the quarterback just handed the ball back to the center, right back through her legs and she took off with it. I thought that might be a helluva play, a trick play we might pull off someday. So I went to Steve Owen, our coach then, and between the two of us we worked it up. We'd line up with just an end next to Mel Hein, our center, on one side, then just before the snap the end would shift into the backfield which would make Mel eligible as a receiver. Well, we pulled it off against the Bears in that game and I think Mel got maybe 40 yards on it. After I had handed it back to him, I spun around faking as if I had the ball, then pretended to trip. Well, all their linemen were convinced I had the ball and several of them landed on top of me. One of them, big George Musso, who was about 270 pounds, was the first one to land and, as he was getting up, he suddenly got this very puzzled look on his face and said, "Where the hell's the ball?" I just looked at him and said, "Next time you want to see me do some card tricks?"

Well, for all of our surprising plays, we still lost. They got a touchdown in the closing minutes and beat us 23–21. But it was one of the greatest games ever played in terms of excitement. I completed twelve passes in that game, two of them for touchdowns. It was a tough one to lose.

We won our division again the next year. For me, it was a really rugged year. In one game, I carried the ball thirty-four times, which then was a league record and, as I think about it, pretty stupid for a quarterback. It wasn't because I wanted to. The reason I had to carry it so often was that Ken Strong had a broken toe, Bo Molenda had a bad back, and there seemed to be something wrong with everybody else who ordinarily carried the ball. We were playing Green Bay that day at the Polo Grounds and we beat them 17–3. At the same time, Strong couldn't kick the ball so I did all the place kicking that day as well. I also returned punts and kickoffs. It was one of the longest, most bruising days I ever encountered in a football uniform.

One of the reasons it was so bruising was that they had a guard by the name of Mike Michalske and he was a tough tackler. Before that, Green Bay had the most brutal lineman in the game, Cal Hubbard. He played tackle and was about 6 feet 5 inches and maybe 270 pounds. He played with the same kind of intensity that Dick Butkus did later. We used to say of Cal that even if he missed you he still hurt you. When he tackled you, you remembered it. I do to this day.

The next week, in a game against the Chicago Bears, I suffered two broken bones in my back and that did me in for the season. Ed Danowski, a rookie out of Fordham, replaced me at tailback. The team went on to win the NFL championship that year. They beat the Bears in that famous game where they wore tennis shoes because the field was frozen. I was there but I wasn't in uniform.

In 1935, I had a contract dispute with the Maras. I decided to hold out. In that last game that I'd played in, in 1934, the one against the Bears, we filled the Polo Grounds. Because I was on a percentage, they had to pay me a lot of dough. As a result, they wouldn't give me the same kind of contract for the next year. Also that year before they had a fund-raising game for Major Cavanaugh, I think that was his name. He was a famous World War I hero, and it was a benefit for him and charity. They had a sellout for it and I donated my entire salary for that game to the benefit. They never said anything about that when contract negotiations came around. I held out but it didn't do me a lot of good. The season started and I kept myself sort of busy scouting for Coach Kipke of Michigan. I scouted teams like Columbia. But finally I had to do something so I came back and played out the year with the Giants. I alternated with Danowski that year but I felt my days with the Giants were over. They were never going to pay me the money I wanted, I knew that.

So the next year I got out of the NFL altogether. Along with a couple of others, I started the American Football League. Ken Strong came along into the new league and so did Red Badgro. We had teams in six cities: New York, Brooklyn, Rochester, Cleveland, Pittsburgh, and Boston. I started the team in Brooklyn and we called ourselves the Tigers. The Cleveland team, the Rams, were later brought into the NFL and after that moved to Los Angeles. The second year of the league, 1936, my franchise moved up to Rochester. We didn't have many big-name players, most were right out of college and they were the ones who didn't make the NFL. We didn't draw very well either in Brooklyn or Rochester and the league fell apart after that season. Those were still the Depression years and we just couldn't make a dent in the NFL—which, incidentally, wasn't doing all that well either.

After the demise of the AFL, I left football. I went back to Detroit, my home town, and went to work for the Ford Motor Company. I was in the sales department at first but soon I worked into a position where I represented the company over at the state capital in Lansing. I was basically a lobbyist for Ford at that time.

In 1946, I opened my own Ford dealership in Detroit. A few years later I opened another one in Denver, Colorado.

I played on a few very good teams in the 1930s. We knew what it was like to win, but we truly worked for it. We were very serious about the game. I still love the game, but because I'm retired now and living in Florida, I guess I watch the Miami Dolphins more than any other team. I also watch the University of Miami, who are very popular down here. And I still follow Michigan. I still have a lot of feeling for that school. I watch the New York Giants, too, but I don't have the allegiance to them that I probably should have. When I look back on it, they treated me fairly well when I was there. I probably wanted more money than I should have gotten, and I can understand why now that I didn't get it. But that's just the way it was in those days.

## Trick Plays

Cliff Battles, who made it to the Pro Football Hall of Fame as a result of his sparkling performances as a tailback for the Boston and Washington Redskins in the 1930s, had many stories to tell about owner George Preston Marshall and the budding franchise in those uncertain times. He often talked about the days when he and the other Redskin players would, at the urging of Marshall, put on war paint before a game and do a little Indian dance to entertain the paying customers. One of his favorite stories, however, had to do with coach Will "Lone Star" Dietz, a full-blooded Indian hired by Marshall to guide the Redskins in 1933 and 1934.

"Lone Star had a bagful of trick plays that he liked to use. We didn't, because most of the time they didn't work. But we had triple reverses and fake fumbles. But the best was a thing Lone Star called the 'squirrel cage.' It was for a kickoff. In those days no one kicked from a tee, and therefore the ball would usually come low and fast, a line drive. Well, with the extra time that afforded us we would sometimes use the squirrel cage. After the ball was kicked to us, we would all run back to about the 10 yard line and form a huddle. The man who had caught the kickoff would hand it over to another player. Then we would all break out running as if we had the ball hidden behind our backs. The player we usually gave the ball to was Turk Edwards, who was over 250 pounds and the biggest man on the team. No one would think that he was carrying the ball. They would tackle all of the backs and ends and the like, and Turk would lumber up the field with the ball hidden behind his back. He got 50 yards or more on a couple of occasions, and the crowd used to love it, even more than when we did our pregame war dance."

## The Bronk

Johnny Dell Isola, a linebacker for the New York Giants in the last half of the 1930s, recalls his first encounter with Bronko Nagurski of the Chicago Bears:

"I had heard a lot about him, but I thought most of it was exaggerated. We were at the Polo Grounds when I first ran up against him. It was first and ten and they gave the ball to Nagurski, up the middle. Well, a huge hole opened and I saw him coming. I put my head down and charged into the hole. We met at the line of scrimmage, and you could hear the thud all over the Polo Grounds. I had my arms around his legs and my shoulder dug into him. It was the hardest tackle I ever made, but I made it and said to myself, 'Well, I guess that will show you, Nagurski!' Then as I was getting up I heard the referee shout, 'Second down and two!' "

George Halas tells about one game in the Bronk's rookie season. It was at Wrigley Field, the home of the Bears and the Chicago Cubs in those days, where the outfield wall was not very far from the endline. The Bears were on about the 2 yard line. Nagurski got the handoff, his head down and

Bronko Nagurski here clearly illustrates his notorious running style: shoulder and head down, knees churning, 230 pounds of unbridled fury hurtling at the enemy like a runaway Mack truck. The NFL's all-time measuring stick for power runners, Nagurski, who wore a Chicago Bears uniform for nine seasons, was also a devastating blocker and tackler. In the background are Bears guard Madison Pearson (26) and halfback Gene Ronzani (6). *(Pro Football Hall of Fame)*

legs churning, and plunged into the line. He blasted through two would-be tacklers as though they were a pair of old saloon doors, and kept on going right through the end zone. His head still down, Nagurski ran full speed into the brick outfield wall, went down, then got up and trotted off the field. As he approached an ashen-faced Halas on the sideline, Nagurski shook his head and said, "That last guy really gave me a good lick, coach."

# 10

# Don Hutson

The "Alabama Antelope," as he was called, Don Hutson was the first end in the history of professional football to inscribe his name in legend at his position as inalterably as players like Red Grange and Bronko Nagurski had at theirs. There simply had never been a pass catcher as swift, as elusive, as sure-handed as he. And therefore he became one of the pivotal figures in the evolution of the passing game in pro football.

A slender, lissome figure on the football field, Hutson stood 6 feet 1 inch and weighed 165 pounds in college and 180 as a pro. He could run the 100-yard dash in 9:7 and, in the words of Greasy Neale, coach of the Philadelphia Eagles, "was the only man I ever saw who could feint in three different directions at the same time." From the time he began playing the game in high school until he finally left the field for good in 1945, Don Hutson routinely confounded and embarrassed defensive secondaries who ordinarily assigned two defenders to him and sometimes even triple-teamed him.

Hutson earned all-American honors at Alabama, and on January 1, 1935, caught two touchdown passes in the Rose Bowl game in which the Crimson Tide demolished a previously unbeaten Stanford team by sixteen points. Curly Lambeau, who watched that game in Pasadena, knew Hutson possessed the precious metal he needed to gild the Green Bay Packers' passing attack.

Lambeau's prescience on that particular subject has never been questioned. In Hutson's eleven-year career with Green Bay, he was named all-Pro *nine* times, and in the process he virtually monopolized all NFL pass receiving records. Several of his benchmarks still stand: most touchdown pass receptions in a career (ninety-nine), most seasons leading the league in touchdown pass catches (nine; the next closest, Lance Alworth, has only three), most seasons leading the league in pass receptions (eight; the next closest, Lionel Taylor, has only five), and the most consecutive seasons leading the league in pass catches (five).

His seventeen touchdown catches in 1942 broke the NFL single-season record of nine, which he had shared with teammate Johnny Blood, and the new record has only been equaled twice since, by Elroy Hirsch in 1951 and by Bill Groman in 1961. That same season, Hutson became the first receiver to gain more than 1,000 yards, his 1,211 eclipsing the NFL mark he had established in 1939 by 365 yards.

Don set another record when he caught at least one pass in ninety-five consecutive games, a mark that would stand for twenty-five years. But Hutson was more than just a receiver, he was an accomplished place kicker as well, and combining that with his touchdown catches he tallied enough points to lead the NFL in scoring five times. And, of course, he was a sixty-minute man, playing defensive end for the first few years of his career before switching to safety.

Even in his final year, 1945, the thirty-two-year-old Hutson led the NFL in pass receptions and in points after touchdowns.

He remained in Wisconsin after leaving the game to operate the Chevrolet and Cadillac dealerships he owned there and to direct his other business interests until he retired in 1984.

I grew up down in Pine Bluff, Arkansas, which is a town of about fifty-five thousand today but when I was living there it was only about twenty-five thousand. That was right in the middle of the Depression. Pine Bluff was basically a farming town, cotton country, and it really felt the hard times. I don't want to say that I was starving to death because I wasn't. My father had a job and we didn't have any real problems, although a lot of other families did.

I was the first Eagle Scout they ever had in Arkansas. That was one of my biggest interests when I was growing up around there. I remember that to earn one of my merit badges, the one for reptile study, I had to go out in the woods and collect different kinds of snakes. Well, I did and put them in cages out in our backyard. I kept them there and took care of them until I got my merit badge and then I took them back out in the woods and let them go. Years later some sportswriter wrote that I had a pet rattlesnake collection as a boy, which, of course, is not the way it was. But I truly liked scouting.

At Pine Bluff High School, they had only two organized sports, football and basketball, and I played both. I hadn't played any football before I got to high school. The thing I remember best from that time was in my senior year when we played the team from Fordyce, another small town down there. Their star player was Bear Bryant. They won the state championship that year. Bear was all-state and he was a highly recruited football player. We were both ends.

I wasn't that good a football player in high school. I'd just started as a junior and hadn't really gotten going yet. But I still ended up getting recruited. There was a fellow from Alabama by the name of Jimmy Harlon who was their recruiter. They drew a lot of their players from Arkansas in those days. In fact, the captain of their team the year they came over to talk to us was from Arkansas. And the year before, they'd taken two boys from the Pine Bluff team. That was just before the University of Arkansas started to have a good team and began to seriously recruit players. When I was in high school, I can't remember Arkansas trying to recruit anybody.

In my senior year, Alabama had their eye on a number of Arkansas boys. Of course, Bear Bryant, but they also wanted a couple from the Pine Bluff team that I played on. One of them was Bob Seawall, a friend of mine. Well, they all got to talking and somehow they decided to bring me along, too. I think they did it primarily because they wanted to keep everyone down there satisfied. Arkansas was quite a football state on the high school level and the coaches at Alabama knew it.

At Alabama, our quarterback was Dixie Howell, a fine college football player and a very good passer. His first year out of college, Dixie was signed by the Washington Redskins, but instead of going with them he went down to Mexico to coach the University of Mexico football team. But it was a bust and he came back the next year. He signed on with Washington, that was in 1937, but they had also signed another quarterback that year by the name of Sammy Baugh. Dixie played backup to him that year and then left football.

I was also on the track team at Alabama, and how that came about is a kind of interesting story. I hadn't planned to go for the sport. You see, at Pine Bluff High School they didn't have a track team so I didn't have any experience with it. So I just didn't think anything about it when I got to Alabama. But later, in my junior year I think it was, our end coach, Red Drew, who was also the track coach, came up to me after a session at spring football practice and said, "Don, I want you to go in and get on a pair of track shoes and shorts because our guy who's running the 100-yard dash here doesn't have anybody to run against. I want you to try to extend him." Well, as it turned out, I beat him by a couple of yards. Red Drew said to me after the race, "From now on, you're running the 100 for us." And I did. That's how I ended up on the team. That was actually the first time I ever had a pair of track shoes on. As a matter of fact, I played baseball and ran track at the same time during my last two years at Alabama. And if they had a track meet and a baseball game at the same time there in Tuscaloosa, they used to schedule the 100 and 220 dashes early so I could run them and then get over to the baseball field by the third inning or so. I got to where I could run the 100 in 9:7 consistently and that was pretty good in those days. The world record, I believe, was 9:5 then and I think Jesse Owens got it down to 9:4 in 1936. We went to the Rose Bowl after the 1934 season and played Stanford. It was the biggest thing in college football in those days, the Rose Bowl. Stanford had a good running game and they had been champions out there on the coast for several years. I believe they were undefeated when we went out there. But we got so far ahead of them with our passing game that they never could come close to catching up. We beat them 29–13. We had a fine team, too, as they found out. I had a good day, caught two touchdown passes. Our other end, by the way, was Bear Bryant that year.

Curly Lambeau of the Green Bay Packers was out there for the game. I didn't meet him at the time, but he was around scouting. Our coach at Alabama, Frank Thomas, had gone to Notre Dame, as had Lambeau. So Curly came out to watch us practice. Thomas would let him in because they were old friends. Curly liked the passing game, too, and I guess he was impressed with what he saw because after that he contacted me about coming to play for Green Bay after I graduated.

Actually, it's a kind of involved story about how I came to be with the Packers. First, Shipwreck Kelly, who owned the Brooklyn Dodgers then, came to Tuscaloosa before we went out to the Rose Bowl. He told me he wanted me to play for Brooklyn the next year. At that time, I hadn't heard anything from Lambeau or anyone else in the pros for that matter. I promised him I'd sign with Brooklyn if he matched any offer I got from another team. It was that simple of an agreement. Well, when I got back from the Rose Bowl, I began hearing from all the teams. This was before the NFL had a draft. I was the equivalent of a free agent, I guess. One of the people who contacted me was Curly Lambeau. Anyway, there was some bidding and as it went up others dropped out. Finally it was just Curly and Shipwreck. Each time, Curly would make an offer, I'd wire Shipwreck and he would match it. Well, it finally got up to three hundred dollars a game, quite a bit of money in those days. When Curly gave me his offer of three hundred dollars, I sent the wire to Shipwreck, but I didn't hear back from him. Curly kept calling me and after about a week went by I sent another wire to Shipwreck, and I didn't hear anything back from him again.

Finally Curly sent me a contract and I just went ahead and signed it. The day I put it in the mail, Shipwreck showed up in Tuscaloosa. He said that he had been down in Florida on vacation, and that he had just gotten the wires forwarded down to him. He wanted to match the three hundred dollar offer. I told him that I couldn't because I'd already signed with Curly and had put the contract in the mail that morning because I hadn't heard from him. Shipwreck said, "Don, I think you at least owe me a chance to meet it."

I said, "Well, hell, I can't. As I told you, I already signed one and it's gone off."

"Don't worry," he said. "Sign a contract with me, too, and let me worry about it." Well, I felt I did owe it to him after our agreement. So I signed one with Shipwreck, too. Later, both contracts were sent to Joe Carr, the NFL commissioner then, to decide which one was valid. The Green Bay contract got to him before Shipwreck's did and so he ruled I should go to Green Bay. And it was probably the biggest break I ever got in football. The reason is that Brooklyn was a grind-it-out team, in the old Ohio State tradition, a "put-out-a-lot-of-dust" operation. But at Green Bay, they had a real good passer in Arnie Herber, and Lambeau was a very pass-oriented coach. He emphasized passing as well as running and so it was obviously a real break for me to end up there.

There's another story about the salary. When I got to Green Bay, Curly told me he didn't want the other players or anybody else for that matter to know how much I was earning. Well, there were two banks in Green Bay in those years and the Packers had an account in each. So, to keep it a secret, I got two checks after each game, one hundred and fifty each, and each was drawn on a different bank up there. Things were done a bit differently in those days.

A most common sight in the eleven years from 1935 through 1945 was the dazzling Don Hutson gathering in a pass. A speedster with seemingly inhuman moves and faultless hands, Hutson was unparalleled as a pass receiver in his time and was also a deadly accurate place kicker. Despite his ordinarily sublime form, there were on occasion a few less graceful moments, such as this one in a game against the Pittsburgh Pirates in 1940. Chasing Hutson is defensive back Merl Condit (1). *(Green Bay Press Gazette)*

I didn't really know much at all about pro football before I got to Green Bay. I never followed it while I was in college. In fact, they never even carried the scores or the standings of the professional teams in the newspapers down in Alabama in those days. So when I got there it was a whole new world, a far cry from the college game. But I got into it pretty quick.

One thing I did when I went with the pros was to modify my equipment, pads, that is. I had my shoulder pads cut down so they were pretty small and less restrictive. I didn't wear hip pads. It was to give me a little more speed, a little better maneuverability; it gave me a little edge, I believe.

We were always working to invent things that would give us a hand up. I worked pretty closely with Arnie Herber and Lambeau to develop some new and different pass patterns. A lot of them that we came up with are the same kind of things that are run today by the pro teams.

I was never nervous, but I was aware that a ballplayer could be cut or dropped from the team. I didn't worry about it but the thought was there. But I got off on the right foot. In our first game, which was against the Chicago Bears, a fierce rival, on the first play of the game I caught a pass for a touchdown, an 83-yard play. They double-teamed Johnny Blood on the play and I got ahead of Beattie Feathers, the Bear defender on the other side of the field and Herber was right on target with the pass. I caught it somewhere near midfield and ran it in. We beat them 7–0 that day. It was a great start for me, gave me a good deal of confidence. After that I didn't spend a lot of time thinking about other ways of making a living.

I made friends with Arnie Herber and Clarke Hinkle when I first got up there. Johnny Blood, of course, was there, too, and he was quite a character. There are certainly enough stories about him, especially about his extracurricular activities. Johnny was kind of a legend around Green Bay by that time. He was about thirty years old by then. But he was still a fine football player, a great athlete.

In the early days I roomed with Arnie Herber up there. He was a fine guy. And Clarke Hinkle, he was one of the most fun-loving guys around. He had this big belly laugh and he was always a pleasure to be with. And what a powerful football player he was. Clarke was as good on defense as he was on offense, and there weren't many players you could say that about. He was a great fullback and a great linebacker. Bronko Nagurski was the same way. I believe he was named an all-American in college both as a fullback and a tackle. He and Clarke used to have some real bang-ups when we played the Bears. Theirs was a great rivalry on the field, but they were good friends and respected each other. Clarke was quite a bit smaller than Nagurski. He was a decent size, 6 feet, 200 pounds maybe, but Nagurski went about 240. But Clarke had heart and he took it to Nagurski all the time. No one else gave Nagurski as tough a time as Hinkle.

Those first couple of years, I played baseball in the spring and summer, too. After I had gotten out of Alabama I signed with the Cincinnati Reds, and I played one year in the Southern League for Knoxville and the next year I moved up to Triple-A with the team from Albany, New York. It had been my plan to allow myself two years to get into the major leagues but that didn't happen. I said to myself, if I didn't, I'd quit baseball and concentrate on other things. I wanted to get into business anyway. When the two years were over, I saw I wasn't going to the majors and so I quit. I didn't quit football, however, because by the end of my second year in that sport I'd been put on the all-Pro team and things were going very well for me.

I was fortunate in having a creative coach like Curly Lambeau, one who really saw the merits of the passing game at a time when just about no one else did. He was a stern coach and there was a big gap between Curly and the players. He didn't mingle with them. He was the coach and that was that. After I left football, we became very close friends. We both had homes in Palm Springs. And he used to ask me to go to the league meetings with him, and I would ordinarily. But in the beginning, he was the coach and I was just an end.

Curly used me as a kicker, too. I'd kicked for Alabama: kickoffs, field goals, extra points. At Green Bay, Curly had me kick field goals, the short ones, and extra points. Clarke Hinkle would kick the longer field goals. I played defensive end, too, for the first few years in Green Bay but then we drafted a boy from South Carolina named Larry Craig, who was a fine blocking back and a helluva defensive end. He took over at that position and I moved back to safety.

In 1936, we won the league championship, played for it in New York at the Polo Grounds. I remember it very well because it was my first championship game. We played the Boston Redskins but George Marshall, their owner, had the game moved to New York City because he was unhappy with Boston and was planning to move the team to Washington the next year. I caught a touchdown pass in the first quarter from Herber and we never gave up the lead after that. We won it 21–6. Of course, it was a big thing for the city of Green Bay. Everybody up there lived and died football. It was the first time a Green Bay team had won the championship since they started having a championship game. It was really something for them to win the title, after all they were just a little town of about twenty-five thousand people then and they won it over teams that came from all the big cities, like New York and Chicago and Detroit and Boston. We came back by train after the game and we got to Green Bay the next day and, hell, the whole town was there to greet us. There was a lot of celebrating, a parade, a banquet. The town was football-crazy and it still is.

We played for the championship again in 1938 and we should have won it again. That was the only game I can remember when an injury really affected me. I had a pulled ligament in my leg which I'd gotten a week or two earlier in a game against the Detroit Lions. I think I only played two or three plays in the championship game because of it, and on those I was just used as a decoy. In all my career, that was the only time that an injury kept me out of a game. We played the New York Giants for the title that year and I felt we were a better team than they were. We should have won the game. We even played better than them that day, but we lost it on a couple of kicks they blocked and were able to take advantage of.

We won our division again the next year and played the Giants again for the crown. This time the game was held in Milwaukee. It was very windy that day, I remember, and passing was difficult. But we got our revenge and shut the Giants out 27–0.

The last championship game I played in was in 1944, and that, too, was against the Giants. We played it in New York. I had a pretty good day, caught some passes and was successful as a decoy on some other plays.

The game I remember most, however, was against Detroit in 1945. We set a bunch of records that day. I caught four touchdown passes and kicked five extra points in one quarter alone. As a team, we scored forty-one points in that quarter. We ended up winning the game 57–21. It all happened because of the wind. I remember vividly how it was blowing straight down the field, like maybe thirty or thirty-five miles an hour. It was all a matter of judging the ball in the air and we were much better at it that day than the Lions. With the wind with us, we'd throw these long passes and I was able to get down there under them. I think their defensive backs didn't think the ball would travel as far as it did. And some-times, when we were throwing into the wind, I'd have to circle back like I was going for a lazy fly ball just as I did when I played center field. There was never another game quite like that, at least one that I played in.

Another memorable moment I had was in New York against the Gi-ants. I used to do the end-around play every so often. I had done that a lot at Alabama, too. Lambeau liked to use it as a surprise. Well, this one day in New York, I came around on it, running like hell, and everybody naturally thought I would just keep on around the end. Everybody on the Giants swarmed over there to cover it, the defensive backs all came rush-ing up, and this right end of ours, Harry Jacunski from Fordham, was standing by himself way down the field. They talk about a "lonesome end," well, let me tell you, he was the most lonesome end anybody ever saw. There wasn't a defender within 30 yards of him. I pulled up and threw a long pass, maybe 40 yards or more, and fortunately it was on the mark and he caught it for a touchdown. It was the only touchdown pass I ever threw in my entire football career.

Besides Arnie Herber, I also worked with another great passer at Green Bay, Cecil Isbell. He would be in the Hall of Fame today if he hadn't quit playing football so early. He only played four or five years. One year, 1942, he threw twenty-four touchdown passes, a record then. I caught seventeen of them, which was another record. And that was in just an eleven-game schedule. That gives you an idea of the kind of pas-ser Isbell was. But he quit playing to take the head coaching job at Pur-due, which is where he had gone to school. If he stayed around the NFL, I believe he would have become one of the game's most successful pas-sers, and his name would be all over the record books, and they would talk of him in the same terms they do of Luckman and Baugh.

In the last few years that I was playing football, I also went into busi-ness up in Green Bay. I had studied business at Alabama and I had always thought of going into business for myself. The first thing I did was build a bowling alley up in Green Bay and after that I went into the finance business as well. There was a lot going on as a result of my off-season business activities and as a result, for several years, I kept an-nouncing that I was going to retire from football and devote my entire time to my business interests. But I kept coming back, until 1945 anyway. It was damn near impossible for me to quit football in Green Bay. You know what the Packers meant to the town and I'd been having some good years. I got the feeling they wanted me to play forever. But the time had come. Before the 1945 season, I told Curly I'd play that year only if he promised not to ask me to play again the next year. He said all right, and he was good to his word. And that was it. I did remain with the team after that as an assistant coach to Curly, working with the ends and the backs.

I lived in Green Bay for about five years after I stopped playing football. Then, in 1950, I moved to Racine, Wisconsin, where I opened a Cadillac and Chevrolet dealership. I operated that until 1984, when I sold it.

A lot of the players used to stay in Green Bay after the season back when I played. There were jobs to be had and businesses to go into. The town loved the team and the players. One who was prominent up there and still is, I believe, is Tony Canadeo. I played with Tony in the early 1940s and he was a fine running back and a very fine fellow. Charley Brock, the center on our team most of the time I was there, also stayed in Green Bay.

We had some very good teams, and I know the city was proud of us. And some really memorable fellows: Herber, Hinkle, Isbell, Canadeo, and, of course, Johnny Blood and Curly Lambeau. We gave them a lot to remember, I believe.

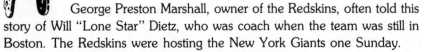

## *The View from the Top*

George Preston Marshall, owner of the Redskins, often told this story of Will "Lone Star" Dietz, who was coach when the team was still in Boston. The Redskins were hosting the New York Giants one Sunday.

"Dietz had heard that Lambeau and Halas had a coach high up in the stands who radioed instructions down to the bench. He thought it was a good idea, so good that he decided *he* would direct the Redskins from the upper deck of the stadium where we played. He had this walkie-talkie-like thing that he could use to talk to another coach on the bench.

"This was the first time he planned to use it. And he had another strategy that day as well. On the sideline just before the game he instructed the team to kick off, no matter whether they won the toss or not. His plan was to get the Giants deep in their territory and hold them there. Then he trotted into the stands and back to the ramp that led to the upper deck. When he finally got to his station, he looked down on the field and saw the Redskins

The Chicago Bears, lined up at a practice session just before the 1935 season. At that time of year, practice was held in a vacant lot behind a factory a few miles from downtown Chicago because the Chicago Cubs were still playing baseball at Wrigley Field. In the photo: backfield *(left to right)* Gene Ronzani, Bronko Nagurski, Carl Brumbaugh, and Keith Molesworth; line *(left to right)* Bill Karr, George Musso, Madison Pearson, Ed Kawal, Zuck Carlson, Link Lyman, and Bill Hewitt. *(Pro Football Hall of Fame)*

lined up to receive the football. He grabbed the walkie-talkie and shouted into it to his coach down below, 'What the hell's going on? I said to kick the ball. Not receive. What the hell are we doing receiving it?'

"There was a pause, then his assistant coach said, 'We did kick. Harry Newman ran it back 94 yards for a touchdown.'"

## *Trivium*

Four of the most famous football names in the NFL's first college player draft, conducted in 1936, were Heisman Trophy winner Jay Berwanger of the University of Chicago, Notre Dame's triple-threat all-American back Bill Shakespeare, Alabama's rugged end Paul "Bear" Bryant, and all-American end Eddie Erdelatz of St. Mary's College. All four, however, declined to sign pro contracts, which in those days offered paltry salaries in the range of $125 to $250 per game for a top rookie, and opted for careers that at least then appeared more lucrative.

# 11

# *Wellington Mara*

Wellington Mara had a unique childhood; he grew up with the New York Giants football team. He was nine years old in 1925 when his father, Tim Mara, a New York bookmaker and close friend of Governor Al Smith and Mayor Jimmy Walker, bought the franchise. He watched the team grow through the wide eyes of a youngster, then through the keen eyes of an expert on player personnel, and finally through the encompassing eyes of a club president.

Wellington was there on the bench with his father and older brother Jack at the Giants' very first game at the Polo Grounds against the Frankford Yellow Jackets. He watched as a gimpy, thirty-seven-year-old Jim Thorpe tried to gain a few yards for the new franchise, and he saw a very talented Hinky Haines direct the team from his tailback position. He found other early greats on the field that day, too, like Guy Chamberlin and Century Milstead. But he also saw the Giants lose their first home game 14–0.

From that moment on, however, professional football would be an integral part of his life. By the time he was sixteen, Wellington was his father's adviser on college football talent and would present him with carefully researched lists of the players that would aid the Giants' cause.

Among his first real coups was the snagging of running back Tuffy Leemans. It was autumn 1935 and Wellington, then a nineteen-year-old student at Fordham University, went to his father and told him that he needed to go to Washington, D.C., on business for the Giants. He explained that there was a fine running back there who the Giants truly needed, a senior at George Washington University. His father agreed, so Wellington wired Tuffy Leemans to set up a meeting, and then went to Washington. When he approached Leemans in front of the gymnasium at

George Washington, Leemans allegedly mistook the tall teenager for someone wanting an autograph. That corrected, Wellington then convinced Leemans of the efficacy of joining the New York Giants. Leemans would remain for eight seasons and become one of the Giants' all-time finest backs.

Wellington Mara pulled many great Giant names from the college pool. Two others he was crucially responsible for were Charlie Conerly, whom he had to lure away from a rich contract offer by Branch Rickey of the All-American Football Conference's Brooklyn franchise, and Emlen Tunnell, the Giants' first black player.

Wellington Mara offers a keen insight into the world of professional football, his world since he was in fourth grade: fan, scout, player personnel director, unofficial team photographer, secretary of the club. He took over the duties of president of the Giants in 1965 after the death of his brother Jack.

**M**y earliest recollection of the Giants was on a Sunday morning, I guess it was in the autumn of 1925 and I was about nine years old. We were coming out of mass and I remember my father saying to one of his friends, "I'm gonna try to put pro football over in New York today." Then I recall going to the game. I don't think my father had ever seen a football game before. I had seen one or two. My brother Jack had taken me to a couple of Fordham games.

During the game, and I've told the story many times, we were sitting on the Giant side and it was a little chilly. My mother complained to my father that we were sitting in the shade. Why couldn't we go over and sit in the sun where we'd be nice and warm? So the next game, and from then on, the Giant sideline in the Polo Grounds was in the sun.

Another thing I remember from those first days was that I wanted to sit on the bench and I got to. I remember our coach, Bob Folwell, a former Navy coach, turning to one of the players on the bench, his name was Paul Jappe, who is still living in Florida, and saying, "Jappe get in there and give them hell!" I thought, boy, this is really a rough game.

My father came to own the Giants in a kind of roundabout way. He was a bookmaker in New York and he was very friendly with Billy Gibson, who was the manager of Gene Tunney, the boxer. My father actually had been instrumental early in Tunney's career. He had been very friendly almost from boyhood with Al Smith and through him with the political organization in New York City and New York State, and boxing at that time was very politically-oriented. My father helped Tunney to get some fights, some bouts, that he otherwise might not have been able to get. Anyway, Billy Gibson came into my father's office one day and brought with him a gentleman named Harry A. March, who was a retired Army doctor. Dr. March had been interested in pro football and its origins out in Ohio, the Canton area. I don't think there was a pro football team in New York at the time, although I've heard that Jimmy Jemail, a columnist for the New York *Daily News*, he wrote The Inquiring Reporter, said that he had a team in New York in 1924, and that my father took over that franchise. I was never aware of that. I only remember that my father said, "How much will it cost?" and that was it. There are two versions of that story, too: one was that it was five hundred dollars, the other that it was twenty-five hundred dollars. I know my father did say that even an empty store with chairs in it was worth that in New York City, so he went for the five hundred dollars or the twenty-five hundred dollars, whichever it was, and that's how he got interested in pro football at that time.

In the beginning, the football team, to put it mildly, was not a financial success. The first year we were bailed out, however, because Red Grange came to the Polo Grounds. I remember that very well. My father had gone out to the Midwest to try to sign Grange. Back then we didn't have a formal rule that said a player had to be drafted. And Red Grange, playing for Illinois, was the eighth wonder of the world in those days. My father went out to see Red Grange around the time he was playing his last collegiate game with the intention of signing him to play for the Giants.

My brother, Jack, who was eight years older, and I were very excited about all this. We got a telegram from my father saying: "Partially successful. Will arrive on train and explain." We didn't really know what that meant. We had already heard that he had been unable to sign Red Grange because Red had signed with the Chicago Bears. As far as we were concerned, he was totally *un*successful. But what he meant was that he had booked an exhibition game in the Polo Grounds with the Bears and Red Grange. The game sold out, more than seventy thousand paid to see that game, and my father made up what he had lost that year. Actually it was my father and just two assistants who sold those seventy-odd thousand tickets out of one small office in the Knickerbocker Building in New York. You know today you'd have ten or twenty people and they'd have to be there for days in order to sell that many tickets. Another thing my father worried about in regard to that game was the weather. It had been very bad all week and he was concerned about it. But about two in the morning on that Sunday a friend of his called and said, "Tim, look out the window. The stars are out."

Still, football in New York was very unsuccessful. My father's friends all told him that he was foolish to stay with it. I remember Governor Al Smith in our house one day when we had heard that the team had just lost rather badly to Green Bay. Al Smith said to my father, "Your team will never amount to anything. Why don't you give it up?" My father looked at my brother Jack and myself and said, "The boys would run me right out of the house if I did." That's certainly one thing that sticks in my mind about those early years. I really think my father was talking more in terms of my brother Jack than myself, however, because Jack was of an age where he mingled with the players, as pals more or less, and I was still in the hero-worshipping stage.

I didn't travel with the team at the start. I was too young. My brother Jack did. I didn't really start traveling with the team until about the mid-1930s. Once in a while I was permitted to take a trip in the early '30s, when I was still in school, if it wouldn't interfere with my Friday afternoon classes.

Money was still tight in the '30s, in fact it was very tight. But at the same time, my father said, among the areas of the entertainment business, sports businesses somewhat prospered during the Depression because they really offered the best entertainment for the money. A football game or a baseball game was great entertainment and a man could get it for his whole family. We did better during those years, the mid-'30s, but we were still just barely breaking even.

Of course, it was a very different game they played then. I remember a couple of things from it that gave an idea of how it was different. I recall the days when you didn't have hash marks, and later when you had them but to get the ball to one of them you actually had to go out of bounds. If you were tackled one yard from the sideline, that was where the ball was put in play. I remember teams having special plays for that. Along those lines I remember Tony Plansky, a tailback from George-town, who had been a great decathlon athlete, drop-kicking a field goal for us from around the 40 yard line that won a game. The thing was, however, that he was way over to the left side of the field and he was ambidextrous and kicked the ball left-footed because he was going from left to right. And the Chicago Bears had this guy who passed the ball behind his back, Bull Doehring.

It was also a one-platoon game then. As Steve Owen used to say, men were men in those days. He was our great coach for so many years and he saw a lot of truly sturdy, talented sixty-minute men who played for and against us. Stamina played a great part of it in those days, and the players had to pace themselves. They couldn't go all out on every play, you just couldn't do that for sixty minutes of football playing time. The player who played opposite you, however, was under the same handicap, but it still was grueling. The individual skills were not as refined as they are today either. Some were, like those of Don Hutson. But still he had to play defense even though his specialty was that of being a great pass receiver, probably as great as any receiver we have in the game today who only has to concentrate on catching footballs. Hutson wasn't able to hang up the statistics the receivers have today because he had to make tackles on defense as well. Arnie Herber, with the same Green Bay team, was a great passer but he wasn't used all the time because he was a poor defensive player. And once a player was taken out of a game he couldn't go back in during the same period of play, so substitutions had to be made very carefully.

Steve Owen was a true innovator. In 1937, he developed his version of the two-platoon system. We had a young team and a very deep bench at the time, and Steve used to change ten of the eleven men at the end of the first period and at the end of the third period. The only one who stayed on the field for the entire game was Mel Hein. He was too good both on offense and defense to take out. One time we were playing the Bears in 1939 and the first period ended with them having third down and two yards to go on our 2 yard line. Steve changed ten of the eleven players and they held.

Unlike today, the stars of those days were relatively anonymous. Mel Hein, as great a player as he was, a Hall of Famer, could walk down Broadway and I don't think anyone would have recognized him in those days. I think players were a lot more closely knit at that time, however. The salaries weren't such that they could have their own homes or apartments. If you had a twenty-five-man squad, probably twenty of them lived in the same hotel. Maybe two or three roomed together. We would travel by train. We'd go to Pittsburgh, for example, at noon on Friday and not get back until maybe noon on Monday. Being on the train so long is another example of how the players were thrown together a lot more back then.

The great majority of our players in those days came into New York during the season and then went back to where they were from after it was over. We used to try to get off-season jobs for as many as we could but we weren't always successful. Most simply went back home. We had a great many boys from the farmlands and they all went back when the season closed up. Steve Owen, in fact, came from Kansas. And, of course, we didn't have the far-flung scouting empires that we have today. A lot of Steve's talent scouting was done through the eyes of people he had played with. They went to football games or coached football teams in Kansas and Oklahoma and Texas and so we obtained a lot of players from those areas.

Steve Owen was an integral part of the Giant organization and he was like a second father to me. He came in as a player, and he was one player who did stay in New York. He married a New York girl and he worked in a coal company that my father owned and then later at the race track during the off-season. I admired him, was greatly attached to him, and respected him. He kind of brought me up in the football business. Starting in the early 1930s, I went to training camp and always felt like he was taking care of me.

Another Giant I remember well was Benny Friedman. He was really our first big star. Friedman had been with Cleveland and Detroit but both those teams had folded. In fact, my father had bought out the remnants of the Detroit team and brought Benny Friedman in here with Roy Andrews, who was their head coach, Steve Owen's brother Bill, and several other players. Benny Friedman made a great contribution to pro football in New York, off the field as well as on it. Several times a week he would go around to high school assemblies in the mornings and give tickets away to promote the game. He really did make an enormous contribution. He was also, of course, a fine player and a durable one. I don't think he ever missed a game because of an injury. Benny Friedman truly deserves to be in the Hall of Fame. The problem there, I think, is that there is a large gap. I don't think enough people on the selection committees remember the guys who were the real pioneers of the game. Friedman was one of a kind and never got the proper recognition.

A Giant deservedly in the Hall of Fame is Mel Hein. I remember very

The cadre of the New York Giants, circa 1940. Second from the right is club founder Tim Mara, flanked by his sons, Wellington (on his left) and Jack (on his right). Next to Jack is coach Steve Owen. Ownership of the Giants was turned over in 1930 to Jack and Wellington Mara, who served as president and secretary, respectively, until Jack's death in 1965. Since that time Wellington has presided over the organization. Steve Owen, a Giant legend, served as head coach from 1931 through 1953, compiling a record of 151–100–7 and winning two NFL championships and eight divisional titles. *(Pro Football Hall of Fame)*

well the first day he came into our camp. But the thing I remember most vividly is when he gave me a black eye. It was in the early '30s, and I was in my early teens. It was one of the first times I had been entrusted to stay overnight at training camp, which was a big thrill for me. I used to get out on the field with the players. Mel Hein was centering to our punter, who was booting the ball downfield. There were players in two lines on each side of Hein, running down under the punts. Every once in awhile Mel would run down, too. I was retrieving the balls as they were thrown back and putting them down in front of Mel. Well, he decided to run down under one just as I was bending over and putting the ball down. He ran right over me. It took my eye about thirty seconds to close tight.

Ray Flaherty was another of our favorites on the team. He was a tremendous competitor. We had two of the toughest players ever at our two ends in those days—Flaherty and Red Badgro—and at the same time they were two of the nicest guys you'd ever meet. Red Badgro was just inducted into the Hall of Fame [1981], and Flaherty has been in for some time. Ray was also an assistant coach for us and later became a fine head coach for the Washington Redskins. I recall one particular incident concerning Flaherty. He hurt his hand in one game, really didn't hurt it badly but the doctor put a big bandage on it. Ray held it like it was broken and in a sling, and he was pretending to be in great pain. Everyone was very solicitous toward him. I don't remember who the player was but it was one of Ray's particular friends and he was helping Ray over to the bench on the sideline. "Are you all right, Ray?" he asked. "Yeah, I'm all right," Flaherty said and then punched his friend in the stomach with his supposedly broken hand.

There was also Harry Newman. Harry was a sort of Benny Friedman clone. We didn't have that term in our vocabulary in those days, but Newman, who came from Michigan, was short, stocky, an indestructible Jewish boy, and a very smart quarterback, just like Friedman. He had a couple of very successful years with us. I'll always remember one thing that Harry did in those days. The rule is still in the book. When a member of the punting team touches a punt but doesn't actually down it, just touches it, the receiving team can pick it up and advance it any time before the official blows his whistle. And even if you fumble the ball and lose it, you would still get the ball where the other guy touched it. Harry Newman picked one up like that in Boston and ran it back for a touchdown. I still remember the Boston player coming off the field and saying, "I'll never do that again. Never again!"

One of the greatest of them all was Ken Strong. He was a fabulous all-around player and he truly deserved to go into the Hall of Fame. Ken Strong had been a great back at New York University in the years when my brother Jack was going to Fordham. That made him a hated rival, of course, but we still thought he was the greatest. We wanted him for the Giants very badly. My father had this employee who was instructed to make every effort to sign Ken Strong. But he failed and we were very upset when Ken signed with the Staten Island Stapletons, who were a key rival of ours. He then came over and beat us a couple of times. We used to play the Stapes on Thanksgiving Day, and it was a big game in New York.

Strong often played without a helmet; he was a great blocker, great punter, great runner, and could pass with the best of them until he broke his hand. When the Staten Island team disbanded, Strong came to us. My father said, "Well, Ken, you are three years too late. I never understood why you went over there for less money than we offered you."

Ken said, "What do you mean?"

"We offered you ten thousand dollars a year."

"No, you didn't. You offered me five thousand dollars."

Apparently our employee was going to pocket the five thousand dollars difference or else he thought he was going to save the club some money and make some points for himself. I don't know which, all I know is that that's how we lost Ken Strong.

Shipwreck Kelly also had a brief career with us. He came to us at a time when we didn't have a very good team. He was a very flashy, colorful player, always did the unexpected. One time he was back to receive a punt for us, caught it, and then punted the ball right back. People talked about it for weeks afterward. He was a very fine player, but he was an undisciplined one. You never knew in which direction he was going to run. I don't know whether he did either. He later went over and became a part owner of the Brooklyn Dodgers. We played against them several times. I've seen him on occasion since then at the race track and once in a while if he's in town he gives me a call. He's a very pleasant, unusual guy. He was a big man about town, which didn't help his football career any.

Then, of course, there was the famous "Sneakers Game" of 1934. It had been very, very cold that week in New York. There was a good amount of snow and the field was frozen. Saturday night, Ray Flaherty, who was one of our assistant coaches and played end for us, called Steve Owen on the telephone and said, "One time when I played at Gonzaga in

college we had a frozen field and we borrowed sneakers from our basketball team and went out and beat a team which was much better than us.
We had a lot better footing." It was an idea, Owen agreed, but it was also
Saturday night and there wasn't much that could be done about getting
the shoes. And on Sunday all the sporting goods stores would still be
closed in New York.

At the Polo Grounds on Sunday morning, the field was completely
frozen. We had a little fellow on the payroll named Abe Cohen, a sort of
jack of all trades. Abe was a tailor by profession and he also worked for
Chick Meehan, who was a famous coach at Manhattan College and was
quite a showman in his own way. Meehan was the first coach to put what
we call satin pants on a football team. He had done that first at NYU in
the days of Ken Strong. Abe was his tailor and made the pants for the
players so that they would fit properly. Steve Owen asked Abe to go up
to Manhattan College, to which he had access—he had a key to their
equipment room and the gym—and borrow the sneakers from the lockers
of the basketball players and bring them over to the Polo Grounds for
our players.

Abe got in a taxi and went to Manhattan. I think he had to break into
the lockers. At any rate he got back around halftime of the game with
nine or ten pairs of sneakers.

Some of the players didn't want to put them on, but those who did
had so much success that eventually most of our players put them on.
Ken Strong, who kicked off for us, place-kicked with the sneakers on and
he lost a toenail on his big toe. In the second half we began moving the
ball. One of the Bear players went over to the sideline and told George
Halas that we were wearing sneakers. "Step on their toes," Halas shouted
to his players.

The following week after the championship game—in those days you
had barnstorming trips after the season was over—the Bears were playing
an exhibition game in Philadelphia, and Steve Owen and I went down to
see the game. We went into the Bears' dressing room, I guess to crow a
little bit, and the first thing we saw was about 24 pairs of sneakers on top
of the lockers. Halas said to us, "I'll never get caught like that again."

The war came along and took the great majority of the athletes out of
the NFL. It threatened to close football down altogether. George Halas
was going back into the Navy and since he was going to be gone from
football he kind of led a drive to cancel the season, call the whole thing
off. George Marshall, Bert Bell, and my father crusaded to keep it going

at any cost, even if we had to play 4Fs and high school players, which we did. I think that it may very well be that playing under those circumstances helped to save the NFL because when the war was over, Arch Ward started the All-American Football Conference. It started at a terrible disadvantage, even though they had some fine teams and excellent players, because we were already established. I think if we had suspended operations for three or four years and then tried to start it up again, the AAFC would have started on more equal terms with us and the league might be a very different one from what it is today.

The game changed considerably after the war. Today the players are so much bigger and faster and the impact when they collide is so much greater. There's been a lot of talk about the artificial turf. I think artificial turf first became popular because people thought it would do away with knee injuries, cleats wouldn't catch in it the way they do in natural grass. There're no statistics to show if it has had any effect one way or the other. But I do think players run faster on artificial turf than they do on grass, maybe a tenth or a fifth of a second faster in a 40-yard sprint, and that difference, with the great weight they carry, results in a dramatic difference in impact. I think that may be why we have more injuries today.

Certainly football was less rewarding financially in those earlier days, but it was surely a lot of fun. I really do believe that. When I got out of college and first started spending a lot of time around the football team, a couple of the coaches and some players and myself would go to play golf one or two afternoons a week because practice would be over at two o'clock. Now they're just getting down to it at two. It's a lot harder work today, more time involved. In the '20s, '30s, and '40s they didn't get salaries in any proportion as to what players get today. Most of the players and coaches had to get other jobs to survive. Vince Lombardi, when he was an assistant coach with us in the 1950s, in fact, had an off-season job with a bank, not only because of the low pay but also because there just wasn't that much to be done by the coaching staff then.

The game was fun in those early days and the men who played it were very memorable. I was very fortunate to have watched it and been involved with it.

# Double Take

George Musso, great guard for the Chicago Bears from 1933 through 1944, recalls the legendary collisions between his teammate Bronko Nagurski and Clarke Hinkle of the Green Bay Packers:

Bobby Swisher (46), a scatback for the Chicago Bears, sets out behind the interference of all-Pro tackle Joe Stydahar (13) in this 1938 game against the Green Bay Packers. The rivalry between the Bears and the Packers is the oldest in the NFL, dating back to 1921, when Curly Lambeau brought his Green Bay team to Chicago for their first encounter with George Halas' Staleys. Chicago won that game, 20–0, and the Bears maintain a slight edge in the series of approximately 150 games.

"Hinkle once plunged into the line and ran past me only to meet Nagurski, our linebacker, head-on. Nagurski hit him so hard that Hinkle was knocked back. He went backpedaling past me back into the Green Bay backfield. But somehow he stayed on his feet and charged right back past me again. It was the only time I ever saw a back go by me three times on one play."

## Welcome to the NFL

Will Walls, an end out of Texas Christian, made his NFL debut with the New York Giants in 1937. In their first preseason game with the Chicago Bears, a team with a reputation for being mean and ugly as well as extraordinarily good, Walls was introduced to the sometimes ungentle and ungentlemanly world of professional football.

On the first play after the kickoff, Walls found himself lined up across from Joe Stydahar, 6 feet 4 inches, 230 pounds, an all-Pro who was then working his way to a niche in the Hall of Fame. Stydahar, who often played without a helmet, was also known as one of the most rugged players in the league.

Walls admittedly was nervous. "I wasn't afraid of him, though," Walls said later, "more curious, I guess, to see if he was as tough as they said."

He was. As soon as the ball was snapped, Stydahar lunged across the line and slugged Walls, knocking him flat on his back.

Walls was stunned and furious and leapt to his feet. Stydahar looked at him dolefully. "Kid, I didn't mean to do that," he said. "Sometimes I just get too excited at the start of a game." He then patted Walls on the back and gave him a reassuring smile.

Walls said something to the effect that he could understand that and returned the smile.

On the next play, the reassured Walls was again face to face with Stydahar, and again Stydahar surged across the line at the snap like an enraged bull. This time it was a ferociously wielded forearm to the jaw that dulled Walls's senses and reintroduced him to the grass of the playing field.

The dazed rookie got up and found Stydahar looking at him and shaking his head. "You've got to stay alert, son," Stydahar said.

# 12

# *Ace Parker*

Clarence "Ace" Parker sat in the locker room at the Polo Grounds before the Brooklyn Dodgers–New York Giants game on December 7, 1941, listening to the radio reports of the Japanese attack on Pearl Harbor. The two-time all-Pro tailback in his fifth season in the NFL shook his head and said, "What do we do now?" Well, first he went out and beat the Giants that afternoon; then he went into the navy and served there for most of the next four years.

Ace Parker had been an all-American at Duke, graduating in 1937. Then he signed with the NFL's Brooklyn Dodgers, the result of a concerted effort to obtain his services by owners Dan Topping and Shipwreck Kelly and their new coach Potsy Clark. Parker had planned to play major league baseball but with coaxing decided to give pro football a try at the same time.

Ace proved to be a much better professional football player. Both a superb passer and an excellent runner, he immediately won the starting job in Brooklyn. And just to prove his worth to the Dodgers franchise, he also excelled at catching passes, returning punts and kickoffs, place kicking, punting, and becoming one of the best defensive backs in the NFL. In 1940, with a runner-up Brooklyn team in the NFL East, he was named the league's most valuable player.

Parker weighed only 168 pounds when he played pro football, not much weight on a body that stood 6 feet tall, and he was not considered especially fast. Still, he could get things done on a football field that very few others could, and many have said that had his career not been interrupted by World War II he would have produced statistics equivalent to those of legends like Sammy Baugh. At the same time, he did well enough to earn his way into the Pro Football Hall of Fame, being inducted in 1972.

Ace Parker kept the Brooklyn franchise alive during the five years before the war, and it in effect disintegrated while he was gone. Its remnants were restructured in 1945 into what became the Boston Yanks, and after that the New York Yankees in the All-American Football League. Parker played a year with each team and then retired. He returned to Duke University and served as a football and baseball coach there during the next two decades.

I was born and raised in Portsmouth, Virginia, which is down by Norfolk, and then I moved back there after I finished coaching. I was about fourteen when I first took up the game of football, played sandlot ball over in a city park in Portsmouth. It was a big thing in the city back then. Every Saturday we'd have pickup games with kids from all over the city. Sometimes we'd have as many as seven or eight teams show up. We didn't have any equipment, just played in our street clothes. Most of us would go home and get our fannies tanned for getting our clothes all torn up.

After that I played at Woodrow Wilson High School in Portsmouth. I was the tailback in our single wing and I called the signals from that position. We played teams from all over the state, even played as far away as Kentucky. That was against a team from Ashland, a great team in the early '30s that had Bert Johnson on it. They called him "Warhorse," and he later went on to play for the University of Kentucky and then the Brooklyn Dodgers and the Bears and the Cardinals up in Chicago. We had a pretty good team in high school, too, were runners-up for the state championship two years in a row.

My parents were the ones who directed me toward Duke for college. It was a highly regarded school in North Carolina and even though we lived in Virginia, my parents were both from North Carolina, my daddy from Wilmington and my mother from New Bern. Another big factor was Wallace Wade, the football coach at Duke. He'd just moved there from the University of Alabama where he'd made quite a reputation for himself. Duke was a fairly young school at the time, that was back around 1933, and they were trying to put themselves on the map so they hired Wallace Wade away from Alabama. He was considered one of the best coaches in the United States at that time and I thought it would be nice to play for him. He wanted me, too, and sent Eddie Cameron to Portsmouth to recruit me. I got a kind of work-scholarship, which meant everything was paid for but that I had to work around the campus. I waited tables in the dining hall all four years there. I also worked at the school's information desk, answering the telephone and taking messages.

As a coach, Wallace Wade was a strict disciplinarian. As a man, he was a great fellow and he and I are still good friends today. He's ninety-one years old now and I visit with him every so often. He was the type of man who expected you to produce from the moment you walked onto the field. Off the field, he'd do anything for you, any kind of help you needed he'd be ready.

One of my most memorable moments at Duke was in a game against North Carolina, our number one rival back then. I ran back a kickoff 105 yards for a touchdown which, I believe, is still a school record there.

After college, I went to the East-West game in 1937. And I also played professional baseball that year for the Philadelphia Athletics under Connie Mack. I played for them both in '37 and '38. I was able to play major league baseball in the summer and pro football in the fall. I started out as an outfielder but Connie Mack converted me to a shortstop. I didn't do all that well for him though. I had two other chances in the big leagues after that, one with the Pittsburgh Pirates and the other with the Chicago Cubs, but I really wasn't quite a major league caliber player. I think I hit about .179 lifetime.

I did much better in football. The Brooklyn Dodgers picked me in the NFL draft in '37, even though I thought of myself as a baseball player first at that time and I told them I wasn't really that interested in playing pro football. But as the season wore on I kind of got to know that my chances of being a good baseball player were marginal. So around August I started to think more and more about football. And the football Dodgers contacted me again. It was Dan Topping and Shipwreck Kelly, the owners, who came to see me. Potsy Clark, their head coach also talked to me around that time.

The pros didn't start football in those days until Labor Day. So I decided to give it a try. I went and talked with Mr. Mack and asked if I could leave the team a little early to play football. Well, they weren't anywhere in the pennant race. They ended up in seventh place in an eight-team league. And it wouldn't have mattered even if they were, the way I was hitting. So he said it was okay and I went up to Brooklyn and then to the Dodgers' training camp.

I did pretty well that first year in the NFL and at the end of it I realized that I was better off in that sport than I was in baseball.

The contract Topping and Kelly offered me that year was twenty-five hundred dollars for the season. They told me at the time that I was the third-highest-paid player in the league. Hell, you can't even talk to a free agent today for twenty-five hundred dollars, much less get him to play in a game for that kind of money.

Dan Topping was a great guy though, and he took a lot of interest in the team. I always felt bad we couldn't win a championship for him. I think we might have if the war hadn't come along. That's when we had Jock Sutherland as our coach and we had just started to win regularly. We just barely lost out to the New York Giants in 1941, lost out on the last game of the season. We actually had beaten the Giants twice that year, but we ended up losing one more game than they did. After that, I went into the military service and so did Jock and several other players and the Dodgers just didn't do very well from that time on.

Shipwreck Kelly was quite a character. You could never tell what he was going to do next. But, like Topping, he was a likeable sort of fellow. He'd do all kinds of things. My rookie year was his last year. He wasn't even planning to play that year. In fact when I got there he gave me his equipment. You see, in those days, you had to furnish your own shoes, shoulder pads, and hip pads, at least in Brooklyn that's the way it was. Well, I didn't know that and when I first showed up I didn't have those things, so Shipwreck gave me his pads because he said he was through with the game. I wore his equipment the entire time I played pro football, all seven years. When Shipwreck came back during the season, he just got himself some other equipment and never asked me to give back what he'd given me. I ran into him in Kentucky a few years ago and I was telling him that one pair of his pads were in the College Football Hall of Fame and the other was in the Pro Football Hall of Fame, shoulder pads in one and hip pads in the other. He got a big laugh out of that.

Later Dan Topping bought Shipwreck out. They were quite a pair though. One time Shipwreck put a lion in Dan Topping's bed. Dan was in there asleep—they roomed together when they weren't out carousing around town—and old Shipwreck snuck in this lion, not a real full-grown one but big enough. When Dan woke up later and saw it he damn near jumped out of the sixth-story window.

When I first came to Brooklyn, I lived at the Knights of Columbus club over near Ebbets Field during the season. Later we trained out in Freeport, Long Island, and I lived out there when that happened. I was

A pair of perennial all-Pros, tailback Ace Parker (7) and tackle Bruiser Kinard (25) were the keystones of the Brooklyn Dodgers in the late 1930s and early '40s. Parker, a triple-threat back, played seven seasons in the pros with a three-year interruption for military service in World War II. Kinard, a pure sixty-minute man, missed only one game in his nine-year pro career. After the Brooklyn franchise folded, both players joined the New York Yankees of the fledgling All-American Football Conference in 1946. *(Pro Football Hall of Fame)*

pretty much still a country boy when I got to Brooklyn, and I was kind of in awe of it when I got there, especially New York City. Seemed I could never find my way around. I guess I was a little afraid of it at first, being so big and all and everybody in such a hurry, but then I got to like it a lot after awhile.

We didn't spend a lot of time in Brooklyn, except to sleep and practice. When we went out, we went over to New York City. We'd go over on Sunday nights a lot after the game to celebrate or whatever, myself and Bruiser Kinard and Perry Schwartz and Herman Hodges and Ralph Kercheval. Those were the guys I ran with mostly, but there were a lot of other good guys on the team, too, who came along different times. We used to go to the Pennsylvania Hotel a lot. It was right across from Penn Station. Glenn Miller and his band were playing there most of the time and we went so often I got to know him pretty well. We also went to Toots Shor's a lot. So did Dan Topping and Shipwreck Kelly. We'd see them in there from time to time. Toots was a great guy and an admirer of athletes. I used to go in there almost every weekend and I knew Toots real well, too. There were always baseball players or football players or movie stars in there and they all loved Toots. He was one of those guys who, if he knew you real well, he'd shout at you, swear at you, but would do anything in the world for you.

Potsy Clark was our coach when I came to Brooklyn. He was an ex-Marine and a lot of times he wanted you to do things the military way. Very strict sort of a guy. He was real short but a tough little guy. He got pretty frustrated with the Brooklyn ballclub because we couldn't win. He'd come there from a winner. Potsy had been coaching over at Detroit, those Lion teams that had Dutch Clark and Glenn Presnell. They'd won the NFL championship one year under Potsy. Dan Topping hired him away to turn Brooklyn into a winner, but we never did get going in those first couple of years. Potsy used to have parties at his house for the players. There was a good feeling of spirit among us.

We broke even in 1938, won four, lost four and tied three. In eight of the eleven games I played sixty minutes in the other three I played about fifty-seven minutes. I had a good year, led the league in passing, but our backfield was riddled with injuries. Without all the players being hurt we might have given the Giants a better run for the division title. We had a couple of really fine linemen in Bruiser Kinard and Ox Emerson. In 1939 we dropped down again, won only four of eleven games.

Jock Sutherland replaced Potsy Clark in 1940. He was quite a coach, changed the whole football team around when he took over. Up until then Potsy would let you do fundamentally what you'd learned to do in college. Now when Sutherland came in you had to adapt and do everything his way, which brought us all together and that's when we started to produce and win. He was a perfectionist, a helluva coach. His first year with us we won eight games and lost only three. We were a much more tightly knit team. We were only a game behind the Washington Redskins in the NFL East and we beat them once during the year. The next year we won seven of eleven games and were just a game behind the New York Giants. In fact we beat the Giants both times we met that year. One of those times was on December 7, the day Pearl Harbor was bombed. We had never beaten the Giants before Jock Sutherland came along, but after he was there we knocked them off three of the four times we played.

Playing football in those days wasn't nearly as formal as it is today. We practiced in the morning and had our team meetings at the end of the morning and that was it. We had the afternoons off and most of us just took it easy, lied around, none of us had other jobs during the season. Everybody had off-season jobs, you had to in those days because you couldn't really get by on what you got paid for playing football. My job was better than most, playing baseball, at least in 1937 and 1938. I also managed in the minor leagues for four years, too. I played and managed at Portsmouth in the Piedmont League up until I'd have to leave and go play football.

Travel was different back then too. No chartered jets. When we played on a Sunday, we'd leave by train the Thursday before it. And sometimes when we went far away, we didn't come back after the game. I remember my first year we went to Chicago to play the Bears and then went over to Fort Wayne, Indiana, and spent most of the next week there and then the next Sunday went up to Pittsburgh to play the Steelers. They would find us a place to practice in some town, at a college or a high school that had a football field, and put us up in a hotel. It was cheaper than moving us back and forth on a train.

That game in Pittsburgh incidentally was really something. The ground was frozen. Potsy Clark gave us a pair of pliers and told us to take the cleats off our shoes and leave them in the locker room. We did and when we came back after warming up we found they had been put on an emery wheel and that they were as sharp as any track spike ever was. We played with them and some of the Pittsburgh players got cut pretty bad that day. We ran right away from them, won the game 23–0. I wondered about that, didn't think it was right, but in those days teams did things like that. Today, of course, they wouldn't be allowed to do that kind of thing.

I never really got hurt bad in football. But Joe Stydahar of the Bears hit me so hard once that I got a concussion. That was about the worst. I still played the next week, though. That actually happened in my first season with Brooklyn. Old Joe taught me a good lesson. It was just at the beginning of the second half. The score was tied and I threw a pass to one of our ends, a boy by the name of Jeff Barrett, who was from LSU. It was a long pass and it looked like Jeff was going to catch it for a touchdown. I raised up on my toes to see if he caught it, to see over the blockers, and that's all I remember until I woke up at the hospital. From then on I never raised up to see anybody catch one.

After the 1941 season, I went into the navy. I went in as a full lieutenant and served for four years, all of it down in Norfolk at the naval training station there. For two years we were restricted to the base. We were in a special destroyer escort program that was highly secret and so we were frozen to the base. I didn't play any football while I was in the service but I did get to play some baseball down there.

When I came back in 1945, I went with the Boston Yanks, which was only a year or so old at the time. It had a lot of the old Brooklyn players on it because Dan Topping's team had gone out of business by 1945. A man by the name of Ted Collins owned the Yanks, but it wasn't very successful. We won a couple of games but lost a lot more and not too many people came out to see us. Herb Kopf was our coach and we had Pug Manders, an excellent fullback, but there wasn't much else.

The next year I went over to the new league, the All-American Football Conference. It had teams like the Cleveland Browns and the Los Angeles Dons and the San Francisco 49ers and the Chicago Rockets. There were some pretty big name players in it, like Otto Graham, Marion Motley, Crazy Legs Hirsch, Frankie Albert, Glenn Dobbs, Lou Groza, Norm Standlee, people like that. I went with the New York Yankees, which was owned by Dan Topping. He brought over a lot of the old Dodgers like myself. There was Bruiser Kinard, Perry Schwartz, and Pug Manders, I remember. We also had Spec Sanders and he was the best running back in the league that year. We won our division, the AAFC East, without any problem. Our record was 10–3–1 and the next closest team was 3–10–1. We lost the championship that year to Cleveland. Besides Graham, Groza, and Motley, they had players like Dante Lavelli, Mac Speedie, Bill Willis, Special Delivery Jones, and of course, they were coached by Paul Brown. They were a wonderful team. They beat us twice during the regular season but only by a couple of points in the title game. We actually had them beat in the fourth quarter but then Graham threw a touchdown pass to Lavelli and they got the lead. We came back, marched on them, but then Graham intercepted one of my passes down in their territory and they won it, 14–9. That was my last professional football game. I retired after the season.

The next year I went back to Duke University as an assistant coach. I was there nineteen years and then I moved to the University of North Carolina for one more year. I was also the head baseball coach at Duke for thirteen years. Sports, I guess you can say, have been a major part of my life.

## Fight Song

Colorful owner of the Washington Redskins George Preston Marshall commissioned this fight song for his team in the late 1930s:

> *Hail to the Redskins, hail victory,*
> *Braves on the warpath, fight for old D.C.*
> *Scalp 'em, swamp 'em.*
> *We will take 'em big score,*
> *Read 'em, weep 'em,*
> *Touchdown, we want heap more.*

## A Novel Way of Passing

John "Bull" Doehring, a running back for the Chicago Bears in the 1930s, was known for a rather unusual passing ability. He could throw a football behind his back as far as most players could overhand. Luke Johnsos, a Bear end in those days, recalls one play in particular. "Bull took a lateral and started out toward the sidelines. He was supposed to throw a long pass to me, but he was in trouble, the defense was all over him. He didn't even have room to raise his arm. I looked away, figuring the play had failed.

Then I happened to look up and there, coming straight into my hands, was the ball. I was so surprised I dropped it. As we were walking to the dressing room later, I asked him how he got rid of the ball."

"Well, they were rushing me so I threw it behind my back."

"And that is what he had done, thrown the ball behind his back. Forty yards. Right into my mitts."

# 13

# *Alex Wojciechowicz*

The young man whose name drove sportswriters and newspaper linotypers to exasperation, Alex Wojciechowicz, known to his colleagues as "Wojie," played center on offense and center and later linebacker on defense for thirteen years in the NFL. In 1950, his last year as a pro, he finally had to cede his two starting jobs, and it took a player the caliber of Chuck Bednarik, then a second-year man, to replace him.

A two-time all-American at Fordham, Wojie was one of the "Seven Blocks of Granite," lining up alongside guard Vince Lombardi. He was the Detroit Lions' first-round draft choice in 1938 and remained with the club for a little more than eight seasons. His hero had always been Mel Hein, the great New York Giants center, and he fashioned his play after him.

In 1946, Wojciechowicz moved over to the Philadelphia Eagles to play for Greasy Neale and to block for Steve Van Buren on a team that would play in three consecutive NFL championship games (1947–49). Neale said of his acquisition, "He is one of the most ferocious blockers and tacklers in the league who manages to use his shoulders, head, arms, hands, legs, and sometimes even fingernails, all at the same time."

Alex was 5 feet 11 inches when he played in the pros and his weight varied from 200 pounds when he first joined the league to as much as 235 at the end of his career, but throughout he maintained exceptional mobility. He justifiably takes his place as one of the game's all-time great centers along with such others as George Trafton, Mel Hein, Bulldog Turner, and Chuck Bednarik.

Alex Wojciechowicz was elected to the Pro Football Hall of Fame in 1968. After he quit playing the game, Wojie returned to New Jersey and spent the remainder of his working years quite successfully in the real estate business.

I came from a little town called South River in New Jersey, which was a factory town, mostly Polish, Russian, and Hungarian families. And God it was a tough town. We were called the "Bricktowners" because we had a brick factory there and so many people worked at it. There was also a nearby town called Milltown where the Michelin tire factory was located and a lot of people from South River worked there too. It was a true blue-collar area.

As a boy, I caddied a lot at the local golf course to earn some money. That's where I developed my love for that game, one that I have to this day. I also had a lot of chores to do around the house. We never had much money as a family. Athletics, however, were very important to me from the start. I used to work out by running on the railroad tracks. I'd run along them stepping on the ties, ran maybe a mile hitting every other one. Then, coming back, I'd hit every one—short, choppy, fast steps.

In those days, my God, I loved all sports. Football, of course, was one of the best to me. But I think I could have made a career for myself in baseball, too. I was fair at basketball and fair at track and field. I threw the discus and the shot put.

I guess I started playing organized football in 1929 when I was a freshman at South River High School. Before that, I'd played touch football and pickup games, I did that ever since I was about eight years old. I played center from my very first game of organized football, for twenty-one years—high school, college, and the pros—that's what I played.

I was only thirteen as a freshman and I wasn't very big then. But we had a coach who was a big help to me. His name was Bill Denny and he turned out to be my guiding light. You see, my father was a tailor and he worked from six in the morning to about ten at night to earn a living for us. Consequently he didn't have a lot of time to spend with me. So I looked up to Bill Denny for a lot of guidance in those days in all aspects of my life. Bill used to take the football players up to Ursinus College, which is in Collegeville, Pennsylvania, where he had gone to school. We would stay there about two weeks in the summer. He did it all for nothing, just for us. We worked out, practiced as a team, ran the hills over there, and we'd have sessions in the evening talking about everything from football to the facts of life. I remember, too, that there was always a great supply of milk and I used to drink about thirteen glasses of it a day. We all had great respect for Bill Denny.

I devoted as much time to baseball as anything else in those younger days. It was my other real love. Our high school baseball team went undefeated every year. I played catcher and batted cleanup and I made all-State. I played against Joe Medwick, "Ducky" they called him, in a central New Jersey league. He was quite an athlete. He was a helluva basketball player, too, would average about twenty points a game and in those days that was a helluva lot. He used to tell me that I should go on directly into baseball instead of football. But I told him that I wanted to get an education first and football was a way that would enable me to do that. Medwick in those days played third base and he also pitched. He went on, of course, to make a big baseball name for himself with the St. Louis Cardinals and was elected to the Hall of Fame.

Because of football, I had a chance to go to a number of different colleges. Bill Denny actually wanted me to go to Villanova because Harry Stuhldreher of Notre Dame's old Four Horsemen was the coach there. And Bill also had a brother over there. But I really wanted to hit the New York scene and I wanted to go to a school bigger than Villanova. I wanted to go to a Catholic school so I picked Fordham. I talked to Jimmy Crowley, who was the football coach there, just once, for about fifteen minutes, and then I told him that I'd made up my mind that Fordham was the place for me. He didn't have to sell me on it. Before that, though, I'd had an idea about going to Dartmouth but they changed coaches that year, that was when Earl Blaik left there to go to Army. I would have liked to have played for Blaik. At the same time, I felt that once a school changed coaches it took at least two or three years to establish the new coach's program. Jim Crowley, on the other hand, was very well established at Fordham. And at that time, Fordham played the best teams in the country. I always wanted to face the best. I looked on it as a real challenge. They gave me a full scholarship there, and so I got the chance.

We built a reputation there as a defensive team. We weren't the original "Seven Blocks of Granite." They had had another line at Fordham back maybe around 1928 or '29 when Tony Siano was the center, and a sportswriter dubbed them with the name. Then when we came along it was resurrected. That actually happened because of what we did against Pittsburgh. We held them scoreless three years in a row, all the games ended in scoreless ties. They had what everyone called the "dream" backfield. Their big star was Marshall Goldberg, a great back who starred later for the Chicago Cardinals. They ran all over every team they played back then: Notre Dame, Minnesota, Southern Cal, Washington, who they beat something like 21–0 in the Rose Bowl. But they couldn't score a point on us in the three years we played each other.

Vince Lombardi, who played guard, became the most famous of the "Seven Blocks," but he never played pro ball. Some of the others besides myself did. Al Babartsky, a tackle, played for the Chicago Cardinals and the Chicago Bears. John Druze went with the old Brooklyn Dodgers and Ed Franco with the Boston Yanks.

Lombardi was an interesting man. I admired Vince because he had an open hand for all the football players, helped a lot of us. Vince was one of the brains of the team, very good scholastically. He helped a lot of us with our studies.

Vince was a classmate and real good friend of Wellington Mara at Fordham. Well's father was Tim Mara, who founded the New York Giants football team. Vince later worked for Well as an assistant coach with the Giants, but Mara never took him on as his head coach. I think he tried to get him after Vince had moved on to Green Bay but by that time it was too late. We never dreamt that Vince would become a coach. We all thought he was going to be a priest. He'd been an altar boy and he was very religious. We thought if he didn't become a priest, he'd become an attorney, as a matter of fact he went to law school for two years. But then he changed his mind. He had gotten married, needed a job, and so he took on coaching a high school team, St. Cecilia's in New Jersey, and I think he stayed there for something like thirteen years.

I liked Jim Crowley as a coach at Fordham, but my personal coach there, the one who did the most for me, was his assistant, Frank Leahy, who later became famous at Notre Dame. He spent an hour with me every afternoon. Frank was the coach of the center and the guards. Every day it was snap the ball and block, snap the ball and block, for a full hour. He had the biggest influence on my development as a center.

There's a little story about Frank Leahy and myself which happened my senior year. In the years before that, when we'd practice, I'd center the ball and he'd go after me and bang me around the head and everything else, really whack at me. After an hour of it, much of the time I'd have a headache. Because of it, I often didn't study too well in the evening. I just barely passed my courses in my sophomore and junior years. So in my last year, I said to him, "Frank, if you keep hitting me around the head like you've been doing, I'll probably flunk all my courses and never graduate." Then I told him, "You know, coach, I never block against you in practice like I do in a game. I go easy on you. In a ballgame, I block like a wild man."

He looked at me very astonished. "What?"

I said, "Yeah, I'm much wilder in a game. With you, what the heck, you're older and a coach and I've got respect for you and so I don't want to hurt you."

He said, "From here on in, you go at me just like you do in a ballgame. Even more so!"

Well, I didn't for the next three or four blocks and he sensed it and got on me about not going after him. I said, "Are you really sure you want me to?" Frank said "Yes," very emphatically. So I went at him as fast and as hard as I could. I don't think he knew what hit him because I really got him good. They had to carry him off the field and for a long time after that he had to go up to Mayo Clinic for treatments for his back. I felt bad about that. That ended his hitting me around the head, however.

Frank and I remained good friends after I left Fordham, and we stayed in touch with each other. As a matter of fact, when he was at Boston College, I damn near got him the head coaching job with the Detroit Lions. Potsy Clark was leaving, so I talked with Fred Mandel, the owner of the team, and told him about Frank. Frank had just had a tremendous year at Boston College, took them to the Sugar Bowl and won it. Mandel said to see what I could do to get him, so I took a little trip up to Boston and talked to Frank. He seemed interested but, as it turned out, the only thing that stopped him from becoming head coach of the Lions was that shortly after I met with him the head coaching job opened up at Notre Dame. Frank was very gung ho for Notre Dame and he preferred to go there when they offered him the job. Before they did, though, Frank had gone over to Detroit and met with Mandel and they had worked out salary figures and everything.

At Fordham, all the top teams came to play us. We'd draw fifty thousand or sixty thousand every Saturday in the Polo Grounds in those days. They'd come from all over to meet us: Southern Methodist, Texas Christian, Georgia, Purdue. We only played one game away in the entire three years I played varsity ball and that was when we went down to play North Carolina.

My favorite moment in a game came when we were playing Georgia one Saturday afternoon. I was backing up the right side of our line and I anticipated a flat pass to the fullback. I was so sure of it I made my move early. And sure enough, the quarterback faked a pass long then wheeled and lobbed it out toward the fullback. I just ran right by him and caught it and headed downfield. I went about 60 yards with it before somebody caught up to me.

We went undefeated my senior year and tied only once and that, of course, was in our game with Pittsburgh. We weren't invited to a bowl game, however. The Rose Bowl chose Alabama instead. I did play in the East-West game that year. That game ended in a 0–0 tie, too. On the East squad we had three starters from Fordham and three from Pittsburgh.

I was drafted by the Detroit Lions in 1938. The first training camp I went to was held in Cranbrook, just outside Detroit. I was sort of awed by the team, the skills of the ballplayers. Detroit was big and good in '38. I thought we should have won the league that year but we lost to the then-lowly Philadelphia Eagles (they were 5–6 that year) the last game of the season and that enabled the Green Bay Packers to win the division title. Then they beat the New York Giants for the NFL championship. But we should have been the ones to do it. The next year we finished second in the NFL West again, and again we were a game behind the Packers.

Dutch Clark was the Detroit coach when I got there in '38. A lot of people didn't like him and I was one of them. No personality, no charisma, he never taught me a thing, neither did his assistants. He just played the basics: running, running, running, running. It's a good thing to be basic but, my God, you need a lot more in the pros. It's a different game than the one played in college, much more sophisticated, but Clark sure didn't seem to know that. Even as a rookie you learned that pretty quick. At Detroit, we had to learn it by ourselves. Clark was no help whatsoever.

The second year in Detroit I had Hunk Anderson and he taught me more than anybody. He was actually an assistant coach to Gus Henderson. We should have won it that year too. We won six of our first seven games. After that, though, there was a flare-up between Hunk and Gus Henderson and they kind of parted. The whole team just sort of blew up at that point and we lost our last four games in a row. After that it was just one coach after another. In eight years at Detroit, I had six different coaches. How the hell can a team do anything with that many different head coaches? Besides Dutch Clark and Gus Henderson, there was Potsy Clark, Bill Edwards, Bull Karcis, and Gus Dorais.

Those first couple of years at Detroit we had some fine talent. There was Bill Shepherd, an excellent fullback; and Lloyd Cardwell, our wingback who made all-Pro; and Vern Huffman, the tailback. We had a heckuva backfield. Ace Gutowsky was there, too, a powerful runner; he was my roommate. He also almost ruined me. One day in practice I tackled him and hurt my shoulder pretty bad. He came through the line, his knees flying in front of him, that wild way in which he always ran. I met him head-on and his knee went into my shoulder and my shoulder went out. It was popped back in place but it didn't get a lot better. From then on, I had to favor my left shoulder because it was never the same. For three years I played with it bothering me, and then I was ready to quit the game because of it. My shoulder and arm would go numb. I really had to learn to play defensive football all over again. I'd been used to tackling with my left shoulder, and now I was forced to tackle with my right. I was arm-tackling, too, a lot of the time instead of shoulder tackling. I was at a big disadvantage.

I told Fred Mandel I thought I'd had it as a player. He then took me over to Chicago to see a Dr. Leventhal, who, as it turned out, actually saved my life. He found eighteen pieces of bone in my shoulder that he then took out. That took care of my shoulder. But he also found a blood clot in an artery in my left shoulder and he operated and took that out as well. The blood clot, he believed, had been caused by the blow. If he didn't take it out, he told me, one day it would get loose, go to my brain, and chances are kill me. Anyway, after it and the bone fragments were removed, my shoulder was fine. But then I had to go back and relearn how to tackle with my left shoulder.

We had strong rivalries in those days with the Chicago Bears and the Green Bay Packers. Both were great teams, but I think we beat them as much as they beat us, at least during the first few years I was with Detroit. The Packers kept winning the division with Don Hutson and "Cece" Isbell and Clarke Hinkle. And the Bears were something else, too, they had three backfields then, one as good as the other. All our games with the Bears and the Packers were physical, bruising ones. I used to go up against Bulldog Turner when we played Chicago and he was a great one. There were some nasty collisions, I remember. He wasn't afraid of me and I wasn't afraid of him, and we became good friends. I was also very friendly with Sid Luckman, the Bear quarterback. We worked together at Manhattan Beach. We still stay in touch.

The most memorable moment from that time was when I scored a touchdown up in Green Bay. I was covering Don Hutson, an almost impossible task, and I knocked him down. We collided but the referee didn't call a penalty. Cece Isbell had already let the pass go. I grabbed it, Hutson was just lying there on the ground looking up, and then I ran it

The mid-man of Fordham's famed "Seven Blocks of Granite," Alex Wojciechowicz went on to become one of the pro game's finest and most durable
centers. He was a two-way, sixty-minute center for his first eight years in the
NFL, spent with the Detroit Lions. During the next five years, spent with the
Philadelphia Eagles, he switched to linebacker on defense but maintained his reputation as one of the game's premier blockers. His trademark, evident here, was
an exceptionally wide stance for a center. *(Pro Football Hall of Fame)*

maybe 30 or 40 yards for a touchdown, the only one I ever scored in thirteen years of professional football.

In 1942, we were just awful, a year I'd just as soon forget. We lost all eleven games that year, in fact we never scored more than a single touchdown in any one of the games. Most of our players had gone off to the army or the navy and we got a new coach that year and he quit after a couple of games. We had no passer at all. The team was a complete nothing. That year I would line up at end every once in a while and I even caught four passes, none of them for much yardage, though. My dream always had been to play halfback but I never got the chance, not even that year.

I left the Lions in 1946. At that time, I had a business going in New Jersey, a distributorship. I was in partnership with Hal Newhouser, he was a pitcher then with the Detroit Tigers. Another pitcher, Dizzy Trout, was a partner, too. We were all on the same bowling team in Detroit and we used to tour the state, too. The franchise we had was a thing called Frigid Mist. It was a refrigerating or cooling kind of counter for vegetables in supermarkets. Well, I had the New Jersey territory and it was going very well, at least at first. In August, however, I had to go back and practice with the team in Detroit. I hired a manager to run the business in New Jersey, but a lot of things started to go wrong, a lot of problems. The motors broke down in the August heat and the vegetables would go bad, and the manager wasn't coping with it all that well.

After three games, all of which we lost, I went to see Fred Mandel and Gus Dorais and told them that my heart was in New Jersey. I was losing my shirt over there, I told them. From my figuring, I stood to lose forty thousand dollars in New Jersey and I was only earning about eight thousand dollars with Detroit. They told me to go back and take care of my business.

But when I got back to New Jersey, I immediately got a call from Greasy Neale, who was the head coach of the Philadelphia Eagles. He said, "You're on waivers now and we're interested in getting you."

I said, "Nope, I don't have any compunction for playing anymore." Well, Greasy offered to raise my salary and said all I'd have to do was play in the games. I wouldn't even have to come to the weekday practices, just show up on Friday and work out with the team and then play on Sunday. I couldn't turn that down.

I could also see that we had the real makings of a championship team there. We had Steve Van Buren, of course, and it looked like everything was going to go great guns. And sure enough we played in three championship games the five years I was there. We had fellows like Joe Muha, Tommy Thompson, Bosh Pritchard, Pete Pihos, Vic Sears, Al Wistert, he was our captain. None of our teams in Detroit were anywhere close to what we had in Philadelphia.

Steve Van Buren was one out of a million. He was my roommate and we raised a little hell together. Steve though was a very quiet, very loyal person. In a game, he would give everything he had. They blocked like hell for Steve because everybody liked him so much. He was gung ho. He'd run 100-yard wind sprints before practice, before anybody else got out there. He'd been one of the top 50-yard dash men in the country when he was at LSU. Besides being fast, he could also carry two or three tacklers along with him.

I remember once when Greasy Neale wanted him to take one more step further on a play to go off-tackle. Greasy was always telling Steve how to run, even after he was all-Pro so many years. Anyway, Steve, I guess, didn't feel comfortable doing it, so he didn't. Greasy said, "Steve, you might be an all-Pro but I'm still the coach here. So it's either you or me. If you don't listen to what I tell you, you've got to go or I've got to go." All of the other players who were standing around there shouted, "Goodbye, Greasy!"

Later on I coached with Steve. It was the Newark Bears who played in the Atlantic Coast League. There were teams in it from Portland, Maine, all the way down to Norfolk, Virginia. It was a good league and we won it three times in a row. The reason I went there was just to help Steve out.

There wasn't a better man around than Greasy Neale, either. On the football field he was tough as hell, stern, he was almighty god out there. But off the field he was one of us. He'd gamble with us, beer up with us, go to the race track with us, play golf, anything we'd do he'd be part of it. He was a very creative coach, too. He created the stuttering T formation. Against Pittsburgh, who used the single wing still, he came up with that swinging line that could go either to the right or the left, and as a result Pittsburgh was never able to beat us during those years. Then he put in what we called the "Greasy Neale Defense" which no team was able to penetrate very often. That's the defense that stopped the T, stopped the whole league in the late 1940s. Using it and with Steve Van Buren, we got to the NFL championship game three years in a row—1947, '48, and '49. It wasn't until we met Paul Brown and his Cleveland Browns from the old All-American Football League that anyone could consistently break Greasy's defense. But Brown came along and put out flankers and spread us all over the field.

In 1947, we played the Cardinals at Comiskey Park in Chicago for the championship. Typically, it was freezing there. We had a real problem, too. We didn't have our regular man to play over the center that day, our nose guard as they would call him today. That was Bucko Kilroy. He was hurt so Greasy had to use a guy who had never played that position before. And the kid had to go up there and play over Vince Banonis, who was one of the best blocking centers around. Well, Vince just blew him out of there, handled him like nothing. And Elmer Angsman would just burst through the middle and be on his way. Angsman ran 70 yards for a touchdown *twice* that day. He set a championship game rushing record, too (159 yards in ten carries). Charlie Trippi ran up the middle for another touchdown, his was about 45 yards. Joe Muha and I were spread out as linebackers and with the nose guard being blasted out we didn't have anybody in the middle to stop Angsman and Trippi and they are two guys you just can't give that kind of running room to. They beat us 28–21. If it wasn't for the problem up the middle, I mean if we had had Bucko Kilroy there, who could hold his ground against anyone, I think we would have beaten them.

We played them for the championship again the next year. That game was played in unbelievably deep snow in Philadelphia. A lot of us thought they were going to postpone the game because of the awful weather. Steve Van Buren was almost late for it because he was coming to the stadium on his own and it was so hard to get through the snowy streets, it was coming down so heavily. I think he ended up abandoning his car and walking or running the last mile to get there. But he made it, barely. Actually he would have been late but the game had been delayed about a half hour because they had to plow the snow off the tarpaulin before they could get the tarp off the field. It was good Steve made it because he scored the game's only touchdown and we won it 7–0. It was in the fourth quarter and he carried the ball six times in a row before he finally got it into the end zone. I was only playing defense by that time in my career, outside right linebacker. In the "Greasy Neale Defense," it was a 5-2-4 alignment. Vic Lindskog was our center in those days and he was a good one.

In 1949, we played the Los Angeles Rams for the title out in California. It was a rainy day, very rainy for Los Angeles, and Greasy had a youngster by the name of Chuck Bednarik playing in that game in place of me. We were playing at the Coliseum out there and expecting maybe sixty thousand people but less than twenty-five thousand showed up because of the downpour. Greasy told me he thought younger ballplayers would probably do better under those rainy conditions so he slotted Bednarik at linebacker instead of me. He would have to cover Tom Fears, who was an all-Pro end, and Greasy felt Bednarik could stay with him better than I could. I was getting a little old by that time. I was thirty-four and Bednarik was just a rookie, just getting his great career started. But I got in the ballgame and I enjoyed it when I did. We won hands down, the score was 14–0. They were not a poor team by any means, not with players like Fears, Bob Waterfield, and Dick Hoerner, their fullback. But we had no trouble with them. Pete Pihos caught a pass from Tommy Thompson for one touchdown and the other came when Leo Skladany, a defensive end, blocked Waterfield's punt in the end zone and then grabbed the ball. That was also one of Steve Van Buren's greatest days, too. He set a new championship game rushing record, he was just short of 200 yards rushing that day.

In my last year, 1950, we played an exhibition game against the Bears before the regular season. Chuck Bednarik was sick so I had to fill in for him on defense at linebacker. And Vic Lindskog, our center got himself injured so I had to play for him on offense. I was thirty-five then and I had to go the full sixty minutes, Greasy told me. My God, I thought. Well, just after the game started I lined up on defense across from Ken Kavanaugh, who was a very fine end. I said to him, "Listen Ken, I'm not going to play dirty or rough or whatever today, just a nice cool game because I've got to go sixty minutes. It's only an exhibition game. So I'll take it easy on you." He said okay, he'd go easy, too. I thought everything was fine but then a few plays later we were going at it easy enough when a Bear halfback came up and blind-sided me. I got a hell of an elbow right in the mouth. Well, we didn't have face masks in those days and he knocked my two front teeth out. It knocked me out, too. When I woke up I was without the teeth and I was furious. After all those years, and there in my last season, I get them knocked out. Well, I had to stay in the game and there was a long way to go. But I was enraged and I played so hard, so did everyone else after that shot, that we beat the hell out of them that day. I wasn't sure who it was who hit me or whether Kavanaugh set me up. So I went gunning for every Bear on the field. I mean I was a wild man. After a while, half of them were running away from me on each play because they knew I was so mad and I was going after them with a vengeance.

After the 1950 season, I retired. I sold insurance and then went into the real estate business. I got my brokerage license and sold real estate in New Jersey after that. I was also a real estate appraiser for the state of New Jersey and I remained a real estate broker until I retired in 1981. There were thirteen years in the NFL and they were memorable. They changed the nature of the game a lot after I left.

## Coach Blood

Art Rooney hired Johnny Blood (McNally) as player/coach for his Pittsburgh Pirates in 1937. The famed broken-field runner and off-field hell-raiser lasted into the 1939 season but was able to win only six of twenty-five games.

Part of the reason, Rooney observed, was that Johnny Blood "wasn't always that dependable. On every team, it is customary for the coach to worry about the players. But when Blood was around, the players worried about the coach, wondering whether he was going to show up.

"Once we played a game out in Los Angeles, an exhibition of some kind, and Johnny missed the train home. We did not see him the whole week. Then the following Sunday I heard that he was in Chicago to watch the Packers, his old team, play the Bears. One of the players on Green Bay asked him why he wasn't with his own team.

"'We're not playing this week,' Johnny told him.

"No sooner did he get those words out of his mouth than over the loudspeaker came the score announcement: Philadelphia 14, Pittsburgh 7."

## Pinpoint Passing

Ray Flaherty, who made it to the Hall of Fame as an end with the New York Giants, was also a fine head coach for the Washington Redskins from 1937 through 1942. The story of his first encounter with "Slingin'" Sammy Baugh, his rookie quarterback in 1937, is a classic.

At the team's first workout at summer camp, Flaherty wanted to see just how good a passer Baugh was. He told Wayne Millner, the Redskins' all-

A notable gathering in the offices of the Pittsburgh Pirates in 1938: coach Johnny Blood *(left)* and owner Art Rooney *(right)* welcome their first-round draft choice, Byron "Whizzer" White, an all-American halfback from Colorado College. To play pro ball, White was allowed to delay acceptance of a Rhodes scholarship. Later he went on to Oxford, Yale Law School, and the U.S. Supreme Court. Despite the efforts of this illustrious trio, Pittsburgh won only two games that year and ended up in the cellar of the NFL East. Art Rooney, who founded the Pittsburgh franchise in 1933, would not experience an NFL championship until Terry Bradshaw and Franco Harris brought the Steelers one in 1974. *(Pro Football Hall of Fame)*

Pro end, to run a short pattern over the middle and buttonhook just behind the middle linebacker. Then he turned to Baugh, "I want you to hit him square in the eye with the ball," Flaherty said.

"Sure, coach," the rangy twenty-three-year-old Texan said and moved into his then-tailback position to take the snap from the center. Then Baugh looked over his shoulder at Flaherty and said, "One thing, coach. Which eye?"

# 14

# Sammy Baugh

Sammy Baugh began beating NFL teams before he even became a pro. As tailback for the College All-Stars in 1937, he tossed a touchdown pass to end Gaynell Tinsley to provide the six-point margin of victory over the reigning NFL champion Green Bay Packers.

Then, as a rookie, he led the Washington Redskins to their first NFL championship and was named that year's all-Pro tailback. Grantland Rice had predicted he would not make it as a pro because the 6-foot-2-inch, 180-pound Texan was "too reedy" and that the bruising pros would undoubtedly "tear his arm off." But "Slingin'" Sammy Baugh stayed around for a total of sixteen years, then an NFL record for longevity. And when he retired, he held practically every passing and punting record in the book.

Ray Flaherty, Sammy's first coach with Washington, said unabashedly after that first year, "He's the best passer in the world." Many others said roughly the same thing. And Baugh made the difficult transition from a single wing tailback to a T formation quarterback with the same virtuosity as Sid Luckman of the Chicago Bears.

George Preston Marshall, Redskins owner, often said Sammy Baugh was *the* franchise in Washington. He also said Sammy was unique: a rangy, ambling young man who personified Texas and whose slow Panhandle drawl, dry wit, and propensity for never mincing words made him one of the most engaging men in the game.

When Sammy Baugh retired from the NFL in 1952, he was thirty-eight years old, old enough perhaps to have been the father of twenty-one-year-old rookie Eddie LeBaron, who that year took over the Redskins' passing duties. And when he took off his famous number 33, Baugh had thrown more passes (2,995), completed more of them (1,693), gained more yardage passing (21,886, or approximately thirteen miles), and passed for more touchdowns (187) than any previous passer in NFL history. His completion percentage of 56.5 was also the best up to that time. Sammy led the league in passing six times, an NFL record which still stands. His completion record of 70.33 in 1945 also remains the single-season standard.

As a punter, he had no peer before, during, or after his tenure with the Redskins. Sammy's lifetime average of 45.1 yards a punt has never been equaled, nor has his single-season average of 51.4 yards. He led the NFL in punting four times, another record which remains the league benchmark.

Sammy Baugh was appropriately honored as one of the seventeen charter members of the Pro Football Hall of Fame. When he finished football, he went back to the Panhandle of Texas to tend his ranch, which by the 1980s had spread to about twenty-one thousand acres.

I got into the pros in 1937. I'd been drafted by the Redskins and went on up to Washington. I thought it was a beautiful city when I got there, but I also thought it was a little too damn big for me. I got used to it but I didn't stay there a damn day longer than I had to. When the football season was over, hell, I'd be on the train home that night. I'd head back to Sweetwater as soon as I got out of the uniform.

They always told this story about how I came to Washington. Some writer wrote how George Preston Marshall, the owner of the club, called me up down in Texas and asked me if I had cowboy boots and a ten gallon hat and that I said no. He was supposed to have told me then to go out and buy the things and that he'd pay me back in Washington, and he wanted me to get off the train wearing them, that he wanted all the writers there to see the Texas cowboy. Well, hell, that's just a made-up story. It never happened that way. I normally wore that kind of stuff. I didn't need him to tell me to wear it and I sure didn't need to go out and buy it. Mr. Marshall wouldn't tell a man what to wear, he wasn't like that. Some writer just made it up and everybody picked it up. Writers like to embellish things like that. After it was written, though, Mr. Marshall got a big kick out of it.

I'd been playing football since I was in third grade. I was born just outside of Temple, Texas, and we lived there through my first year of high school. Then we moved to Sweetwater where I finished high school. In Temple we had organized teams in grammar school and it was a big pastime around there.

I started out as an end but when I was a freshman in high school we had such a sorry team that our coach kept changing people around to different positions. He found out I could throw the ball better than any of our backs so I ended up as our passer. And I stayed in the backfield ever since.

I used to practice by throwing a football at a tire hung from a tree in our backyard, but as I think about it now that probably didn't help all that much. You really need to throw it to somebody who is moving, not just some tire swinging back and forth. If you could get a tire to move as fast as a man running down the field it might work, I guess, otherwise the tire doesn't do a damn bit of good. But I did spend a lot of time throwing at one when I was a boy.

I worked at punting a lot, too. Every day in the summer I used to go over to our football field for an hour or so and I'd just kick the ball from one end of it to the other. I'd punt, trot down and get the ball, and then punt it back. I spent a lot of time working at kicking the ball out of bounds, too, angling it so I could get it out of bounds inside the 10 yard line. I was usually by myself when I practiced kicking but sometimes I could talk a friend into coming along.

Football was very popular in Texas in those days, the 1930s, just as it is now. In Sweetwater, it was a major sport. Our high school team played teams from all around the area, like Abilene, San Angelo, Big Spring, towns like that. It was very organized.

When I was in high school I was also playing with a semipro baseball team in Abilene, which is about thirty-five or forty miles from Sweet-water. Well, one day we were playing TCU's baseball team and Dutch Meyer, who was the coach of their team, came up after the game and told me he'd like me to come to Fort Worth and go to TCU. I was a senior in high school that year. Dutch was also the assistant football coach. He went back and talked to Francis Schmidt, the head football coach, and said he thought that I might make a good football player, too. Then they got back to me and told me I could play football, baseball, and basketball at TCU, and as it turned out I did play all three sports there.

I got a scholarship but it didn't pay for everything, as I recall. But you could sign a note there at the school and get the rest of the money and then pay them back later after you got out of school and were earning some money.

Dutch Meyer was the freshman coach when I went to TCU and then in my sophomore year he was moved up to head coach. I played a lot as a sophomore but still I was kind of a backup to our captain who played the same position as I did, tailback. I did all the punting, though. What I remember best about that year was when we went down to Houston to play Rice, which was the best team in the conference that year. Everybody said we were going to get beat but we whipped 'em, 6–0.

When I got through with college, I had a job in Pampa, Texas, up in the Panhandle near Amarillo, playing semipro baseball. That year we went to the Denver *Post* tournament and played an all-star Negro team from the east, who ended up winning it. They had all those good Negro baseball players like Cool Papa Bell and all that bunch. They'd win it every dang year. Rogers Hornsby was playing on a team in it, too, and I guess he was scouting for the Cardinals on the side. He was about forty or forty-two then. I played against him in one game and after it he signed me to a contract to go to spring training with the St. Louis Cardinals the following year.

After the tournament in Denver, I played in the college All-Star game up in Chicago, that was 1937, and we beat the Green Bay Packers. We were the first all-star team to beat the pros. We had some good players on that team: Gaynell Tinsley from LSU, an end who had a good career after with the Chicago Cardinals; Ed Widseth, a tackle who later played for the Giants; and Johnny Drake, a good running back from Purdue who played a few years after with the Cleveland Rams. Drake did the best job of any of us in that game because he had to cover Don Hutson, which was quite a job. That was the first time I was ever in Chicago. Gus Dorais was our coach. Bud Wilkinson also played on that team. The next year I played in the All-Star game, too, but as a Redskin and we got beat. The score was 28–16. We just couldn't stop old Cece Isbell that night. He'd just got out of Purdue and was on his way to the Packers.

My first year with the Redskins we won the NFL championship. I didn't find pro football all that different from what we played in college. A lot rougher, sure, but they used pretty much the same dang things we did in college, like the single wing and the double wing. We also used the spread formation, what they call the shotgun now.

One thing I especially remember from when I first started with the pros was that there wasn't a lot of protection for the passer. I did all our passing and I know it sure as hell. That's one rule Mr. Marshall finally got changed. I remember when he called me in and asked me if it would help if he could get a rule through that would protect passers. I said, "Heck, yes. It probably would let me play ten years longer." You see, in '37, there wasn't really any protection whatsoever for a man throwing a pass. The other team could go after you until the whistle blew. In other words, you'd complete a pass to a fellow out in the flat and he'd take off running, back and forth across the field maybe, and the rushers would be going after the passer all the while. In those days, they'd want to put the quarterback on the ground regardless, even though he's got nothing to do with the play by that time. Mr. Marshall got the rule changed so that they had to lay off the quarterback after he threw the ball. Just stop and think about it, before that, hell, they'd chase you all over the field, maybe 30 yards, until they got their hands on you.

I liked Mr. Marshall a lot. I thought he was a real fine businessman. And he did a lot for the league, he and Mr. Halas from Chicago. They were the two who'd get the things done that needed to be done. They got a lot of the rules changed for the better of the game. Mr. Marshall was also quite a showman. I especially remember how he'd always bring a Santa Claus in at halftime of the game just before Christmas. He'd do it a dang different way every year. Once it was on a sleigh. Another time he was going to parachute one in but the wind was blowing so much that the Santa Claus missed the stadium and landed on a house about a block away.

Mr. Marshall signed me to my first contract in '37 and I got eight thousand dollars for the year. That was a lot back then and I found out later that some of our best players, guys like Cliff Battles, an all-Pro, were only making about three thousand dollars. I was very fortunate.

And we had some damn fine ballplayers on that Washington team. Battles was at least as good as any running back in the league if he wasn't the best. Turk Edwards was an all-league tackle. We only had about twenty-two ballplayers, which meant you had to do a helluva lot of playing with that few number of players. Wayne Millner from Notre Dame was a fine receiver and so was Charley Malone. I used to like to throw to our backs, too, especially Battles and our wingbacks and we had two fine ones in Wilbur Moore and Ed Justice. Wee Willie Wilkin was another really good lineman, so was Jim Barber, a tackle, and Steve Slivinski, a guard. It was as good a team at the end of the '30s as any in the league, I feel.

That first year I roomed with Wayne Millner and he was my best friend on the team in the earlier days. Later Dick Todd and I roomed together and after him it was Harry Gilmer from Alabama for a couple of years. We lived in hotels and our biggest entertainment, at least mine anyway, was going to movies. Hell, I saw more movies those years in Washington than I have in the rest of my life combined. There was a story some writer wrote that all I liked to do was play pinball machines.

Sammy Baugh often said that the life of an NFL tailback was not an easy or a comfortable one, an observation clearly demonstrated here during a game against the New York Giants in 1942. But Slingin' Sam was as indestructible as he was talented. The great passer, punter, and defensive back endured sixteen seasons— eight as a tailback and, eight as a T formation quarterback. When he retired after the 1952 season, he owned virtually every passing and punting record in the NFL. From 1937 through 1952, Baugh was indeed *the Washington Redskins franchise.* (*Pro Football Hall of Fame*)

Hell, I never played one in my entire life. Some of those writers just made things up. It sure did surprise me, reading some of those things they'd write about me.

We beat out the Giants that first year to get to the championship. And they had a good team, players like Mel Hein and Tuffy Leemans and Ed Danowski. But that championship game against the Bears was something else. It was played on the worst field I've ever played on in my life. The game was at Wrigley Field in Chicago. A week or so before that they had a playoff game there of some kind and it had rained and got real muddy. Hell, they just chewed up that field. Well, when we got on it, it was snowing and the ground had froze up. There were all these little frozen balls of mud, hard and sharp as rocks, all over that damn field. They cut the living hell out of you when you hit the ground. A lot of people got chewed up pretty bad that day. We won the game by a touchdown, I think the score was 28–21. Despite that damn field I had a pretty good day. Wayne Millner and I teamed up on a couple of long touchdown passes and I got another to Ed Justice. We won it in the fourth quarter, scored two touchdowns and came out on top.

When I first started playing professional football, it was a defensive game. Today, with the two-platoon system, there's much more offense, it's a much more wide-open game. Back then a lot of damn good offensive ballplayers were eliminated because they couldn't play defense well enough. If they only had to play offense, they might have become stars. But there just wasn't any such thing as a specialist in those days. You had to be able to play both ways and play both damn well.

Today's game is a helluva lot speedier than the one we played. Wide receivers are just wide receivers and they only have to play half the game. They get plenty of rest in between times. When we played and the fourth quarter came around, everybody, and I mean everybody on the field, was dog-tired. We paced ourselves and we had gimmicks to help us in that. For example, if I knew on a play that I was going to throw to the right, I might shorten the pattern for the men on the left so that they didn't have to run so far, maybe have them just go out in the flat or maybe down about 7 yards and hook. You just couldn't run men in those days like they do today because they didn't get out of the game to rest. Today, hell, you lose the ball and you're on the bench resting and when you come back in you're fresh. I always felt it was important for the quarterback to look after his players. I would never send a man deep unless it was absolutely necessary. You had to protect your players.

They did things in those days that they would never do today, too.

They had a thing called a "bootsy" play where everybody would run over one man. They'd use it every now and then to take care of somebody who was getting a little dirty in the ballgame. They'd waste a play just to teach him a lesson. On the snap everybody would go after him who could get to him, and it usually set the fellow on the right track. I expected to get knocked around and I did, as a quarterback and as a safety. But in sixteen years playing with the pros no one really went after me other than just in the normal way, although the normal way before they got that rule changed to protect the quarterback was pretty rough.

I actually liked to play defense. Hell, when I'd punt a ball I'd be about the third or fourth man down the field to make the tackle. You see, they couldn't touch the punter so I could just kick the ball and get the hell down the field while all the others were blocking each other. I got knocked out doing that once though. We were playing the Bears and I punted and was racing down the field, about to make the tackle, when I caught Sid Luckman's knee in the head. He was blocking for the returner, I guess. Anyway I was out for about half the game.

I think the single best team I ever played on was the Redskins of 1940 and we were the team that got beat so badly by the Bears in the championship game that year, 73–0. We'd beat them a couple of weeks earlier and thought we were going to do it again. I know Mr. Marshall did, but as it turned out it must have been the longest afternoon of his life. They got out in front early. I think it was Bill Osmanski who made a long run for a touchdown when they first had the ball. We came right back after that, moved on down the field, and I thought we had a touchdown when I threw to Charley Malone. He was in the end zone and he dropped it. It was one he normally never would have dropped, fine receiver that he was, but for some doggone reason this time he did. The sun blinded him maybe for a second or so and anyway we didn't score. After that we couldn't get going at all, just got further and further behind. We tried gambling, we had to try to catch up, and they hurt us more when we had the ball than when they did, I think. Every time we gambled, we lost. If it was fourth down and 5, when we'd normally punt, well, hell, we'd have to go for it. And we wouldn't make it. Or we'd try a dangerous pass and they'd intercept. Hell, they were laying for us because they knew we'd have to pass. We had three passes intercepted and run back for touchdowns that day. Talk about catch-up football, we threw fifty-one passes that day and eight of them were picked off by the Bears. The Bears threw ten passes all afternoon. Nothing ever went right for us the whole damn day. I remember after the game some writer came up to me and asked if I thought if Charley Malone had caught that pass for a touchdown in the first quarter the outcome would've been different. I said, "Hell, yes, the score would've been 73–6."

Two years after that we played the Bears again for the championship. That was in 1942 and we had just about the same two teams and this time we beat them 14–6. They still had Sid Luckman and Bulldog Turner and Ray Nolting and Danny Fortmann. They were pretty big favorites after winning two straight world championships but we beat them.

In the 1943 title game we played the Bears again, but that time we lost 41–21. I got whacked early in the game, knocked out. I couldn't remember anything. I was still in there but I was calling plays we'd used the year before. Then they took me out and at the half were asking me all these questions about all kinds of damn things, and I don't remember if I could answer them or not. I finally went back in during the fourth quarter. I had a concussion, they told me later.

I switched from a single wing tailback to a T formation quarterback in 1944 and that was the most difficult thing I'd ever had to do in my football career. It was tough for the whole team. No one had ever played it before. Mr. Marshall got Clark Shaughnessy to put it in for us. He'd put it in for a lot of ballclubs: the Bears, who were the first to use it, and I think he also got Green Bay and the Pittsburgh Steelers to using it. Well, we just had no experience at all with it and everybody was confused. After about a year or so we got it down pretty good. The hardest parts were the simple things, like just taking the ball from the center, turning and faking to one man, and then giving it to another. You had to have such precision working out of the T. You had to learn different steps, fakes, moves. Hell, I remember talking to Sid Luckman one time and he told me when he switched over to the T at the Bears he darn near cried it was so damn frustrating. But he sure learned it and, of course, became one of the great ones at it. Actually the T was good for me. I'd played about ten or eleven years of single wing ball, counting college, and I figured I only could go maybe another year or two as a tailback. Hell, I was getting beat up and hurt all the time, and my shoulders and knees were getting beat up pretty bad by that time. Never had a broken bone but I was hurt a lot. But with the T formation I didn't take such a beating and that enabled me to play another seven or eight years. Altogether I got in sixteen years with the Redskins and four at TCU, which is a pretty long career in the game.

I played under a lot of different coaches in Washington: Ray Flaherty, Dutch Bergman, Dud DeGroot, Turk Edwards, even Curly Lambeau in

1952, my last year, but the strangest one of them all was Admiral John Whelchel. He was a retired admiral and he'd coached at Navy. Not a bad fellow, the admiral, but he didn't get along with Mr. Marshall. That was in 1949 and we didn't have a very good ballclub that year. A lot of our good players were getting old and some had retired. One time, after a practice, Mr. Marshall, who had been watching it, came up to myself and a couple of other players in the locker room and said he wanted to talk to us. We went out and got in his car and as he's driving along he turned to me and said, "Why aren't we winning more ballgames? Are you guys doing what Admiral Whelchel is telling you to do?"

"Of course we are," I told him.

"Why?"

"Hell, he's the coach. You hired him to coach us and we're doing what he says."

He ate us all out right there. It was really something. He yelled, "What're you doing that for? That's what's ruining a good ballclub. Christ, I hired him as a disciplinarian, not a goddam coach."

The old admiral didn't last the season, and we didn't win many games that year. I got a big kick out of Mr. Marshall. I used to negotiate my own contracts with him. I'd go in and tell him what I wanted and he told me what I was going to get and that was it.

After I'd been with the club some years, I used to go to the Kiwanis Clubs and the Lions Clubs and things like that with Mr. Marshall. He'd give these talks and he was a very entertaining man. He'd ask me to come on along. At those affairs they'd ask him questions after his talk and I remember one time he was asked why he didn't have any colored ballplayers. That was when black players were just coming into the NFL and most of the teams already had them. In fact Washington was *the* last team to get any. His answer was he'd start using Negroes when the Harlem Globetrotters started using white basketball players. But he finally came around and started using blacks. When all the teams started using blacks, I think that's when football picked up a great deal.

I got hurt early in the 1952 season and didn't play very much. I was thirty-eight years old by that time. So I figured I'd just hang it all up at the end of the season. I came back and played in the last two games and we beat the Giants and the Eagles. Then it was back to Texas.

There were a lot of things that went along with playing football in those days, things you wouldn't have got to do otherwise. I went out to Hollywood to make a movie, I remember, called *King of the Texas Rangers*. I played King.

I was out there for about six weeks and we made it at Republic Studios where they used to make all those westerns with Gene Autry and John Wayne. What I remember best was talking to all the people who worked on the picture, behind the scenes. They all told me they didn't like Gene Autry, that he was through, and that this new youngster was going to take it over and be the big star—Roy Rogers. He'll run Autry out of the business, they said. He did, I guess, but Autry didn't do too badly for himself either, I'd say. But it was all pretty damn confusing out there. They'd give me a script to read and tell me to read a certain part of it the night before. So I'd study that part the night before and, hell, the next day they started shooting someplace else where I hadn't even read. I didn't even know what it was about and they'd say "Don't worry!" and they'd shoot it anyway and somehow we got through it. I never knew just what to expect. I'd just get up in the morning and get down to the studio by six and we'd shoot the damn movie and then I'd go back to this little apartment I had. I didn't even see very much of Hollywood the whole time I was out there. I didn't really care if I did. I made another movie out there, too, a football movie called *Triple Threat*. It had other fellows in it like Bob Waterfield, Sid Luckman, Charlie Trippi, Steve Van Buren, Bill Dudley and a lot of others. But it wasn't any *Gone with the Wind*.

I did some coaching at Hardin-Simmons after I got out of pro ball. Then Harry Wismer, the sports announcer who owned the New York Titans in the AFL, ran out of people to coach his team. He used to announce our games on the radio in Washington when I played and I knew him pretty well. He asked me to come up to New York and coach and so I did. That was in 1959. I coached there three years. But I never liked coaching like I liked playing the game. Coaching took up most of the damn year. I liked playing the game in the season, then going back home and ranching the rest of the year.

I've had my ranch since 1941, added to it a lot along the way. In my football days, I'd play like three and a half months and the rest of the time I'd run my ranch. It's about forty miles from Sweetwater and maybe fifteen from Rotan. We breed and raise cattle. Recently we've gone to a Beefmaster breed, that's a three-way cross between a Hereford, Brahma, and a milking Shorthorn. We have seven hundred mother cows at all times. It's a good life.

I enjoyed the years I spent in pro football. I played with a fine bunch of boys when I first started, then another group would come along and they were equally fine, and then another. I was there a pretty long time, saw a lot of different faces come and go. Today, I'm both a Washington

Redskins fan and a Dallas Cowboys fan. Love them both. But when they play each other, I've got to admit, I'm on the side of the Redskins.

## Best Friends

George Preston Marshall's wife, Corinne Griffith, the movie star, told this story in her book, *My Life with the Redskins*. After a Bear player had taken a punch at Marshall's prize quarterback, Sammy Baugh, the Redskin owner stormed down onto the field and began a violent argument with Bear coach George Halas. As Mrs. Marshall tells it:

"Somehow they had been pushed over to the Bear bench in front of our box. Halas was saying: 'You dirty_____, get up in that box where you belong. It's too bad it ain't a cage. Now laugh that off.'

" 'You shut that_____mouth of yours, or I'll punch those_____gold teeth right down that red throat!'

"One of the Bear players started for him. George (Marshall) seemed to think that a good time to leave. He stomped back to the box, snorted as he sat down and, of course, took it out on me.

" 'What's the matter with you? You look white as a sheet.' "

" 'Oh, that was awful!' "

" 'What was awful?' "

" 'That horrible language. We heard every word.' "

" 'Well, you shouldn't listen.' "

" 'Oh, you. And right in front of ladies. . . . And as for that man Halas!' " Every hair of George's raccoon coat bristled. 'He's positively revolt——'

" 'Don't you dare say anything against Halas,' George was actually shaking his finger under my nose. 'He's my best friend.' "

## Little Scuffles, Large Pains

Was it a rugged game, the one they played back in the 1930s? Consider this account from the *New York Times* of the 1938 NFL championship game between the New York Giants and the Green Bay Packers:

"What a frenzied battle this was! The tackling was fierce and the blocking positively vicious. In the last drive every scrimmage pile-up saw a Packer tackler stretched on the ground. . . . As for the Giants, they really were hammered to a fare-thee-well.

"Johnny Dell Isola was taken to St. Elizabeth's hospital with a spinal

In this poignant scene on the Washington Redskins bench in 1943, the pain and anguish that often are such an inherent part of the game of professional football are forever captured in the face of Sammy Baugh. *(Pro Football Hall of Fame)*

concussion that just missed being a fractured vertebra. Ward Cuff suffered a possible fracture of the sternum.

"Mel Hein, kicked in the cheekbone at the end of the second quarter, suffered a concussion of the brain that left him temporarily bereft of his memory. He came to in the final quarter and finished the game. Leland Shaffer sustained a badly sprained ankle.

"The play for the full sixty vibrant minutes was absolutely ferocious. No such blocking and tackling by two football teams ever had been seen at the Polo Grounds. Tempers were so frayed and tattered that stray punches were tossed around all afternoon. This was the gridiron sport at its primitive best."

(The Giants, incidentally, won the game, 23–17, with the winning touchdown coming on a pass from Ed Danowski to Hank Soar.)

# *Jim Benton*

Long, lean Jim Benton stood 6 feet 3 inches when he came out of Arkansas to play for the Cleveland Rams in 1938. He quickly established himself as an end with adhesive hands and the talent for making diving, leaping, seemingly impossible catches. His misfortune, however, was to play in the same era as Green Bay's legendary receiver, Don Hutson, and he was therefore doomed to live forever in the great Packer's shadow.

Benton played all but one of his nine NFL seasons with the Rams, the exception being 1943, when that team suspended operations for a year. Benton was picked up by the Chicago Bears and helped them in their successful quest for the NFL title. During his career, Jim had the good fortune of being on the receiving end of some of the game's premier passers: Parker Hall in Cleveland, Sid Luckman on the Bears, and Bob Waterfield with the Los Angeles Rams.

As a rookie, Benton was the fifth most productive receiver in the league, trailing such already established pass catchers as Hutson, Gaynell Tinsley, and Charley Malone, and his average gain per catch of 20 yards was the best in the NFL. In 1944 and 1945, only Don Hutson caught more passes. The battery of Waterfield and Benton produced 303 yards on ten passes in the game in 1945 against the Detroit Lions which clinched the NFL West for the Rams. No other receiver in NFL history has gained that many yards in a single game.

In 1946, the first year Don Hutson was out of the league, Benton led the NFL in receptions (sixty-three) and yardage gained on them (981) and was named to the all-Pro team.

Over his career, Benton caught 288 passes for 4,801 yards and forty-five touchdowns. When he retired after the 1947 season, only Don Hutson exceeded him in those three pass catching categories. With those impressive credentials, Jim Benton went back to Arkansas to pursue a variety of business interests.

Arkansas was as good a football state as any when I was growing up. The sport was very popular and practically everybody followed the local teams. I was born in Carthage, but when I was two years old my dad was elected sheriff of Dallas County and we moved to Fordyce, a small town with a population of maybe thirty-five hundred down in the southern part of the state.

That's where I had my first exposure to the game. I guess it was in the third or fourth grade. We'd have makeup games at recess. But when we were in the fifth grade we had a regular team, we'd play the sixth grade, and then when we were in the sixth grade we'd play the fifth and the seventh grades.

Fordyce was an avid football town and it developed a program for the youngsters, especially those in the seventh and eighth grades. I played at Fordyce High School all four years.

We played all over the state. I remember we'd go up to play Central High in Little Rock, which incidentally was the only high school in that city even though it was the capital and by far the largest city in the state. Central is the same school where they had that integration crisis, when Governor Faubus called out the National Guard in 1957 to stop some Negro students from entering the school and President Eisenhower sent in federal troops. Anyway, we played them in 1930 and beat them 34–0, even though it was by far a much bigger school. We also played Pine Bluff in those days, which, year in and year out, was the top team in the state. That's where Don Hutson played his high school football, where he grew up. But that 1930 Fordyce team beat Pine Bluff and Don Hutson 50–12. Hutson scored both of Pine Bluff's touchdowns that day and he played the game with a broken hand. I was on the Fordyce team but I was just a freshman and watched the game from the bench. One of the stars of that Fordyce team was Paul "Bear" Bryant, who went on to coach at Alabama. He played end on offense and tackle on defense and was some ballplayer himself. We also had two backs, the Jordan twins, who were great high school ballplayers, and my older brother, W. R., played tackle. W. R. went on to Arkansas and made all-Conference there.

There were several reasons I decided to go to Arkansas. One of the biggest, I suppose, was that my brother was playing up there and he had a lot of influence on me in those days. They also came down to Fordyce to recruit me. Some other schools did too: Alabama, Tulane, LSU. I thought seriously about going to LSU and even went to their campus in Baton Rouge. In those days I was about 6 feet 3 inches and weighed about 180 pounds, kind of a skinny, raw-boned type. It was okay for my position, end, I guess. But as it turned out, I went to see LSU play in Shreveport and ended up talking with the coach of Arkansas, who they were playing that day. He was Fred Thomsen and he was a brilliant coach. He was one of the pioneers of the passing game. He talked to me and asked me to come up to Fayetteville and visit the school. I had a good feeling about it when I got there and, I must say, the players up there impressed me. I watched them work out and a lot of them talked to me afterwards. So I figured that would be the best place for me, especially because of the emphasis on the passing game, with me an end and all. I never regretted the decision.

When I was at Arkansas in 1936, a junior, we played Texas at Little Rock. It was the last game of the season and the winner of it would take the Southwest Conference championship. We were the underdogs, but we beat them in the rain and mud, 6–0.

The next year it came down to the final game of the season, too, only this time we were playing Rice at Houston. Well, at that time, no team had won the Southwest Conference title two years in a row. We really wanted to set that record. All we had to do was knock off Rice. And we had them beat with twenty seconds left to play in the game. But they had the ball, fourth down and 10 on about our 20 yard line. They were using the Notre Dame box formation and they had a wingback by the name of Ollie Cordill, who was 6 feet 3 inches and very good. He played a year with the Cleveland Rams later and I played against him again in the NFL. Anyway, we knew they were going to go to Ollie, we even knew what play they were going to use. We called a time-out and talked it over. It was a pass play they used a lot, had a lot of success with. The end would run a post pattern and the wingback would run an out-and-up. Jack Robbins, our tailback, was also a fine defensive back. He had Ollie covered beautifully when Rice ran the play. Well, Ernie Lane, their tailback, was a great passer, and he ran out to the right, rolled out looking to pass. He saw Ollie was covered but threw it in desperation anyway. I was our left end and I played off a block from the fullback and just as Lane threw the ball I leaped and the ball grazed my middle finger. It went a little off-course as a result. If it had been on course as he threw it, Jack Robbins would have intercepted it or knocked it away. But instead Ollie was able to turn around, go up, and grab it in the end zone. They got a touchdown and won the game and we lost the conference title.

We had a fine group of individuals at Arkansas, not just fine ball-players but fine human beings. Jack Robbins, our tailback, was a true triple threat. We played out of a short punt formation and used the single wing. Jack could pass, run, and kick the ball, and he was touted for all-American our senior year. But he hurt his knee and missed three or four games and that knocked him out of the running. We had another very good back in Dwight "Paddlefoot" Sloan. They called him Paddlefoot because of the way he ran, kind of with his toes turned out. Paddlefoot played in the pros just like Robbins and myself. He went with the Chicago Cardinals first and then played for the Detroit Lions.

Paddlefoot was a character. I played against him in the NFL. I remember in my first season with the Cleveland Rams we were playing the Cardinals in Cleveland. I was going down on a punt and Paddlefoot, who played safety and tailback, was back to receive. I timed it just perfectly and just as he caught the ball I nailed him. Wiped him out. I'll never forget it. He was just sitting there on the ground, the ball cradled in his lap, and grinning at me. He was a great grinner. But I knew he'd get even. And he did. A little later it was the third quarter and they needed 8 or 10 yards for a first down. They were on the 40 or 50 yard line and I rushed old Paddlefoot real hard. It was one of those situations where I got through from the side, the end position, and so old Paddlefoot moved up in the pocket and I just rushed on by him. He took off the same way I'd come in, the same exact path and ran about 40 yards. When we lined up for the next play Paddlefoot was looking right at me and he had that same damn grin on his face.

We never made it to a bowl game while I was at Arkansas, and I sure was disappointed about that. When I was a junior, that was the first year of the Cotton Bowl in Dallas and they didn't have the agreement then that the winner of the Southwest Conference would automatically be the host team. We had won it but TCU was second that year and TCU had Sammy Baugh as their star. So the Cotton Bowl officials decided, probably rightly so, that because Sammy was such a big draw in Texas that they'd invite TCU. Consequently we didn't get to play in it. The next year they had the rule in effect and we didn't get to go because we lost to Rice on that last game of the season. Had we gone we would have played Colorado and that was the year they spotlighted Whizzer White, who was all-American and, of course, went on later to become a Supreme Court justice.

I played in the East-West game after the college season and then in the All-Star game up in Chicago. In the first I played on the West squad and the game ended in a 0–0 tie. Paddlefoot Sloan was also invited to that game but Robbins wasn't, probably because he missed those games during the regular season.

In the All-Star game I played only about three minutes. We practiced for a week or two at Northwestern University before it, and Bo McMillin coached us. Cecil Isbell was the star of the game and we beat the Washington Redskins, 28–16.

That year, 1938, I was drafted by the Cleveland Rams. I was young and naive when I arrived there, had a lot to learn about the world. I mean I had the idea that when I signed the contract I was just automatically going to be on the squad. Well, of course, it doesn't work that way. I'd gotten married that last year at Arkansas and had some very definite responsibilities. Shortly after, my wife got pregnant and, as it turned out, it would be twin boys. I got to the Rams training camp at Berea, Ohio, at Baldwin-Wallace College, and I got to listen to them talking and suddenly I realized how many players they were going to have to release. There were seventy-five or eighty ballplayers trying out and they were only going to keep maybe thirty-three or thirty-five. There I was with a pregnant wife and I knew I just had to make that team. You've got to remember that back in those days it was really difficult to find a job of any kind. Anyway, when I got there after the All-Star game, I looked at my competition at end and felt I had a pretty good shot at making it. But I didn't take any chances. I worked like hell at that first training camp. I did make it, thank heaven. I had a per-game contract, not very secure in that they could release you anytime they wanted to. I was paid $150 a game which probably was about average for a rookie. I heard talk that Don Hutson, who was already well established as a star and an all-Pro, was making only $250 a game. You heard a lot of stories or rumors like that and you didn't really know who started them. Probably the owners.

We had a very young team, all the players were in their early twenties. That was only Cleveland's second year in the NFL. The year before they were 1–10, but there were some changes made and in 1938 we beat the Chicago Bears twice, and they were quite a powerhouse at the time. We beat them in back-to-back games in fact and that knocked them out of the race for the West division title. We won four games that year in total. We used the single wing like most teams in the NFL then. I didn't

Rams end Jim Benton makes one of his patented diving catches in this 1946 game at the Los Angeles Coliseum against the Chicago Bears. It was the Rams' first year in Los Angeles after leaving Cleveland. Benton played eight years with the Rams and one with the Bears, and as a pass catcher was considered second only to Don Hutson. No. 66 on the Bears is Bulldog Turner. *(Jim Benton)*

start the first game. We played Green Bay to open the season and lost, but after that I won a starting position. And I had a pretty good rookie year. I think I led the league in average gain per reception, 20 yards per catch.

In the off-season, I usually ran my bowling business. I had a bowling alley in Pine Bluff. One year, however, I worked in a steel mill in Cleveland. Another couple of years I went back to Fordyce. By that time my daddy was county judge and he wasn't in real good health. I went back to help out and I got a job driving a gravel truck for the county. I did the loading and the unloading, and when I went back to the Rams for the season I was really in good shape.

In 1941, I dropped out of the pros and went back to Fordyce. I had a chance to coach back there, and like every football player I truly wanted to coach a team. So I left the Rams and took the job. It was at the high school there. We played all the big high schools and ended up winning six games and losing two, I believe. Everybody was pretty pleased about it, but I found that financially I just about starved to death back there in Arkansas. So, in 1942, when the Rams asked me to come back, I did. Dan Reeves was heading it then and they offered me a much better contract than I'd had before.

Dan Reeves was a fine man. He bought into the Rams in 1941. I never negotiated a contract directly with him, it was ordinarily with Chile Walsh, who became coach and later general manager under Dan. All the players liked Dan. He had their interests at heart, I believe.

In 1943, because of the war, the Rams dropped out of the NFL. The players that were still around went with different ballclubs. There were only eight teams in the league that year, four in each division, and one of them was a combination of the Philadelphia Eagles and the Pittsburgh Steelers. The next year the Steelers combined with the Chicago Cardinals. Anyway, I was drawn by the Chicago Bears for the 1943 season. I sure was lucky because they had a fine team and we won the league championship that year. I also thought they were a great organization. They treated me just fine and I really enjoyed that year in Chicago. George Halas was gone, he was in the navy. Luke Johnsos and Hunk Anderson and Paddy Driscoll did the coaching and they did a terrific job. Luke was a really smart offensive coach and he was responsible for a lot of our success that year.

That was the same year that I had applied for a commission in the navy because I figured for sure I'd be called up in the draft any day. They turned me down because of a heart murmur they found. When I heard about that, I seriously thought of quitting football. I told the coaches in Chicago about it and that I thought I ought to quit. I mean if I couldn't serve in the navy because of my heart, it didn't seem to me that I should be playing professional football. They said, "Let's have you checked by a specialist." Well, they did and he checked me every Monday morning after our Sunday game. He told me I had a heart murmur all right and that he couldn't really understand how I could play with it. But then he said it didn't seem to be doing any damage and that I might as well play but I should be sure to get a lot of rest at the same time. Well, I decided to play out that year and then retire.

When the season was over, the Bears tried to buy me from the Rams. Rights to all of us were still held by Cleveland because they had only suspended operations, not folded up. The Bears only had a right to me for that one year while the Rams were out of business. The doctor told me the heart murmur wasn't a factor to worry about anymore. I wasn't so sure so I went to another doctor in Arkansas and he said he thought I could play, too. Then the Rams, who were back in business in 1944, offered me a contract that was about twice what I'd been making. So I went on back up to Cleveland and I never had any heart trouble since.

I really enjoyed that year with the Bears, though. That was the year Bronko Nagurski came back, and let me tell you, he was a horse. What I remember best was the Cardinal game, the last one of the season. I had the flu and didn't even suit up for the game, but I was on the bench. In that game against the Cardinals, Nagurski was playing tackle on offense and defense and the Cardinals got ahead of us by about two touchdowns. So they moved Nagurski to fullback and he won the ballgame for us. He ran the ball down their throats. Any man who could play like he did that year after being in retirement as long as he had been had to be something special.

There's another thing I remember about Bronko. Frankie Sinkwich was the tailback for Detroit that year. He was a fine back and Detroit was a real good team. In fact, of all the players I went up against the toughest to tackle were Sinkwich, Steve Van Buren, and Tony Canadeo. It was almost impossible to get a clean shot at any one of them and it was really difficult to bring them down one on one. But Nagurski could freeze Sinkwich. I don't know what it was about Bronko but he had this thing over Sink. I mean Sinkwich would run with the ball and when Nagurski would zero in on him old Sink would just freeze up and Nagurski would nail him every time. Nobody else in the game could do that to Sinkwich.

We didn't have much of a team in 1944, most everybody was off to the war. The game wasn't nearly as good that year with so much talent gone. I remember one game when we were playing Card-Pitt, the merger of the Cardinals and the Steelers. They were worse than everybody and didn't win a single game all that year. They had a back by the name of John Grigas, a fullback, one of those 3- or 4-yard runners, powerful, with good balance. They started a drive down the field and made maybe five or six first downs. And then on this particular play they really opened a hole up and Grigas rambled through it for 7 or 8 yards and then all of a sudden I saw one of our players, Rattlesnake Matheson, a linebacker, come running back through the same exact hole with the football. Those kinds of things happened a lot in 1944.

In 1945, however, we had a good team, won the West division and then the NFL championship. Bob Waterfield was a rookie that year but already a great quarterback. He was a strong leader, quiet, never said a lot, but that didn't affect his being a leader. Waterfield was also a great clutch player. When you needed something, he'd come through. He and Sid Luckman of the Bears were the two finest quarterbacks I ever played with. Bob was married to Jane Russell at the time, the movie star. She used to come to the games and probably got more attention than the team did on the field. The first game we played in Cleveland that year, against the Cardinals, they had a get-together after it for the players and sportswriters and she was there. Bob introduced her to all of us. Bob got a lot of good press after that.

In the championship game of 1945, we faced the Washington Redskins. They had Sammy Baugh but he was hurt and only played in the first quarter. The game was played in Cleveland and it was only about five degrees above zero. They had put hay on the field and a tarp on top of that for about two weeks before the game to keep the field from freezing. They removed it just before the game but by the first quarter the open end of the stadium, the one near Lake Erie, was frozen, and by the second half the field was totally frozen.

They had a rookie covering me, Bob DeFruiter, and he was having a heckuva time. I ended up having a very good day. Waterfield hit me for a touchdown near the end of the first half to put us ahead 9–7. We got a safety earlier when Baugh threw a pass from his own end zone and it hit the goalpost. The goalposts were on the goal line in those days and if a passer hit one it was an automatic safety.

The touchdown pass to me was a 38-yarder. All in all, I caught nine passes that day for 125 yards. Jim Gillette, one of our halfbacks, caught an even longer touchdown pass from Waterfield, about 45 yards. He ran a pass pattern right down the middle. Myself and the other end ran sideline patterns and Waterfield hit him right on the button. We won the game 15–14. I heard later that even though we won the NFL championship Dan Reeves still lost something like fifty thousand dollars.

After that we moved to Los Angeles and I must admit I liked it a lot better out there than in Cleveland. The weather was sure a lot better and as a team we had a lot better support from the fans. Of course we had to travel a lot further than any of the other teams. We went by train and sometimes by airplane in those days. Because we had to travel so far to play back east or in the midwest, it took a lot out of us, something other teams didn't have to worry about.

We played against some mighty good teams after the war. The Bears were always tough, with Sid Luckman, George McAfee, and Bulldog Turner. And the Cardinals got real good around then. They had the dream backfield, that's what it was called—Charlie Trippi, Pat Harder, Elmer Angsman, and Paul Christman. The team that gave me the most difficult time, however, was the Philadelphia Eagles. They would always double-cover me. Steve Van Buren was always on me, he played safety on defense, and there would always be a defensive halfback, too, sometimes it was Jack Banta others it was Bosh Pritchard. They really were tough on me. That Eagle team was really something all the way around. Besides Van Buren, who was everybody's all-Pro, they had Tommy Thompson at quarterback, Pete Pihos was one of their ends, and linemen like Alex Wojciechowicz, Vic Sears, Al Wistert, and Bucko Kilroy. They went to the championship in 1947, my last year in the pros.

After I retired from football, I stayed in the bowling business until 1954. I also did some coaching. For three years I was the head coach at Arkansas A&M, which is the University of Arkansas at Monticello today. I loved coaching. In 1951, my first year at A&M, we won eight games and lost only two. We won our conference that year. In 1953, we won it again.

I also helped out in the pros, too. In 1948 I helped coach the Ram receivers. That was Tom Fears' first year in the league, and I knew right from the start that he was going to be a great one. He led the league in pass receptions his very first year. And I never saw a player with more desire than Tom Fears. George Halas also had me come to the Bears training camp in the early 1950s to work with their receivers, and they had some good ones around then, guys like Ken Kavanaugh and Jim Keane.

All told, I played professional football for eight years, and they were good ones to remember. I was glad to be a part of it.

## *The First TV Game*

Jim Campbell, author, editor, and director of communications for the NFL alumni, wrote of the first pro football game ever televised:

It was October 22, 1939 . . . The Philadelphia Eagles versus the Brooklyn Dodgers.

The game was played in Brooklyn's Ebbets Field before 13,000 . . . The Dodgers with the help of three 40-yard-plus field goals by Ralph Kercheval, subdued the Eagles, 23–14. Two records were established that day—Kercheval's 45-yard field goal was the season's longest, and 6-foot, 205-pound Brooklyn fullback Ace Gutowsky eclipsed Cliff Battles' lifetime rushing mark when a brief appearance netted him 7 yards for a new standard of 3,399 yards. Pug Manders and Ace Parker also were Dodger standouts. . . .

For the Eagles, coached by Bert Bell, back Franny Murray ran and passed well all day and scored on a short sweep. Bill Hewitt, playing without a helmet, caught a six-point pass from 5-foot 7-inch, 150-pound Philly back Davey O'Brien.

But so far as anyone can tell, none of the players knew the game was being broadcast to the approximately one thousand TV sets in New York City.

"I didn't know about it," says Ace Parker today. Bruiser Kinard, Brooklyn's outstanding tackle, agreed: "I certainly wasn't aware of it."

The announcer for the game was Allan Walz, a former New York City Golden Gloves champion and NYU football star who did the sports for (the NBC station) W2XBS.

"I remember the game," said Walz. "Pro football was a great game to do by television. . . . It was late in October on a cloudy day and when the sun crept behind the stadium there wasn't enough light for the cameras. The picture got darker and darker and eventually it went completely blank and we reverted to a radio broadcast. . . .

"We used two iconoscope cameras. I'd sit with my chin on the rail in the mezzanine and the camera would be over my shoulder. I did my own spotting and when the play moved up and down the field, on punts and kickoffs, I'd point to tell the cameraman what I'd been talking about and we used hand signals to communicate. The other camera was on the field, at the 50 yard line, but it couldn't move so we didn't use it much.

"Producer and director Burke Crotty was in the mobile unit truck and he'd tell me over the headphones which camera he was using. There wasn't a monitor up in the broadcasting box, but there was one on the field. I never really understood what that was for, but I think Potsy Clark (Brooklyn's coach) insisted on it. He was experimenting with scouting by television, I think.

"Afterwards, I'd interview players, but it was too dark by then to do television and the players probably thought I was just another of the radio men there."

# 16

# *Sid Luckman*

A key to the character of Sid Luckman is found in the fact that he turned down several college scholarship offers at academically lesser schools and chose Columbia, where he would have to work his way through four years, because he felt he would get a much better education there. He did, and he also played a fine game of football for that Ivy League school, ending up an all-American halfback in 1938.

George Halas, owner and coach of the Chicago Bears, followed Luckman's football fortunes that senior year with more than casual interest. He saw in Luckman, who was both a fine runner and a good passer, the qualities he felt were necessary for the complex T formation he was infusing into the Bears' scheme of things. Luckman not only had the physical talents, but he had a brilliant, absorbent mind; he was quick to read defenses, decisive, a natural leader, and a dogged worker. Halas said he saw all that in Luckman, and so he went after him with a passion and signed him.

The transition from a single wing tailback to a T formation quarterback was a very difficult thing, but after apprenticing as a halfback for part of his rookie year, Luckman made it and, of course, became the game's first great T formation quarterback. In his twelve years with the Bears, he guided them to five league championship games and to four NFL titles. He was an all-Pro five times in an age when the NFL could boast quarterbacks of the caliber of Sammy Baugh, Cecil Isbell, Tommy Thompson, Bob Waterfield, and Paul Christman.

His greatest single effort was on "Sid Luckman Day" at the Polo Grounds in New York in 1943, a special tribute to the Brooklyner who had done so well after leaving that city's mean streets. His mother was in the stands for one of the very rare occasions on which she watched him play the violent game of football, and gifts were bestowed before the game.

Luckman was deeply touched. Then he went out and destroyed the New York Giants by throwing an NFL record *seven* touchdown passes that afternoon in a 56–7 triumph. To this day no one has thrown more touchdown passes in one game, although several passers have since tied it.

When Sid Luckman retired in 1950, he had thrown 1,744 passes for 14,686 yards and 137 touchdowns. Sid was inducted into the Pro Football Hall of Fame in 1965, with the third class of enshrinees.

With the same qualities that made him a masterful quarterback and team leader, he became an eminently successful businessman in Chicago after retiring from football. But even while building his business empire, he kept his hand in football as an assistant coach at various places, from the Bears to Notre Dame, teaching the intricacies of T formation quarterbacking. And he remained a close and devoted friend to his coach and mentor, George Halas, up until Papa Bear's death in 1983.

W here I grew up in Brooklyn, New York, we used to play football, stickball, and baseball all the time. But football was my favorite. We played right out there on the city streets. We used to wait for the cars to pass, then we'd start playing. It was in Flatbush by a place called Erasmus Hall High School.

How I got from there to Columbia was a rather interesting story. I don't want it to sound like a braggadocio, but I'd done pretty well in high school, in football and scholastically, and I had a number of college scholarship offers. Some of the people in the neighborhood around that time took me over to see the Columbia-Navy football game. It was a very interesting game, played at Baker Field. After the game was over, the people who had taken me there brought me in to meet the coach of Navy and then into Columbia's dressing room to meet their coach, Lou Little. I'd heard a lot about him. He'd been to the Rose Bowl with Columbia a few years earlier. And right away I could see there was something about the man; he had a certain charisma, a certain air about him. I felt from the start if I could spend four years with a man like that it would enhance my life.

Later I was contacted by a man named Littauer, who was once a famous football player from Columbia and was now a doctor, and a man named West. They asked if I'd be interested in going to Columbia. They were the first to talk to me about Columbia, although I had talked to people from other schools. Well, I was very excited because I was really desirous of going to Columbia because of Lou Little. After they contacted me, it had to be determined if my grades were good enough to get in, because it was a very difficult school then just as it is now.

I met Lou Little again and after the second meeting I was certain Columbia was the place where I wanted to matriculate. I wanted both to play football and to get a good education. Coach Little wanted that for me, too. He said football was just a means to enhance your life. When I think about it, though, I guess it was not really the university I chose, although I love it with all my heart; it was the person, Lou Little, who had such a tremendous charisma, that I really chose. He reminded me very much of Franklin Delano Roosevelt, with the pinch glasses.

Columbia was not giving any scholarships in those days, however. Other colleges were but the Ivy League wasn't. So I'd have to find a way of working my way through school. The tuition in those days was about three hundred and fifty or four hundred dollars, plus living expenses. I did know that it was a good school scholastically and that it would surely help me later on when I would go into business.

As a football coach, Lou Little was tremendous. It was very difficult for him. Admissions were very strict at Columbia. He couldn't get the players that other schools outside the Ivy League could. I was the biggest back he had, and I weighed only about 178 pounds then. Our line averaged only about 170 pounds. I was the tailback in the single wing. But I called the signals. It was a very unusual situation because he never had a real chance to prove how good a coach he was. The boys he had were just not on a par with the teams we were playing against. And so when we went into a game, even though we fought with all our hearts, we were always up against opponents who were bigger and stronger.

I played against a lot of good players in college. Bob MacLeod of Dartmouth was an all-American, a tremendous running back. Hal McCullough of Cornell was very good. Brud Holland was an end and also from Cornell and was terrific.

Then I went with the Bears. It was kind of interesting how that came about, too. George Halas wrote me a letter, saying he might like to have me play for him in Chicago. I answered it saying I didn't have any desire to play professional football. I'd taken a lot of punishment as a tailback in college, and I knew how rough the pro game was.

Coach Halas had come up to watch Columbia play. The Bears were playing the New York Giants the next day at the Polo Grounds and he came with Luke Johnsos and a few other of his assistant coaches. He sat in the press box and apparently after the game he made up his mind that I could fit into his system, the T formation, which he was just beginning to develop. With it the quarterback did a lot of spinning and handing off and as a tailback I did a lot of that. I guess he decided I might work as a quarterback in his system. You see, his quarterbacks, Carl Brumbaugh and Bernie Masterson, were getting a little old, and there weren't many people around who understood what quarterbacking was in those days. There just weren't any quarterbacks then as we know them today. Nobody else in the pros was using the T formation. So he wrote me that letter and I wrote back that I wasn't interested.

Then Coach Halas called Lou Little who talked to me for him. Halas also made a trade sending Eggs Manske to the Pittsburgh Steelers and giving them his first round draft choice for their first round draft choice— they had the first pick that year. Then he called Lou Little again. After that he came to New York to see Lou Little, and the three of us got together. I reiterated that I hadn't the least interest in playing professionally and that I'd just gotten a wonderful job. I also told him that I didn't think I, as an Ivy League player, was good enough or could possibly get good enough to play pro football. He was very insistent, however, that I at least give it some serious consideration. He came back again and by that time I'd gotten married. We had a little apartment. He came over to visit with me and my wife, Estelle, at the apartment. Estelle made dinner for the three of us. Afterwards he made me a very fair and equitable offer. Later he said to me that I was the only player he had to truly talk into playing professional football. He had the contract with him, handed it to me, and I signed it. Then he walked around the table and kissed Estelle on the cheek. He sat back down and lifted up a glass of wine and said, "You and Jesus Christ are the only two people I'd ever pay that much money to." I think it was five thousand or six thousand dollars at the time. But that was the most money he'd ever paid anybody except for Red Grange. So I joined the Bears.

It was a very difficult transition from playing tailback at Columbia to quarterback for the Bears. The signal-calling was diametrically opposite. The spinning was very difficult because you had to be so precise and so quick. They don't do it today like we had to do it. We had counterplays and double-counters and fakes. It was very hard for me to adjust, to get my hand under the center, and to get back and set up.

Coach Halas had made up his mind that I would play quarterback but he started me off at left halfback. Then every day he had his former quarterback, Carl Brumbaugh, work with me for about two hours after practice. Carl taught me the setting up, the spinning, all the different ramifications and fundamentals of the T formation. We worked very hard during the day, and then at night I'd go home and study the play book with Mrs. Luckman. I felt I had to get to know better what the guards and tackles did or were supposed to do. I wanted to have a better understanding of what the overall picture was when I was in the huddle.

Finally, after the fifth game, I got my chance at quarterback. Coach Halas loved to start players in games in the city they were from, the reason being because there was no television back then, it gave them a chance to play before their hometown fans. He reasoned they would be fired up and do better. So he started me in the New York Giants game, at halfback. There were a lot better halfbacks on our team than me in 1939, fellows like Ray Nolting and Bobby Swisher. It was a nice gesture and enabled my hometown folks to watch me play. Well, during the course of that game at the Polo Grounds, the Bears were behind 16–0. It was in the third period and we weren't moving the ball very well. The Giants always had a great defense with Steve Owen as their head coach. Coach Halas, who always called me son, walked over to me on the sideline.

"Son," he said, "Are you ready to go back in?"

I said "Okay, coach."

"All right, son, I want you to go back in at quarterback."

Well, that was the single most intense nervousness I've ever known in football, even more so than a world championship game. That *one* moment, in my hometown with my mother there—she only saw me play a couple of times before that—Coach Little was there, all my friends, and there I was trying to be a T formation quarterback, a position I'd never played in a game before. There I was in New York, at the Polo Grounds going up against the Giants. It was almost like a dream. And the good Lord must have put his arm around me that day. Bob MacLeod, from Dartmouth, who I'd played against in college, was at halfback for the Bears at this particular time. He came back in the huddle and said to me, "I can beat my defender if you want to try a long one, Sid." I always liked to listen to people in the huddle so I said, "Sure, Bob." I called a stop and go and he went in motion. It was a play very similar to the ones they run today. Coach Halas had us running plays just like they do today, just as imaginative. Men in motion, split ends, double tight ends. Everything you can think of, he was doing in those days, forty years ago. The T formation really should be called the Halas formation because he made it into a science and brought it into the game of professional football. Anyway, MacLeod goes in motion, made his fake on the defensive back and then shot around him. I threw a long wobbly pass. It was too short and MacLeod had to come around, circle back, and he did and just took it right out of the Giants' defender's hands. It looked like a sure interception, but Bob took it away and kept right on going around him all the way for a touchdown.

A little while later I called a play to throw to another of our backs, Bobby Swisher, who was from Northwestern. It was a little screen pass and he grabbed it and ran 65 yards for another touchdown. We still lost 16–13, but the next day the people back in Chicago read about how I threw two touchdown passes. Everybody said, "Hey, that's great." They didn't know I really hadn't had a damn thing to do with it. It was Mac-Leod and Swisher who made those plays.

Then the big test came when we played Green Bay two weeks later. Coach Halas started me this time at quarterback and we beat them 30–27. They were a real powerhouse that year and went on to win the title. That was the second-most exciting, pressure-filled time I experienced in football. The pressure came from the fact I was playing at quarterback, but also because for the first time I was going against people like Don Hutson and Clarke Hinkle and Arnie Herber and Cecil Isbell. They'd been heroes of mine before, and I never honestly expected to be playing as a pro against them on a football field. And I looked at their line, me who had been used to playing against linemen in the Ivy League who weighed 170 or 180 pounds. And all of a sudden here are guys weighing 250 or 260. I just couldn't believe that there were those size athletes. I sort of got into the groove after the game got started, though. That was the start of my career really as a T formation quarterback, and it worked. We had a great team that year with linemen like Joe Stydahar and Danny Fortmann and George Musso and such great runners as Bill Osmanski and Joe Maniaci. It was the beginning of the Bear dynasty.

Coach Halas came up with the finest material around, the best players. He chose them himself, using his own draft system. He got the manpower and he was the only one using the T. He was way ahead of the game. Everybody was trying to copy him, but they were behind. Then, of course, the war came along and broke up that tremendous dynasty. It would have continued for years, the Bear dynasty, but we lost so many greats like George McAfee, Bill Osmanski, Ray Nolting, Danny Fortmann, and, of course, Coach Halas himself.

Halas in those days was probably the toughest coach in the game. They talk about Vince Lombardi being tough but Halas was just as

"Papa Bear" George Halas gives his fair-haired boy, Sid Luckman, a little tousle during a game at Wrigley Field in Chicago in the 1940s. In 1939, Halas converted Luckman from a tailback into the pro game's first T formation quarterback. In his twelve years of calling signals for the Bears, Luckman also proved to be one of the game's all-time great quarterbacks. A five-time all-Pro, he led the Bears to five NFL championships. Halas and Luckman maintained an almost father-son relationship until Papa Bear's death in 1983. *(Pro Football Hall of Fame)*

tough. And he had down all the finesse of the game as well. I remember he used to give us nineteen seconds in the huddle, said we had to be out to start the play no later than nineteen seconds, which left us eleven to get the play off. He had everything down to a science. He demanded perfection. He was a perfectionist himself and we had to work twice as hard just to be half as good as he was. His whole life was football. He worked seven days a week, from nine in the morning until ten or eleven at night. He was truly dedicated and he wanted total dedication from everyone associated with the team. Leadership, drive, and knowledge of the game, those were his keynotes.

We played offense and defense in those days. It was very different from today. You couldn't today, not with the kind of players you go up against who are so fast, so big, so strong. Wide receivers, for example, have such great speed. I as a defensive back couldn't compete with them. When you played all the time, sixty minutes, you never thought a thing about it. In high school, college, the pros, you simply played offense and defense. It was the game. We never realized that someday it would become a game of specialists. In those days there weren't any substitutions like now; if they took you out of the game you couldn't come back during that quarter. Which also meant you couldn't have any plays sent in like they do today. It was a 15-yard penalty if a play was sent in from the bench so I had to call all the plays myself. It was truly different. I mean here I had to cover as a defensive back a receiver like Don Hutson or Jim Benton of the Cleveland Rams or later Tom Fears when the Rams were in L.A. It was a problem. And while you were doing that you were also thinking about what you were going to do as soon as you got the ball: what kind of plays you would call, what kind of series you would plan. In other words, your mind had to be functioning all the time. You had to stay a little bit ahead of the game.

And you had to stay healthy, in good shape to go the distance. It was a very rugged game. They hit hard, played hard. I remember some very tough tacklers: Mel Hein of the Giants, he was one of the all-time greatest, Baby Ray at Green Bay was another, and Fred Davis of the Redskins, who later played for us at the Bears, and Wee Willie Wilkin, another great lineman for the Redskins who was not very "wee"—he was about 6 feet 4 inches and 260 pounds.

The Bears had many of the true greats of the day, however, like George McAfee. You'll never find a guy who can run better than he did. And Bill Osmanski, Bullet Bill, an incredible powerhouse, and Ray Nolting who could hit a line as fast as any man I've ever seen. I could go on and on about the Bears of those days: Joe Stydahar, Danny Fortmann, George Musso, Lee Artoe, Dick Plasman, George Wilson, John Siegal, Norm Standlee, Joe Maniaci. They were all all-Stars. And look at the pass catchers I had: Ken Kavanaugh, an uncanny football player, as were Jim Keane and Harry Clark and Dante Magnani.

I was at the right place at the right time. And I have to thank Mr. Halas for that. If I'd have been a tailback or signed with another team, which I probably would not have done, I don't think I would have been able to stay in the league for twelve years as I did with the Bears. As a quarterback in the T formation, however, I was able to stay.

One of my most vivid memories is, of course, the 1940 championship game against George Preston Marshall's Redskins. It was the greatest display of psychological impact ever given to a football team. That was one of the things Halas was marvelous at. He had a great way of building you up for a game. Well, we'd lost to the Redskins 7–3 in the regular season. The game was played in Washington a few weeks before. We had pretty well dominated that game, just a few breaks went against us. Then on the last play of the game we were on the Redskins' 7 yard line. Bill Osmanski was our fullback and I called for a pass to him over the center. He was just about to catch the ball, it was just a short pass over the goal line, and as he went to grab it the defensive back knocked his hands down and the ball just bounced off his stomach. Well, the official was standing right there, and it was clearly pass interference. But for some reason or another he didn't call it. We screamed about it but that didn't help.

We vowed that we would even it up when we met again. Well that meeting was the championship game. It also was played in Washington. We took the train from Chicago on Friday night, and normally the boys would be playing cards or something like that. But this time everybody had their playbooks out. Nobody was laughing or horsing around. You could actually feel the tension in the air.

We arrived in Washington on Saturday morning and went out to practice that afternoon. Coach Halas ran us through a very short drill and after it we had a players' meeting. Later that afternoon Sammy Baugh and I went on national network radio and talked about the game. Now Sammy is a very humble, very decent man. We wished each other luck, may the best team win, that sort of thing. When the radio show was over I said, "Sammy, it's going to be quite a game."

He said, "Yeah, I know, but we're ready for you."

"We're gonna have a lot of fun out there tomorrow," I said.

The headlines in the newspapers Saturday night, however, said the Bears were crybabies. This had come from George Marshall. He said something to the effect that ever since they whipped us in the regular season, all we did was cry about how we were robbed by the officials. We were just crybabies, quitters, he said. Coach Halas, of course, saw it, and took it out of the newspapers. Then he had the pages blown up. I don't know how he did it on a Saturday night. He must have found some printing company who could do it. Anyway, around the whole dressing room when we walked in were these blown-up newspaper stories.

Then he made his classic speech, one of the most memorable of my life. He said, "Gentlemen, I know," and he looked us right in the eye, "this is the best football team ever assembled. I know it. You know it. Now I want you to prove to the American public that you are as good as *you* know you are, as good as *I* know you are. And more importantly I want you to prove to Mr. Marshall and the Redskins that what they think of you is not true." He pointed around the room at the newspapers on the wall. "Look at this, this is what he thinks of you, what the Redskins think of you. All you great players, players who I respect, look at this. We have never cried in our lives. No one can talk that way about us."

Then it was over. And I tell you there was never such a surge for the door. I tell you we almost broke the damn door down.

He had given me some plays to run if the Redskins were using the same defense that had worked against us before. It had worked well then and Halas wasn't going to let it happen again. If I saw a similar defensive lineup, we would compensate: McAfee in motion one way, Nolting in motion the other, whatever, to beat that defense. We knew if they used the same defense we had them. We'd planned against it the entire week before the game. And they used the same defense.

It was just one of those incredible games. We were perfectly prepared for it. Halas had seen to it. We were motivated. And we won 73–0.

Another great memory was of Bronko Nagurski. When I first saw him, I saw the nearest thing to the most perfectly built, strongest human being I'd ever met. He had such tremendous power. He had played in the '30s, become a legend, then he came back to training camp in 1943. He came back to play tackle for us. The Bronk was thirty-four or thirty-five then and had been out of the game for about six years. It took him a little while to get back into the swing of things. A couple of our coaches, Hunk Anderson and Luke Johnsos, later decided to try him again at fullback in the last couple of games. And that came back to him, too. When I handed him the ball, I could just sense the power. He would take it with just such a great burst as he went into the line. In one of the games, against the Redskins, I was walking off the field with Sammy Baugh afterwards and I said, "Sammy, can you imagine what he must have been like in his prime?"

Sammy said, "I remember. He was the most powerful human being I ever played against." And I might add Bronko Nagurski was also one of the finest gentlemen you'd ever meet.

In 1946, the championship game we played against the New York Giants was the most vicious football game I'd ever played in in my life. There was the toughest tackling, the fiercest blocking, the hardest running. What happened was, somehow or other, there was this supposed gambling situation. The night before the game one of the Giants, Merle Hapes, a back, was suspended, and Frank Filchock, their quarterback, got in trouble but he was allowed to play. Steve Owen, their coach, told me afterwards that he'd never seen a team who wanted to win a game more than the Giants did that one. They wanted to win it for those two fellows accused of the gambling. They wanted to show all the fans that it was on the up-and-up. Especially Frank Filchock, he was playing and he wanted desperately to show that he wasn't involved. They felt they had to win to save face. And it was a real brawl. They gave us a helluva tough battle. But we finally won it, though.

One of the most memorable plays I ever had in pro football occurred in that game. We had a play called "Bingo keep it" where I ran with the ball. Halas didn't care if I ran with the ball but he didn't want me to do it too much during the regular season. In the championship game, that was another matter. If I got a bad bruise I'd have the rest of the year to get over it, not just a week, like in the regular season. Well, it worked like this. McAfee was such a tremendous threat as a runner, the best breakaway back in the game, they always had to watch out for him. And he had been running well off left end all day in that championship game and the Giants were always looking for him. So, in the middle of the fourth period, I took a time-out and went over to talk to coach Halas. I said "Now?" He knew the play I meant. We'd talked it over before the game.

He nodded. "Now."

So I went back out and called "Bingo keep it." When I got the snap, I faked to McAfee who went around the left end with the defense in hot pursuit. Everyone was chasing McAfee so I just danced around right end with the ball and then along the sidelines for a touchdown. Nineteen yards. That was one of the few times in my life I ran for a touchdown. It was a real thrill for me.

We won that game 24–14, despite how hard the Giants played. It was especially wonderful in that Coach Halas was back, his first year after spending four years in the Navy. It was a great team we had, just like the dynasty before the war. I played a few more years after that and we were in it each year, very close, but always a little short, and that game with the Giants turned out to be the last championship game I played in.

## *Playing the Goalpost*

In 1942, Don Hutson set an NFL record by catching seventeen touchdown passes. He was also in the midst of setting a record of touchdown passes in consecutive games when he ran up against the Chicago Bears at Wrigley Field.

The Bears, a powerhouse that would not lose any of their eleven games that year, were winning 38–0 in the fourth quarter. Bear coach George Halas, secure in his impending victory, was also determined to snap Hutson's touchdown reception streak, remembering no doubt how Hutson had burned the Bears so often in the past.

With two minutes left in the game, Green Bay had no chance to win. But they were on the Bear 20 yard line and trying to keep Hutson's record alive. Cecil Isbell threw three straight incompletions, principally because Hutson was covered by three Bear defenders: George McAfee, Harry Clark, and Dante Magnani. But on fourth down! Pat Livingston, sports editor of the Pittsburgh *Press*, described it aptly:

"Then came the most incredible premeditated play I ever saw on a football field. . . . Lining up as a flanker, harassed by three Bears, the cagy old Alabaman ran a simple post pattern, diagonally in on the twin-poled uprights, Bears convoying him, stride by stride.

"As the four men raced under the bar, Hutson hooked his elbow around the upright, stopped abruptly, flung his body sharply left, and left the red-faced Bears scrambling around in their cleats. He stood alone in the end zone as he casually gathered Isbell's throw to his chest."

## *Music, Maestro*

Redskin owner George Preston Marshall is remembered as one of the game's most illustrious showmen. "Football," he once said, "is a game of pageantry. It derives as a spectacle from the gladiator shows of the Ro-

Washington Redskins owner, the irrepressible George Preston Marshall *(right)*, presents a lifetime pass to Redskins games to President Harry S. Truman. Looking on is NFL Commissioner and former co-owner of the Pittsburgh Steelers Bert Bell. Marshall launched the Redskins in Boston in 1932, moved them to Washington in 1937, and brought show biz to the NFL with marching bands, fight songs, and assorted halftime entertainments during his thirty-eight-year career as head of the Redskins. Bell served as commissioner from 1946 until 1959. *(Pro Football Hall of Fame)*

mans. . . .It is strictly amphitheater. Its great success is due to the color surrounding it. It needs music and bands. Football without a band is like a musical without an orchestra."

So Marshall put together a 110-piece marching band for his Redskins, outfitted them in elaborate Indian costumes, including headdresses, and turned them loose at every Washington halftime. He also reinforced their act with sidelights that ranged from trained animal acts to having a Santa Claus parachute into the Redskins' stadium the Sunday before Christmas.

Jack Mara, son of Tim Mara, the New York Giants' founder, always liked to tell this story to describe Marshall and his priorities. The Giants were to play the Redskins on a Sunday afternoon in December one year when a freak and heavy snowstorm left about a foot of snow on the playing field. A few hours before the game, Mara stood on the sideline surveying the situation and wondering if it would be possible to play a game under such dire conditions. His thoughts were interrupted when he saw Marshall trudging across the field through the knee-high snow.

When he reached him, Marshall clapped Mara on the shoulder and said reassuringly, "Don't worry, they're coming. They'll be here in plenty of time."

"Snowplows?" Mara asked.

Marshall looked at him in disbelief. "Snowplows, hell, I'm talking about overshoes for the band."

# 17

# *Tony Canadeo*

Tony Canadeo learned to play football on the sandlots of Chicago, then took his rough-hewn skills two thousand miles west to Spokane, Washington, where he refined them at Gonzaga University. He became known as the "Gray Ghost of Gonzaga," a nickname that would follow him into the pros.

A tailback by definition, Canadeo did just about everything on a football field. He ran with the best of them, he passed, he was a fine receiver, he returned kickoffs and punts, he punted, and he was a bruising defensive back. Curly Lambeau got word of this multi-threat football player and, despite the fact that he played at a relatively minor college, thought he might be just the back to relieve an aging Clarke Hinkle in the Green Bay Packers' lineup.

Canadeo was not the Packers' first-round draft choice in 1941—a fullback named George Paskvan was—but he made the team and earned a starting berth. Canadeo joined a veteran backfield that consisted of Hinkle, Cecil Isbell, and Hal Van Every. At 5 feet 11 inches and 190 pounds, he was an average-size back for the 1940s, but he was acknowledged as one of the fiercest competitors in the game.

In 1943, with Cecil Isbell gone from Green Bay, the onus of the passing game fell on Canadeo, and he teamed up ably enough for Don Hutson to lead the league in pass receptions, yardage gained on receptions, and touchdowns on pass catches.

Because of military service, Tony missed the only Packer championship game in which the team participated during his eleven-year career in Green Bay (1944).

When he came back, however, he established himself as the squad's premier running back although he still occasionally threw the ball. In 1949,

Tony became only the third back in NFL history to gain more than 1,000 yards rushing in a single season. His 1,052 yards, an average of 5.1 per carry, put him in the same enviable league as Beattie Feathers (1,004 in 1934) and Steve Van Buren (1,146 in 1949).

Tony Canadeo gained 4,197 yards for Green Bay between 1941 and 1952, ran for twenty-six touchdowns, passed for sixteen, and caught five TD passes. When he left the game in 1952, only Steve Van Buren and Marion Motley had rushed for more yards than Tony in all NFL history. He was inducted into the Pro Football Hall of Fame in 1974. After his football days were over, Canadeo remained in Green Bay, carving another career in the steel business.

I began playing football on the northwest side of Chicago where I grew up. We had neighborhood teams in those days, the middle of the 1930s, and we'd play each other, sandlot games, but they were actually played in the parks.

The first time I really got into it in an organized way was in high school. I started out as an end but as a sophomore they switched me to a back. I went to Steinmetz High School, which was in the Public League. In Chicago they had two leagues, the Public and the Catholic, and both had a large number of schools.

Around the time I played, there was another fellow in the Public League who was immensely popular, Bill DeCorrevont. He played for Austin High School and he was really something special, a tremendous football player, the best in the city. Bill matured a little faster than the average guy. He was fast and strong. Everybody in the city followed him, followed what he did on the football field.

I never played against DeCorrevont, but I saw him play. We should have played him, though. Our team ended up in a tie for the division championship with the team from Schurz High School. Well, in those days, they didn't have a playoff system, they just flipped a coin. We lost the flip and Schurz played Austin for the Public League championship. DeCorrevont and Austin won it and then they went on to play the champions from the Catholic League. That was the highlight of the year in Chicago back then for high school football. It was called the Kelly Bowl, the game for the city championship, named after Mayor Kelly, and it was played at Soldier Field. And this is the truth, when DeCorrevont played that year in that game more than a hundred thousand people were in Soldier Field for it. Bill went on to play for Northwestern and then, after the war, he was in the NFL, mostly with the Chicago Cardinals and Bears, I think, but he was not the star in the pros that he'd been in high school.

After that I went to Gonzaga University, which is a Jesuit college like Marquette or Fordham. It was out in Spokane, Washington. It wasn't the most natural place for a kid from Chicago to end up, and I got there in a kind of round-about way. You see, there weren't a lot of recruiters around in those days and the few that were looking at Chicago high school players were looking for guys like DeCorrevont.

I had an older brother who was a football player and a CYO boxing champion and he was on a scholarship up at St. Norbert College in De Pere, Wisconsin. Some of the people he knew there were transferring to Gonzaga to play football out there. There had been a Gonzaga grad coaching at one of the high schools up there in Wisconsin and he kind of recruited them for Gonzaga. I went up to St. Norbert to see my brother and the school, and I got acquainted with these guys who were going out there and I learned about the school.

I didn't have any other offers, and I actually didn't have one from Gonzaga either. But I was told if you went out there and made the team, you would be given a full scholarship. So, myself and some others decided to give it a try.

There were about seven of us who left from Chicago. This was 1937 and one of the guys had a 1927 Packard and we all piled into it and headed out there. It's about two thousand miles away and it took us seven days to get there because we had a breakdown about every two hundred miles. We shipped our stuff ahead, which is how we could fit seven of us into that old touring Packard. You can't imagine how much oil that car used on the trip.

That year there were about ninety freshmen trying out for the team at Gonzaga. And it was pretty serious stuff because if you didn't make the team, and only about thirty would, you either had to pay your own way through school or go back home.

Mike Pacarovitch was the coach out there then, and he took a good look at all the freshmen. It was kind of scary. Here you had all the pressure of trying to make the football team and at the same time it was my first real experience with being away from home, and it was two thousand miles away as a matter of fact. You were lonely and homesick at the same time and there was a lot of competition. At first I didn't think I was going to make it, not when I saw how many were trying out. But I guess I got a little lucky in one of the intra-squad games and ran a punt back for a touchdown and then in another I ran a kickoff back for one, too. After that I was pretty secure.

I started on the freshman team. We played other freshman teams from schools like Washington State, Montana, and Idaho, and we played the regular varsity teams from smaller schools like North Central Teacher's College. So I got my scholarship but still you were required to work at the school. All the athletes waited tables in the dining hall. You would work a week, then have a week off, alternating like that all through the school year.

Going out there opened up a lot of new things to me. It was the first time I'd ever seen a mountain. And I went fishing for the first time in my life out there.

I moved up to the varsity the following year. There we would play teams like Santa Clara and St. Mary's down in California and Oregon and some of the other smaller state schools out around there. We even played Texas Tech once. I remember my senior year we played Detroit University, that was in 1940, and they were quite a good team. They had just beaten Texas Christian, which was a pretty highly regarded team in those days. Gus Dorais was coaching Detroit that year and he, of course, later went on to coach the Lions in the NFL. Well, they came up to Spokane and we beat them, 13–7, I believe the score was. I was fortunate to have a good game that day, I scored both our touchdowns. As a result of it, I ended up with the Green Bay Packers. Gus Dorais, who knew Curly Lambeau quite well, told him about me and that's how I ended up being drafted by them. If it wasn't for Gus, I'm sure Lambeau would never have heard of me or at least not given me much thought, coming from a small school like Gonzaga.

We did have a definite touch with the pros out there, however, because Ray Flaherty, who was head coach of the Washington Redskins, was a Gonzaga grad and he used to bring his team out there for their summer camp training. I got acquainted with him and he told me he wanted me for the Redskins. He did a lot of recruiting, that is finding people out there in the Northwest. He got Mel Hein for the Giants when Ray was still playing for them and he got Max Krause for them, too. Max was a fine running back from Gonzaga. Later he got Ed Justice and George Karamatic for the Redskins, both were Gonzaga grads, too.

Flaherty told me that he thought I'd do well with the pros and that he wanted me. But he said he was going to kind of sneak me through the draft. He said I was a sleeper, being from Gonzaga, and that the other teams, chances are, hadn't heard of me. He would just grab me late in the draft, he said. Well, the Packers took me before he got the chance because of the good things Dorais had told Curly Lambeau about me.

There were two others in our backfield at Gonzaga when I played that went into the pros, too, Ray and Cecil Hare. They were brothers and both of them ended up with the Redskins.

The most famous Gonzaga grad, however, was not a football player. He was Bing Crosby and every time we went down to California to play against Loyola of Los Angeles or Santa Clara, he would throw a big party for us. He would get one of the big halls in the Hollywood Roosevelt Hotel or some place like that. He'd have the football team and the priests who came down with us and he'd bring out all kinds of beautiful girls from the studios. He'd be there with his wife, and it would be quite a party. The first time I saw him actually was when I was a freshman. They brought him back to Spokane and gave him an honorary degree in music. He was certainly generous to us.

Our coach, Mike Pacarovitch, was a good friend of Bing's and he had a good sense of humor. I'll always remember one of his pregame pep talks to us. We had not been playing up to par and we had to play St. Mary's, which had a very big team and a very good one that year. Well, both teams come out of their locker rooms and go down this same tunnel to the field. He told us to go out and do our best. "Now get going," he said, "but if you hear a loud noise in the tunnel behind you, get the hell out of the way because that's St. Mary's coming out."

I went to Green Bay in 1941, which incidentally is right near De Pere where I first found out about Gonzaga. When I got there they wrote about me and kept the nickname I'd gotten out in Washington. A writer there had dubbed me the "Gray Ghost of Gonzaga." The ghost part was because I was a rather elusive runner, he said, and the gray was because I was prematurely gray. Anyway, it stuck with me.

Ending up in Green Bay was pretty much a shock to me. I thought if I had any chance in the pros at all it would have been with the Redskins because of Ray Flaherty. But, as it turned out, it was undoubtedly the luckiest thing that ever happened to me because I truly enjoyed playing for the Packers and I grew to love it up in Wisconsin. And I've lived there ever since.

After I was drafted by the Packers, they sent me seventy-five dollars for expenses to get to Green Bay. That was about the train fare from

Spokane in those days. Well, I didn't use it for the train. There was this good buddy of mine, Buck Baker, a tackle on the football team, who had just gotten married. Like me, he had stayed out there during the summer and worked. We used that seventy-five dollars to help him on a honeymoon trip. He and his bride and I all drove back to Chicago in his car. They honeymooned and I was along with them, didn't sleep in the same room but otherwise we were together. They stayed with me in Chicago for a few days and then went on and I got up to Green Bay from there.

I had seen the Packers play against the Bears at Wrigley Field in Chicago, but I had never seen their home field until the first day I arrived on it for practice. I was really nervous. There was Don Hutson and Clarke Hinkle and some of those other boys who were known to be tremendous ballplayers. I got a room in the Union Hotel up there and after I made the team I moved over to the Astor Hotel where most of the players stayed. At the Astor two of us would room together and I believe the cost was seven or eight dollars a week. We'd eat across the street at the YMCA, that was about the most reasonable place around.

My first roommate was Lee McLaughlin. He was from the University of Virginia, a guard, and he was a rookie, too. The next year I roomed with Larry Craig who had gone to South Carolina. After the war, I roomed with Bruce Smith from Minnesota and after that with Dick Wildung, a great tackle, who was also from Minnesota.

Those first couple of years I went back to Chicago after the football season. I had a job down there with a company called Revere Copper and Brass. It was really just a laborer's job, lifting things, moving things, bull work.

In 1943, I got married. My wife, Ruthie, and I stayed in Green Bay that year until I had to go into the service. That was the same year that earlier I decided I was going to get a raise from Lambeau. He was a real bull when it came to that kind of dealing. But I told my wife, "By golly, I'm going to get more money this year." I told her that he wasn't going to talk me out of it. If I had to, I was going to put cotton in my ears so I couldn't hear anything he said. I was just going to hold out and that was it. Well, I went off, and when I came back I told Ruthie, "You know what? I'm goll-damn lucky to be playing for this team!" Curly was a hard man to get a dollar out of.

The veterans didn't have much to do with you when you were a rookie. But it was a little different after you made the team that year. I remember one game where we were playing the Cleveland Rams. They had a real fine end by the name of Jim Benton. Well, we had a certain

Tony Canadeo (3), one of Green Bay's all-time greats, exhibits one of his varied football talents here as he breaks through the Los Angeles Rams defense in a 1947 game. Ram pursuers include linebacker Riley Matheson (11) and tackle Clyde Johnson (8). Canadeo could do just about anything on a football field with consummate skill: run, pass, receive, play defense, return punts and kickoffs, and punt the ball. He spent eleven years with the Packers (1941–52), with a one-year intermission for military duty in World War II. *(Pro Football Hall of Fame)*

coverage designed for him. On one play where he caught a pass, I ended up closest to him after it. Actually it was Clarke Hinkle who was supposed to have been covering him but he fell down or something. At halftime, Curly just crawled all over me about why I hadn't been on Benton. Hinkle stood up and said, "It wasn't his man, it was my man." That's the kind of person Clarke was, a helluva guy. I only played with him for one year and then he went into the military.

Don Hutson was another fine fellow, a regular guy. And a smart one, he always had a lot of business deals going. We still see each other from time to time, sometimes play golf together. Some of the others I palled around with were Lou Brock, not to be confused with the baseball player, and Andy Uram and Charley Brock. They were a great bunch of guys. And we had a lot of things to do up there. There were the usual bars where the players hung out after a game. And a lot of us got into sailing.

I was chiefly a running back up there. But in 1943, Cecil Isbell left us and I got the passing job. I had done some passing before that, sometimes we had platooned our backfield and when Isbell was out I was the tailback. We used the single wing then and sometimes the Notre Dame box. There wasn't free substitution then but sometimes Curly would change things around in the backfield. But in '43 I did most of the passing and Irv Comp, who was a rookie that year out of a little school called St. Benedict's, was my backup. I was better as a runner than a passer, and when I came back after the war that's where Curly used me to his best advantage. I played defensive halfback, too, that's the equivalent of corner back today.

Our biggest rivalry back then was with the Chicago Bears. In 1941, they called them the "Monsters of the Midway," which is what they were. That was one of the greatest Bears team ever. It was the one who killed the Redskins the year before in the title game, 73–0. Golly, they had Sid Luckman and George McAfee and Norm Standlee and Bill Osmanski and Hugh Gallarneau and Ray Nolting and Gary Famiglietti. These were all great backs, all on the same team. And they had Bulldog Turner and Danny Fortmann and Ray Bray in the line. And Ken Kavanaugh was one of the best ends in the game.

We played them even-up that year, however. Both of us ended up with records of 10–1. They beat us once at home and we beat them down in Chicago. But they beat us at a playoff game in Chicago for the division.

Our first game of the year my rookie year was against the Bears and I remember it very well. I was back to receive the opening kickoff and I got it and brought it back out. Well, I got hit and let me tell you, I really got hit. I came up bleeding like a horse. I went back and stuck my head in the huddle and said, "This is a helluva way to make a living." I was bleeding from the lips, they split my lips right open. We didn't wear nose guards in those days and that was part of the problem, the other part is that that was the way those Bears played. George Halas turned out one helluva rugged team.

It was a brutal game that we played, not to say that it isn't today. But ours was pretty bloody. Another team that we had some pretty fierce encounters with was the Detroit Lions. We were playing them once on Thanksgiving Day, and it was a grudging game with neither of us going anywhere. Tobin Rote was our quarterback, he was a rookie that year. Big Ed Neal was our center and he went about 300 pounds. Well, we were inching our way down the field and we got to about the 10 yard line of Detroit. I was playing fullback that year because Ted Fritsch was hurt. Neal got to thinking about our situation and he came back to the huddle and told Rote, "Run it up my butt." He felt he could move their nose guard, Les Bingaman, who was also about 300 pounds, out of the way. Being the fullback, that meant me running it up his butt, which also meant running into 600 pounds worth of battling fury at the line of scrimmage. The first time I went there at Neal's suggestion I got my head chopped down to about my shoulder blades. I came back to the huddle to Neal and said, "I don't think this is going to work."

He said, "Don't worry, run it again. I slipped."

So the next time I go, Christ almighty, they straightened me up like I was a log. This time I go back to Neal and said to him, "You come back here now and I'll go up there and you can run it up my butt." By this time Tobin Rote stopped listening to Neal and he called a pass play to Larry Coutre, one of our halfbacks, and it worked and we scored. I'll tell you, though, that Les Bingaman could leave you with an incredible amount of bruises.

In 1944, I was in the military but I still got to play in three games that year for Green Bay. I was in the army, stationed down at Fort Bliss, Texas. And while I was there my son Bob was born and I was given emergency leave to go back and be with my wife. I had been playing on the Fort Bliss football team and therefore I was in pretty good shape. Well, I hitched a ride home on a B-17 which got me to Detroit and from there I got another army plane, a DC-3, that got me to Green Bay. I was a corporal at the time. Anyway, I got home and Ruthie was fine and so was the baby. As soon as Curly Lambeau heard I was back in town he contacted me and said he wanted me to play. Remember, players were pretty scarce in those war years. He got permission from the army for me to play while I was on furlough. So I practiced with the team during the week and we went out and played the Cleveland Rams the first week I was back. That was in Green Bay and I really felt it that day, I guess I wasn't in as good a shape as I thought I was, but still I gained about 110 yards rushing that day. Well, Lambeau was real pleased and he said afterwards, "That was great, now next week we go to Detroit."

I said, "Hell, you might be, but I'm not. I'm home on furlough." Well, I still went and we beat Detroit and they flew me right back to Green Bay after the game. The next week we played the Bears down in Chicago and we lost to them. After that game, the team went back up to Green Bay and I got on a train and went back to Fort Bliss. Green Bay, of course, went on to win the NFL championship that year. By the time I heard about it, a week or two after the title game, I was in England in an antiaircraft unit with the army. After that I went to mainland Europe and eventually into Germany. We handled 90-millimeter guns and 40-millimeter guns. We went all the way across Europe until the war was over. I finally got home in January of 1946 and I went back to the Packers that year.

I was still pretty young in '46 and in decent shape so it wasn't too bad. I had a good amount of time to get myself ready. I also had played football while I was in the army. We even played while we were in Europe. I remember playing against the 101st Airborne. They had Dick Hoerner, a helluva fullback who later played with the Los Angeles Rams. We were stationed in Munich, Germany, at the time.

Don Hutson was gone after I got back. He retired from the game. As a result, teams played us a little differently. We really missed him, I must admit. He stayed around and helped coach, however.

It was in 1947 that Lambeau switched our offense to a wing-T. The concentration was on running the ball and I loved it. The formation gave me more freedom, it relaxed me more. And we did real well with it. Our team was a good one that year. We had Indian Jack Jacobs, a good quarterback, and Nolan Luhn, a fine end, and Dick Wildung, one of the best guards in the league. But that was also the year the Chicago Cardinals were so good and they won our division. They had Charlie Trippi and Pat Harder and Elmer Angsman. They beat us twice that year. There were a number of really great teams around then. The Bears with Sid Luckman were still a powerhouse. And the Rams had Bob Waterfield and Jim

Benton. And, of course, the Philadelphia Eagles with Steve Van Buren and Tommy Thompson, they were especially tough.

The next year we had that big incident with Curly Lambeau. After one of our games, he fined the entire team. It was against the Chicago Cardinals early in the season. We lost by a couple of touchdowns and he claimed we hadn't been trying, so he docked us a week's salary, which was a big chunk to all of us. Everybody was really ticked off. But we thought we'd get the money if we played well the next week against the Rams. Well, we did, shut them out 16–0, but we didn't get the money from Curly. After that we all were twice as mad and everything went downhill from there. We didn't win another game all year, lost seven straight. After the season, Lambeau gave us back the money, though.

The next year, it was even worse. We won only two of our twelve games and ended up in last place in our division. That was Lambeau's last year in Green Bay. He resigned after the season and the Cardinals hired him. The team was really flat. Surprisingly, though, I had my best year running and gained over 1,000 yards. Jug Girard was our quarterback that year and he was a native Wisconsin boy.

Gene Ronzani took over for Curly and he installed the Bears' T formation. I got off to a bad start with Gene, not because we didn't like each other, but because I was holding out that year. After I gained that 1,000 yards the year before, I thought I'd get more money. I think I ended up getting a thousand or two more and that was it.

Ronzani knew a helluva lot about football. He was trying desperately to rebuild the football team and that was a pretty tough job. We didn't do very well my last three years in Green Bay. The last one, 1952, wasn't as bad as the others. In fact, we were right up there until Thanksgiving Day when Detroit gave us a real whomping. Then we lost the next two games and ended up 6–6 for the year.

I was thirty-three years old that year and I could tell I'd lost at least a step or two. I felt it was time to retire. Actually I'd had another job with a steel company in Chicago, called Production Steel. In 1952, I was giving a talk in Oshkosh and one of the people at it came up afterwards and told me about this company and said they needed a man up in Wisconsin to represent them. I went to Chicago in March and they offered me the job. They asked if I wanted to play football still and I said that I'd like to for at least another year, and they said that was fine with them. Gene Ronzani said it was okay with him if I had the other job. The company kept me on my draw during the season, too, even though I wasn't selling for them during that time. Maybe on Mondays after the games I'd make a

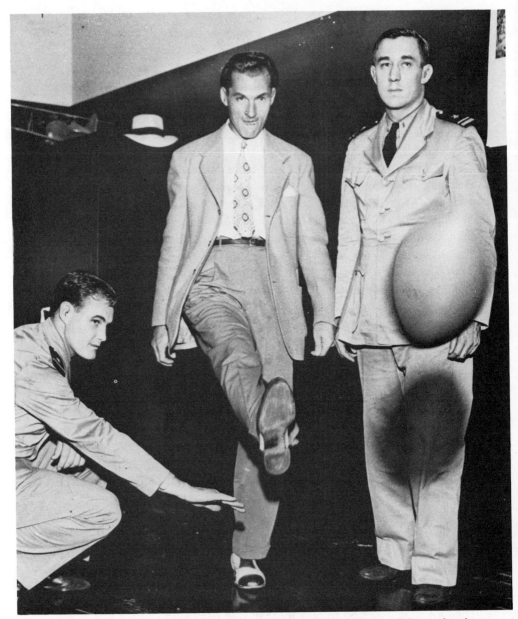

Don Hutson literally kicks off a U.S. Navy drive to recruit new flying cadets in the early days of World War II. Looking on is Lt. J.G. Jay Berwanger, former Heisman Trophy winner and the first player selected in the NFL's premiere draft in 1936 (although he chose not to play in the pros). Holding is Ens. Claude York, who also had a fine college football career. More than six hundred NFL players served in the military during World War II, and twenty-one were killed in action. *(Official U.S. Navy photograph)*

few token calls, that was all. I stayed with them a long time after that. But around 1978 I went on my own and opened Canadeo Metal Sales, Inc. I represent a number of steel companies in Wisconsin.

I stayed in the Green Bay area ever since I left the Packers, and, yes, I still am an ardent Packer fan.


## *The First Draw Play*

Buckets Goldenberg, who at 5 feet 10 inches and 220 pounds played both in the backfield and on the line for the Green Bay Packers from 1933 through 1945, claims to be the victim of the game's very first draw play. He tells it this way:

"I had noticed that whenever Sid Luckman [the Chicago Bears' quarterback] planned to pass he would drop his left foot back. When I saw him do that, I would yell to a teammate to cover for me and I would barrel right in. I got to be pretty successful in getting Sid until one day Bulldog Turner realized what I was doing. He persuaded Luckman to fake a pass and hand off to Bill Osmanski. It went for a nice gain and the draw play was born."

# 18

## *Bill Dudley*

"Bullet" Bill Dudley they called him, although he was far from the fastest of backs. When he passed, he threw the ball sidearm. He had the most unorthodox place-kicking style in the game. And he was a mere 5 feet 10 inches and 175 pounds when he joined the Pittsburgh Steelers in 1942.

But Art Rooney knew what he was doing when he made the University of Virginia tailback his first-round draft choice that year. As a rookie, Dudley established himself as the best running back in the NFL, leading the league in rushing, punt return yardage, and producing the best average for kickoff returns. In his very first minute of play as a pro, he raced 55 yards for a touchdown against the Philadelphia Eagles. Dudley was almost single-handedly responsible for taking the Pittsburgh team, last-place in the NFL East in 1941 (1–9–1), and turning it into a second-place contender in 1942 (7–4); and for his efforts he was an easy choice for all-Pro.

Dudley spent much of the next three years as a flight instructor and then as a pilot in the Pacific theater of operations. He returned for the last four games of the 1945 season and in that brief span managed to score more points (twenty) than any other Steeler in that hapless team's ten games.

The following year he made all-Pro again by leading the league in rushing and punt return yardage as well as interceptions, just to prove he was as adept at defense as he was on offense.

But Dudley did not get along with his coach, the stern Jock Sutherland, and at the end of the season he shocked Steeler fans by quitting the game. Sutherland made no attempt to woo him back, instead putting him on waivers. The Detroit Lions quickly went after him and offered Bullet Bill the most lucrative one-year contract since Red Grange in 1925, a one-year salary of twenty thousand dollars. He played three-years in Detroit and then another three with the Washington Redskins.

During his career and despite his noticeable lack of speed, he was a dazzling runner. In 1950, he ran a punt back 96 yards for a touchdown—at that time the second-longest in NFL history. In 1947, he had raced 84 yards with another punt and in 1946 he had carried an interception 80 yards for a touchdown.

Between 1942 and 1953, Bullet Bill Dudley rushed for 3,057 yards and nineteen touchdowns, caught eighteen touchdown passes, and threw six, chalked up 1,743 yards returning kickoffs, and 1,515 returning punts. He intercepted twenty-three passes, carrying two of them in for touchdowns, and he maintained a 38.2 punting average. Dudley kicked thirty-three field goals and 121 extra points, accounting for an overall total of 484 points in the NFL log book. All of it was more than enough to get him elected to the Pro Football Hall of Fame, and he was formally inducted in 1966.

After football, Bill Dudley returned to Virginia, where he forged a highly successful career in the insurance business and also served as a state senator.

I was almost a Christmas baby in 1921, born on December 24 in Bluefield, Virginia. It's a small town in the southwest corner of the state, right on the border of West Virginia. I grew up there and went to Graham High School, what they call a Class D school, the lowest-size school in the state. There were less than two hundred students when I went there but we had a football team with maybe twenty-five players.

I was fourteen years old when I began playing football there, stood about 5 feet 8 inches and weighed about 138 pounds. They all tried to discourage me from playing, said I was too small. But I made the team as a junior and played pretty well my senior year. We played teams from other towns in the area, most of them were coal mining towns. I was only sixteen when I graduated from high school.

Actually I'd been playing football for as long as I can remember, maybe six years old. I just naturally gravitated toward it. We'd play neighborhood sandlot games. And I always used to look at the sports magazines which had pictures of the big-name football players of the day. I always loved Pathé news, too, they'd show newsreels of football games. I remember especially watching the Four Horsemen of Notre Dame—Layden, Miller, Stuhldreher, and Crowley—and seeing Knute Rockne.

My hero was a little quarterback from Michigan, Harry Newman. Being small, too, I could equate myself with him. I think Newman was only about 5 feet 8 inches and not much heavier than I was in high school.

There was a junior college in Bluefield, too, and it had a football team. And in one of those years while I was in high school, 1935 or '36 I guess, they had a fellow by the name of Pete Young who was the leading scorer in the nation. I used to go to all the games, climb the fence and sneak in. My older brother Jim also played for that junior college team. Later he went to Washington and Lee and played there, too.

When I finally made our high school team they didn't have a pair of football shoes small enough to fit me. We usually traveled to our games in people's cars. About five or six fathers would drive and we'd pack five kids in each car and go off. We only had one coach, no assistants. I played quarterback and did all the kicking. I even kicked field goals which was kind of rare for high school in those days.

Our coach was a man named Marshall Shearer and he taught me how to place kick. He had played football under Bo McMillin at Centre College and they had a quarterback there by the name of Red Roberts. Well, he kicked in an odd way but it worked. He just stood next to where he was going to kick from and brought his leg back like a pendulum and kicked the ball. He never took a step forward before kicking it. Coach Shearer told me it was easy to learn but I didn't think so and I really didn't think I could kick that way. But you do what the hell your coach says if you're smart and I did it. I kicked that way even in the pros. I think the longest one I ever kicked without taking a step was about 33 or 34 yards. The longest when I took a step, which I did on the longer tries as a pro, was somewhere around 48 yards.

The University of Virginia was the only school to offer me a scholarship and that came about on a piece of luck. I had tried to get one from VMI and VPI but they all felt I was too small. I also tried Washington & Lee, where my brother had just come home from. He had to drop out because he ran out of money and he wasn't on a scholarship, but they turned me down, too.

Well, after graduating, I was working on a Nehi soda pop truck in the summer and I met up with my coach one day and told him I didn't think I'd be going on to college because my family couldn't afford to send me. Another fellow who Coach Shearer had played football with at Centre was Matty Bell and he was then the head coach at Southern Methodist. My coach wrote him and recommended me. "Send him out," Bell wrote back. But I didn't have the money to get to Dallas, so nothing ever came of it.

There was another person interested in me too at the time, Dr. Jack Whitten, who was from Tazewell and represented that county in the Virginia legislature. He was a good friend of my father. He talked to my football coach who told him he thought I could play college football if I got the chance. Then one day I got a telephone call from Coach Shearer: "Bill, there's a gentleman named Frank Murray, who's the coach at the University of Virginia, visiting Dr. Whitten. He's looking at some ballplayers from the area and the Doc told me to bring you over to talk to him." So I went over to talk to him. Frank Murray was quite a man, he was inducted into the College Football Hall of Fame in 1983. He also had a doctor's degree in philosophy and a master's in English. I spent about an hour with him and he had a long chat with my high school coach, who told him I was a good place kicker. Well, that was a mark in my favor. He told him I hadn't missed an extra point in the last two years. Coach Murray had lost a couple of ballgames at Virginia recently because they had missed some extra points. Well, he didn't say anything that day but about two weeks later my father got a letter from him which said that they were offering me a five-hundred-dollar scholarship. In those days that was enough to take care of my tuition, books, room, and board. It said the scholarship would be good as long as I maintained my eligibility as a football player.

Virginia was a wonderful school. They were very strong on academics. A perfect example is what happened to me at the end of my junior year. I had just been elected captain of the football team for my senior year and I'd been named to one of the all-American teams as a junior. Well, seventy-five was a passing grade in those days and in sociology I had gotten a seventy-eight at the end of the first quarter. Coach Murray warned me that if my grade went down below seventy-five I'd have to go to summer school to regain my eligibility. Well, all I needed was a seventy-two in the second quarter to average a passing grade of seventy-five. But when I received my grades, it said I only got a seventy.

So I went to Dr. Hoffer, my sociology professor, and said, "Doctor, would you mind regrading my examination paper?"

"Oh, Mr. Dudley, do you think I made a mistake?" he said.

"Sir," I said, "I don't know."

"Well, what did you get the second quarter?"

"Sir, a seventy."

"And what did you get the first quarter?"

"A seventy-eight."

"Well, what does that give you for the course?"

"Sir, that only gives me a seventy-four."

"And what does that do to you?"

"Sir, it makes me go to summer school."

"I'll see you there. Good day."

Being captain of the football team or an all-American didn't mean anything down there. The priority was education and that's why it's such a wonderful institution. I went to summer school and got about a 90 and so I was able to play my senior year.

It was at Virginia where I got the nickname "Bullet," which was a great misnomer because I wasn't very fast. In fact, there have been more articles written about how slow I was. I think my best time in the 100-yard dash was something like 11:2. But I did have a good takeoff, a quick start, and for the first 30 yards or so I was right on beat. But I'd been doing well at Virginia and when you get written up, sportswriters are always trying to put some kind of moniker on you. First it was the "Bluefield Beacon" and then "Beacon Bill" and finally "Bullet Bill."

In 1940, when I was a junior, we had a pretty good team. After the season, we had a choice whether we wanted to play Tennessee the next year. Well, Tennessee had been one of the top teams in the country for three straight years. They didn't lose a game in 1940 until they were upset by Frank Leahy's Boston College team in the Sugar Bowl. I was captain and I got everybody to vote for playing them. After the vote, Coach Murray asked me why I wanted to play a team like Tennessee. I said, "Well, coach, they're one of the best and I like to play the best." He kind of shook his head and walked away. We went over to Tennessee and played them and they beat us. I ran the second-half kickoff back for a touchdown, however, and that's one of my most memorable times in college ball.

My most memorable game was against North Carolina that year. Virginia hadn't beaten the Tar Heels in nine straight years. But we beat them that day and I had one of my best games ever. I ran for two touchdowns, one was about 60 yards, and then I faked a punt and ran 89 yards for another. With extra points I believe I scored twenty-two points that afternoon. And we all felt pretty good about finally defeating North Carolina.

Our team that year was a good one. We used a new formation and we surprised a lot of people. Coach Murray had gone up to Washington the year before to watch the NFL championship game between the Redskins and the Chicago Bears. That was the one where the Bears beat them 73–0. Coach Murray talked to George Halas sometime afterwards and then he put in the T formation. We were the first team in the south to use it.

We had a slightly different slant. We actually started out with me at quarterback, taking the ball directly from the center. I had been the tailback in our single wing and had called the signals. But then Coach Murray told the team we were going to use a kind of bastard form of the T. Another player would line up over the center as quarterback and I'd be behind him where a tailback normally would have been. Then just before the snap, he'd shift or spin to one side or another and the ball would be centered directly to me. Coach Murray felt they couldn't utilize my running ability if I lined up at quarterback in the T formation. I was also able to quick kick from the tailback position.

I had no idea that I'd end up playing professional football. I was only 5 feet 10 inches and 175 pounds when I graduated from Virginia. But then Pittsburgh drafted me in the first round, which was quite a surprise. Actually I was planning on going into the service, in fact I was sworn into the Naval Air Corps in May 1942, but due to the fact that I wasn't twenty-one yet my parents had to sign the papers, too. But without the papers, that was nullified. Then I signed to play with the Steelers. The draft board was on my tail by that time so I took the Army Air Corps exam, passed it, and was sworn into it. But I didn't have to report until after the football season.

Bert Bell, who later became the NFL commissioner, signed me to the Steeler contract. He was Art Rooney's partner in 1942. It was for five thousand dollars, which was a ton of money in those days.

We had a pretty good football team in 1942. I got the starting job at tailback and we ran second to the Redskins, who, of course, had Sammy Baugh. They beat us twice that year.

Still, we were a very improved ballclub. I had said to Bert Bell when I was signing my contract, the first one, "If we have a good year and I do, too, could I get a bonus?"

"Oh Bill, you wouldn't need a bonus," he said.

"Maybe I wouldn't need one but I'd like one."

So he said, "Bill, if we have a good year, you'll get a bonus."

Bullet Bill Dudley, carrying the ball here for the Pittsburgh Steelers against the Washington Redskins in 1946, was not the fastest of backs, but he was one of the most wily, clever, and elusive runners of the 1940s, and he could break the long ones along with the fastest backs in the league. Moving in here with high but dubious hopes of tackling Dudley is defensive back Dick Poillon; other Washington defenders shown are guard Bill Ward (21) and end Ed Cifers (43). Bullet Bill was also a fine place kicker and an exceptional defensive back. He played three years each for the Pittsburgh Steelers, Detroit Lions, and Washington Redskins. (*Pro Football Hall of Fame*)

Well, we did, and I did. I led the league in rushing and made all-Pro. But I didn't get a bonus and I went off to the military.

I went to Florida for basic training. After that I went to San Antonio, Texas, for what they called pre-preflight training and for preflight training. I actually got my wings at Ellington Field in Houston. I wanted to fly P-38s but word came down that I wasn't going to the war zones but instead would be an instructor. So they sent me to Randolph Field just outside San Antonio. They asked me to play football there and so I did.

Randolph Field was kind of the West Point of the air corps in those days. We had quite a football team down there. I played the entire 1944 season. I especially remember one game when we were playing the Third Air Force. Charlie Trippi played for them. Hap Arnold, who was a famous general, came down to talk to both teams at halftime. It was the only time in my life that I've seen two football teams in the same locker room at a halftime. Anyway, Hap Arnold was the commanding general of the air force and he strode back and forth in front of us. "I appreciate what you're doing," he said. "A lot of you have been complaining about not being able to get overseas and fight. Rest assured, that when this season is over, in thirty days, all of you will receive your orders to go overseas."

And that's exactly what happened. I went to Saipan, but I wasn't a big hotshot pilot. I only flew two missions and both of them were supply missions. I didn't see a Jap plane.

We didn't lose a ballgame in 1944. We beat Trippi's team and everybody else. We had a guy by the name of Pete Layden, who later played for the New York Yankees, and Jack Russell, he played for the Yankees too. After the season, some of us were sent out to March Field to play for them in an exhibition game at the Coliseum in Los Angeles against the Washington Redskins. Sammy Baugh was there and they beat us by six points. We played college rules for the first half and pro rules during the second. It drew a huge crowd.

I got out of the service in 1946 and went back to Pittsburgh. I'd kept in touch with Art Rooney and I had the greatest respect for him. He was really one of the finest men I've ever known and was practically a second father to me. He told me that he very much wanted me back in Pittsburgh. I'd also heard from Bert Bell who was also still there. They were a little nervous, I think, because the new league, the All-American Football Conference, was forming. I'd already had two offers from them, one was from the Los Angeles Dons, the team owned by Don Ameche, and the other was from the Buffalo ballclub, the Bisons.

I went to Pittsburgh to meet with Mr. Bell and Mr. Rooney and we sat down to talk. Mr. Bell handed me a contract which he had already signed and so had Mr. Rooney. There was a blank space where the salary figure was supposed to be. "Bill, here's a contract, you fill in what you think you're worth."

So I wrote in twelve thousand five hundred dollars. That was a lot of money in 1946. "Bill, you filled it out within five hundred dollars of what I thought you would," Mr. Rooney said. "I thought you'd write in twelve thousand dollars." I don't know whether the idea was Rooney's or Bell's, but I signed the contract and got twelve thousand five hundred dollars.

Jock Sutherland was the coach at Pittsburgh in 1946 and we had some run-ins during that time. It really wasn't feuding in the full sense of the word. I think the press, however, made it sound like a real feud. One incident that was written up, which was true, occurred at practice one day. I was not the greatest passer in the world, and Jock had been on my back about it. We were both strong competitors. He was extremely stern, and I had my own ideas, too. This one day at practice I was having trouble hitting some of my receivers during pass drills. Sutherland made a remark like, "What in hell's wrong with you! Can't you hit any of your receivers?"

I made the remark back, "Well, if you put different colored jerseys on the defenders I might do better." They wore the same colored jerseys as the offense.

Well, with that, he walked over to me and said loud enough for everyone to hear, "Are you coaching this football team?"

"No, sir, I'm not," I said.

"Well, then you'll take orders like everyone else." And he stomped away. That was all there was to it that day. But the next week we did have different colored jerseys for the defense.

On the other hand, Sutherland was the best coach I ever played for. He knew what it took to win, he knew how to get the job done. Despite the fact we didn't get along, he was the person, I believe, who made me the league's most valuable player that year, looking at it in retrospect. He got me to go out and play some intense football. I ended up leading the league in rushing and pass interceptions in 1946.

We had another incident that year where Jock told me that the rest of the players didn't get along with me, either. I was very upset. I went to

Art Rooney and told him that if all that was true I wanted him to trade me. He said it wasn't and that he didn't want to trade me. I went to several of the ballplayers and found out that it wasn't true, either.

I also got hurt a number of times that year. Between that and the workouts that Sutherland put you through, and believe me, he worked you to the bone, I decided at the end of the year that it just wasn't worth it anymore. I wrote a letter to Art Rooney and to Sutherland and told them I was quitting the game. I think I said in it that I just couldn't take the punishment any longer. Hell, I was playing tailback in the single wing, handling most of the running and passing, I was punting and kicking off, I returned punts and kickoffs, I played defense, going close to sixty minutes every game. Your body can only stand so much, and mine was only about 160 pounds by the time the season ended. I didn't really want another year with Jock Sutherland, even though he was a great football coach.

I went back to Virginia to coach the backs, but that didn't last. The Detroit Lions obtained rights to me and Gus Dorais, their coach then, talked me into coming back. He came to Charlottesville and he convinced me to come back. I was still hurting from a knee injury that I'd gotten in the last game of the 1946 season, and I told him I really couldn't play. Well, their contract offer was for a lot of money. But I really didn't think I could play. Gus asked if I would be willing to go out to California to talk with a doctor, a specialist, about it. They would pay my way. I said I would but only if he agreed that I could play that I would get a three-year contract. It was agreed. I also told him that I was getting married, and he said fine, that they would pay the expenses for both myself and my wife to go to California. That was our honeymoon.

The doctor out there checked my knee out thoroughly and told Gus and Mr. Mandel, the owner of the Lions, that as far as he was concerned I ought to be all right. He said there was some damage to the knee but nothing that would keep me from playing. So they signed me to a three-year, no-cut contract at twenty thousand dollars a year. I guess I was the highest paid ballplayer in the league at the time.

Gus Dorais was a fine man. He had his hands full with the situation in Detroit in those years, it was turmoil. And that same year, he had lost a son, drowned right in front of his mother. It was terribly tragic. And Gus, I don't believe, was up to coaching that year. But he gave it a shot. Anyway, we were not doing well at all and midway into the season there were a lot of rumors that Gus was about to be fired. Well, this one Sunday we were about to play the Chicago Bears. Gus came into the locker room before the game and gave us a really short pre-game pep talk. "We're here to play the big, bad Bears," he said. "And we're going to get the hell kicked out of us, get on the train, get drunk, go home, and get fired. Now let's go out there and have some fun!" We did get beat that day, too. Gus didn't get fired after that game but he did at the end of the season. In the nine years I was in professional football, I had eight different coaches.

Bo McMillin replaced Dorais at the Lions in 1948. There was new ownership of the franchise as well. At the end of the 1949 season, McMillin traded me to the Washington Redskins. I hadn't had a good year in 1948 and I was on my way downhill. So was Sammy Baugh at Washington, he was about thirty-six years old by 1950. We had some talent with Harry Gilmer and Choo-Choo Justice but we didn't do very well as a team that year.

Actually before I was traded I had agreed with the new Detroit ownership to play for them and to take a pay cut. I knew I was not as fit as I once had been and I thought it was only fair. I agreed to play for Detroit for twelve thousand, five hundred dollars a year. But then Bo McMillin traded me to Washington.

Herman Ball was the coach at Washington then. I sat down with him in the Redskins office to sign a contract and he said, "Bill, I can't pay you the kind of money Detroit offered."

I said, "Okay, Herman, let's forget about it. No hard feelings." And I walked out. He called George Preston Marshall, the Redskins owner, who in turn called me and asked me to meet him for lunch at this Greek restaurant. I met him and his general manager. Mr. Marshall came in wearing this very expensive suit. He was impeccable, very impressive. He said, "Bill, you're going to be playing for the first time for a football team that knows what it's doing. We're here to win. We've got a reputation of being a winner. Now what's this stuff I hear that you can't get along with Herman?"

I said, "Sir, there's nothing to it that I can't get along with Herman. I can get along with him just fine. It's the salary issue." He raised his eyebrows like he didn't know what I was talking about. So I said, "Mr. Marshall, being the astute businessman that I know you are, I'm certain you talked with Mr. Anderson in Detroit [the new Lions owner] and that he told you that I'd agree to play for a pay cut. The twelve thousand, five hundred dollars was not my ordinary salary. It was the pay cut. That's what I agreed to play for. I've taken a cut but I will not play for a penny less."

He looked across the table at me. "That's a lot of money no matter how you look at it," he said. "You know we have Sammy Baugh."

I said, "Sir, I've never asked question one about what anybody else got. I just talk about what I should get, and that's the way I feel."

He hit the table with his fist and said, "All right, go tell Herman to give it to you." And that was it.

I got to know Mr. Marshall pretty well and he was quite a man. I remember he once told me, "The biggest problem in football or in any business for that matter is paying big money to mediocre talent. No one ever lost any money paying top dollar for top talent."

I played with Washington through the 1953 season, although I missed the 1952 season. Around that time, in fact earlier, I was thinking about getting out of the game.

While I was in Detroit in the late 1940s I went to work for the Ford Motor Company in their training program. I was in the tractor division. It was 1948, I believe, and as part of it I used to have to get up at 5:30 in the morning to be out on a farm at 6:30. That's how you learned about tractors. I also worked for them in the spring of 1949, but it ended when I was traded to Washington.

When I went with Washington, I moved to Lynchburg, Virginia. After the 1950 season I went to work in the insurance business. My brother, the one who had played for Washington & Lee, was already well established and he offered me a job. I started in the insurance business there for four hundred dollars a month.

In 1952, I got out of professional football and went up to Yale to coach. I was their backfield coach that year. Herman Hickman hired me but then he left. I went back and played another year of pro ball. Then I stayed in the insurance business for the rest of my life. I also got involved in politics in Virginia and served in the state legislature, representing the city of Lynchburg.

I didn't give up football entirely. I did some scouting for the Lions first and afterwards the Pittsburgh Steelers. I remember, I signed Ken Willard to a contract for the Lions but they lost him to the San Francisco 49ers. And I signed another boy, a linebacker from Duke by the name of Mike Curtis, but he ended up with the Baltimore Colts. I signed both of them on the very same day and the Lions lost both of them. I just did it for the fun of it, the scouting, just to keep my hand in the game, so to speak.

I still see a lot of the old ballplayers. Sammy Baugh, who I roomed with at the end of our careers in Washington, is still one of the all-time great guys. We've played in the same golf tournaments. The most enjoyable is the Hall of Fame Golf Classic, which involves people from all sports. In one recently there was Eddie Arcaro, Bill Russell, Whitey Ford, Bill Dickey, and all kinds of others. Del Miller, a harness racer, and I won it one year. Sammy Baugh and Tom Harmon won it another year. It's nice to keep in touch with the people you played with.

I still cheer for all the teams I played for. I'm for Pittsburgh and Detroit and Washington. I guess my truest sentimental feelings lie with Pittsburgh on account of my association with Art Rooney and his family. I got to know them so well, and they are such fine people. But I saw a whole cross-section of the league with the different people I dealt with: owners, coaches, players. It was a wonderful time to have been in the NFL, to have played the game the way that it was.

## Pep Talk

Bronko Nagurski played tackle for the Chicago Bears in 1943 after he came out of retirement. But in the last game of that season, an important one against the Chicago Cardinals, in the snow, the thirty-five-year-old Nagurski was taken aside by coach Hunk Anderson. Hunk wondered if Nagurski could break open the game with some powerful rushes, as he had done so often in his prime in the 1930s.

Nagurski went into the game as a fullback and spoke to Bear center Bulldog Turner in the huddle. Later Bulldog told the gist of the conversation: "Damnedest pep talk I ever heard in my life. He told me, If you don't want to block for me, all right, but just get out of my way or I'll break your back."

## Belled

Games between the Detroit Lions and the Chicago Bears have long been known for their assorted violences. In one of those encounters in the 1940s, Bullet Bill Dudley was having an especially good day running against the

Bears. Finally, a frustrated Bear lineman, Fred Davis, trying to get hold of the elusive Dudley, swung a thunderous forearm and caught the Lion back on the side of the head.

Dudley was decked but got up woozily and was helped to the sidelines by a teammate. "Where am I?" he said to coach Gus Dorais and the Lion trainer.

"In Chicago," the trainer told him.

"What's the score?"

"14–0, we're ahead."

"Am I married?"

"You are."

"Oh!"